MW01069426

SPORTOPEDIA

illustrated by

MARK LONG

written by

ADAM SKINNER

WIDE EYED EDITIONS

CONTENTS

BALL SPORTS

RACKET SPORTS

ATHLETICS

GYMNASTICS

WATER SPORTS

MOTOR SPORTS

TARGET SPORTS

COMBAT SPORTS

SPORTING EVENTS

Humans have been taking part in sport for as long as they have walked the planet. Whether competing individually or as part of a team, people have always had a desire to test themselves against one another.

And with hundreds of sports now on offer, there is something for everyone. Each is unique, demanding a wide range of different skills – some might require speed and power, others intelligence and mental strength. But there is one trait that links them all: anybody can take part.

Sport rarely discriminates; it does not care who you are, where you come from or what you have. In fact, some of the most recognisable sports stars have come from the poorest parts of the world. Pelé – the greatest footballer who ever lived – was born into extreme poverty in Brazil but lifted the World Cup as a 17-year-old, while Jamaican sprinter Usain Bolt is the fastest man on earth and has won eight Olympic gold medals despite growing up without easy access to drinking water. Even disabilities have not stopped people achieving sporting greatness. It is the ultimate level playing field, where natural talent alone is not enough. Athletes spend years trying to reach the top, honing their craft through dedication and hard work.

But it is not just about winning or being the best. Sport promotes physical well-being, teamwork and discipline. It has provided us with some of history's most memorable moments – from opposing soldiers laying down their weapons to play a game of football on Christmas Day during World War I, to American swimmer Michael Phelps winning a record 23rd Olympic gold medal in 2014 at the age of 31.

This book is a celebration of sport and a reminder that you can take part in any of them. Ultimately, it is about playing. Just look out of your window on any given day. Your local park will be full of people doing just that and there is nothing to stop you joining the fun.

Who knows, maybe you will lift the World Cup or win an Olympic gold medal one day!

BALL

SPORTS

FOOTBALL

Football is the world's most popular sport!

Known as 'the beautiful game', it is played by more than 200 million people in over 200 countries.

People have playing football since around 2 BC but the modern game was created in England when the Football Association formed in 1863. They laid down the basic rules and founded the English Football League, a competition which is still going strong today.

It requires skill, strength and fitness but can be played by anyone with a ball and a bit of space. That is why it is loved by millions!

Games at the top level might be played in mega stadiums and feature some of the best-paid athletes in the world. But many of them grew up playing football on the street or in parks on Sunday mornings. The basic aim of the game is to score more goals than the opposing team. Players kick – or 'head' – the ball around a grass pitch and try to score by putting it in the opposing net. Goooooooaaaaallll!

POSITIONS

GOALKEEPER

ROLE: To stop the opposition from scoring using any part of their bodies, including their hands
SKILLS: Agility, quick reflexes, safe hands

DEFENDERS

ROLE: To stop the opposition from scoring
SKILLS: Strong, good at heading, fast

MIDFIELDERS

ROLE: All-rounders, skilled in defence and attack
SKILLS: Passing, tackling, shooting, setting up goals by 'feeding the forwards'

FORWARDS

ROLE: Mainly responsible for scoring goals
SKILLS: Finishing, positioning, heading, strength

THE PITCH

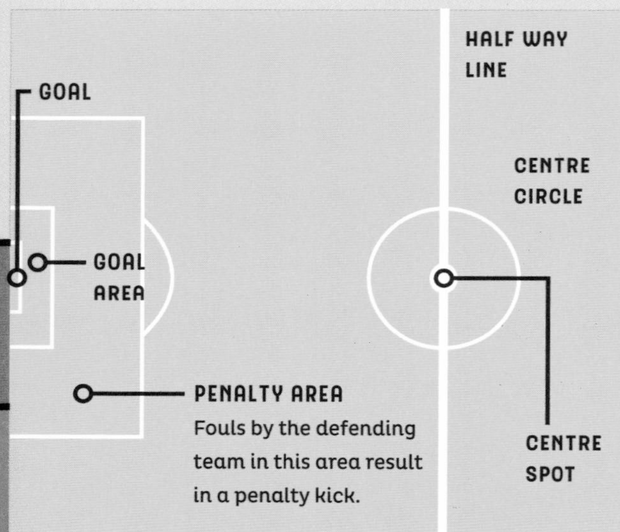

GOAL

Made of metal; the crossbar is 2.44 metres high, with posts 7.32 metres apart. Football teams used to keep track of the score by making a nick in the post each time a goal was conceded, hence the phrase 'to score a goal'.

TOUCHLINE

If the ball touches an attacker before crossing the line, a goal kick is awarded, but if a defender touches it last, a corner is given.

PITCH

Not all pitches are the same size. A grass pitch must be between 90-120 metres long and 45-90 metres wide.

RULES

» Teams of 11 players – ten outfield players and one goalkeeper – move a ball around a pitch with their feet or head and try to score goals.

» A goal is scored when the ball crosses the goal line, between two posts and under a crossbar.

» Only the goalkeepers can touch the ball with their hands – and only in their own penalty area.

» Matches last 90 minutes, divided into two 45-minute halves. Teams switch sides at half-time.

» Free-kicks are awarded for fouls or if players touch the ball with their hands outside the penalty area. A penalty kick is awarded for fouls and handballs inside the penalty area.

» A player is offside and a free-kick called if the ball is passed and there are not at least two players between them and the goal.

» Extra-time is played in some competitions if scores are level after 90 minutes. If neither team is in the lead after extra time, there is a penalty shootout.

REFEREE

The 'ref' enforces the rules along with two (or four) assistants.

CARDS

Breaking the rules can lead to a yellow card, while serious fouls result in a red, meaning the player is sent off. Two yellow cards equal a red. Colombian player Gerardo Bedoya holds the record for the most red cards ever received: 46!

KIT

BOOTS

Football boots have studs that grip the grass.

BALL

Made of leather; 70 centimetres in circumference. The first footballs were made from inflated pig bladders!

NET

Captures the ball when a goal is scored. There were no nets in football until 1891.

FACTS OF THE MATTER

- Every four years at the World Cup, international teams battle for the world's biggest prize. Brazil is the most successful nation, with **FIVE WORLD TITLES**.
- Brazilian legend **PELÉ** was just 17 years and 249 days old when Brazil won the World Cup in 1958 – the **YOUNGEST** ever player to do so.
- England's top division, **THE PREMIER LEAGUE**, is the world's most watched league. It formed in 1992 and has more than **4.7 BILLION FANS** today.
- Teams often pay huge fees to buy players from their rivals. In 2017, French giants Paris Saint-Germain paid **£198 MILLION** to buy Neymar from Spanish side Barcelona – the highest transfer fee any team has ever paid.
- More than **700 MILLION PEOPLE** – more than twice the population of America – tuned in to watch a televised Premier League match between Manchester United and Liverpool in 2015.
- The **FIRST** international match ever was played in 1872 between Scotland and England. It ended in a 0-0 draw... but marked the beginning of a hotly-contested rivalry that's lasted to this day.
- Football originated from old English versions of the game. These could be violent affairs – pitches were the size of **ENTIRE VILLAGES** and everyone joined in!
- Argentinian goalie, **AMADEO CARRIZO**, was the first to wear gloves while goalkeeping during the 1940s.

PENALTY SPOT

Penalties are taken here, 11 metres from the goal.

GOAL LINE

The whole ball must cross this line for a goal to be scored. Goal-line technology was recently introduced to help referees with close calls.

SHINPADS

All players are required to wear shinpads for protection.

SHIRT

Each team has its own unique strip featuring particular colours that are worn season after season. Often, they carry the label of their sponsor.

BALL

Footballs used to be made exclusively with leather, which could become soggy and heavy. Today's modern synthetic balls keep their shape – and 'bounce' – much better.

GLOVES

Gloves help the goalkeepers grip the ball and protect their hands.

BASEBALL

'America's pastime' is one of the oldest professional sports.

Its roots can be traced back to 18th-century England, where it probably evolved from older bat-and-ball games such as cricket, rounders and stoolball. But the USA is responsible for the way the sport is played and organised today. American baseball teams were some of the first in any sport to start paying their players and the game's present-day rules were invented there.

America's Major League Baseball (MLB) is also the biggest competition in the world and its influence has spread to countless other regions, most notably Central and South America, and East Asia.

Baseball is played by two teams of nine, who take turns to 'bat' (hit a ball) and 'field' (defend the field). They try to score runs by hitting the ball and then running around four bases without being caught or fielded out. Swing like you mean It!

PITCHER

The pitcher throws a pitch overarm from a raised mound to the home plate 18.4m away. Cleveland Indians pitcher Bob Feller is credited with throwing a record fastball at 173.6 km/h back in 1946!

HOME RUN!

A home run is the best shot in baseball. It happens when the batter blasts the ball so far – usually over the outfield wall – they are able to run around all four bases.

Each runner 'on base' also advances to the home plate, so some home runs can result in a whopping four runs being scored for the batting side.

BAT

League bats are made from wood, whereas college bats are metal.

CATCHER

One of the toughest jobs in baseball! The player crouches behind home plate to catch the ball from the pitcher and direct defensive play.

KIT

FIELDING GLOVE

Has separate fingers and a deep 'pocket' with open webbing on the side for trapped dirt to fall through.

BASEBALL CAP

This unique style was first worn in the 1860s. The peak protects the player's eyes from the sun.

BATTING HELMET

Worn to protect the batter's head. Ear 'flaps' were introduced in 1983.

UNIFORM

Teams have a 'home' kit (often white) and an 'away' kit (darker). Originally, coloured stockings identified the teams.

OUTFIELD

Outfielders stand here. Their main job is to catch 'fly' balls hit into the air, and to throw the ball to the players on base.

DIAMOND

The name for the field where the game is played. 'Father of Baseball' Alexander Cartwright was the first to draw this diamond shape back in 1845.

FIRST BASEMAN

Ideally tall and left-handed so they can easily throw the ball in-field, the first baseman fields the area near first base.

BALL

Just 23 centimetres in diameter, the stitching on a baseball can measure up to 1.5 kilometres long!

FACTS OF THE MATTER

- The U.S. military designed **GRENADES** during World War II to be the same size and weight as a baseball. The sport was so popular, they believed any young American would be able to throw it properly.
- One of baseball's earliest recorded games involved members of the **PRINCE OF WALES'** (later to become King Edward VII) family, at an indoor match played in London back in 1748.
- References to early baseball were made in Jane Austen's 1798 novel **NORTHANGER ABBEY**. The main character, Catherine Morland preferred 'cricket, base ball, riding on horseback and running about'– not very ladylike for an Austen heroine!
- The rules of modern-day baseball were set down by the **KNICKERBOCKER CLUB** of New York – one of the first-ever organised baseball teams. For example, until 1872, pitchers used to pitch underarm.
- Approximately **70 BASEBALLS** are used per game. Just think how many that adds up to in a season!
- The final game of America's Major League Baseball is the **WORLD SERIES**. The New York Yankees have won it a record 27 times.
- African American players were banned from playing in the Major League for the first half of the 20th century. That led to 'Negro leagues' being formed, where some of the **WORLD'S BEST PLAYERS** could be found.
- Hot dogs are the most popular food eaten by baseball fans. In fact, America's Hot Dog and Sausage Council estimated **21,357,316 HOT DOGS** were eaten in the 2014 Major League season!

THE FIELD

SECOND BASE

THIRD BASE

FIRST BASE

PITCHER'S MOUND

FOUL LINE
A foul is called if the batter hits the ball straight over this line.

HOME PLATE
The batter stands here, ready to hit the on-coming pitch.

PRESIDENTIAL FIRST PITCHES

In 1910, President William Howard Taft become the first president to throw out a ceremonial first pitch – a tradition that lasts to this day, although declined by President Trump in 2017.

RULES

» Both teams bat for nine innings. An inning ends when three players on the batting team are out.

» If it's a tie after nine innings, extra innings are played until a team wins.

» The pitcher 'delivers' the ball overarm.

» The batter tries to hit the ball to 'get on base', and then become a runner.

» Runners stop at bases and advance when the next batter hits the ball.

» A run is scored when a runner reaches home plate.

» If the batter hits the ball over the outfield wall, the batter and any runners automatically advance to the home plate. This is called a 'home run'.

» The pitcher can get the batter out by throwing three strikes.

» A 'strike' is when the batter swings and misses or fails to swing at a legal pitch.

» A pitch is illegal if it is thrown outside the strike zone. If four illegal balls are pitched, the batter walks to first base.

» The batter is out if a fielder touches the base before they can run to it.

» The batter is also out if they hit ball in the air and it is caught by a catcher.

CATCHER'S MITT

This is much deeper than other fielders' gloves, almost bucket-like to help catch the batter 'out'.

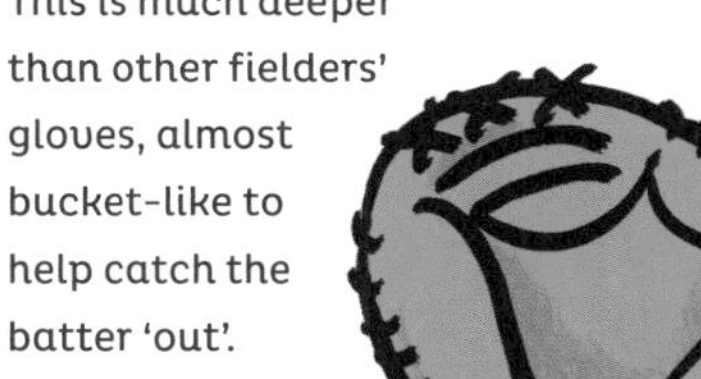

PITCHER'S GLOVE

No holes in the webbing hide the pitcher's grip, and the direction of pitch, from the batter.

FIELD HOCKEY

The ancient Greeks were among the first to play hockey, back in 510 BC.

It was revamped and modernised in Scotland during the 19th century and has developed into one of the fastest team sports around, often drawing comparisons with football. In fact, it is sometimes called 'football with sticks'!

Two teams of 11 players use hooked sticks to hit, push and 'dribble' a hard ball around a pitch and try to score goals by getting it past the goalkeeper. The team with the most goals at the end of the game is the winner.

Hockey has been an integral part of the Olympics since 1928, and nowadays, it is thought that more than three million people play hockey across five continents. Jolly hockey sticks indeed!

POSITIONS

GOALKEEPER

ROLE: To stop the ball from going in goal!
SKILLS: Bravery and quick reflexes

DEFENDERS

ROLE: Split into centre-backs or full-backs, defenders stop opposition attacks and set up counter-attacks.
SKILLS: Positioning and strength

MIDFIELDERS

ROLE: Linking play between defence and attack
SKILLS: All-rounders. They often set the tempo.

FORWARDS

ROLE: To score goals!
SKILLS: Wingers are often very fast and good at crossing to the central attackers, who score

GAELIC ROOTS

An old version of field hockey, called 'shinty', is still played in the Scottish Highlands. The rules are closer to Irish hurling, as players are allowed to use the two sides of their stick, and play the ball in the air, both of which are illegal in field hockey.

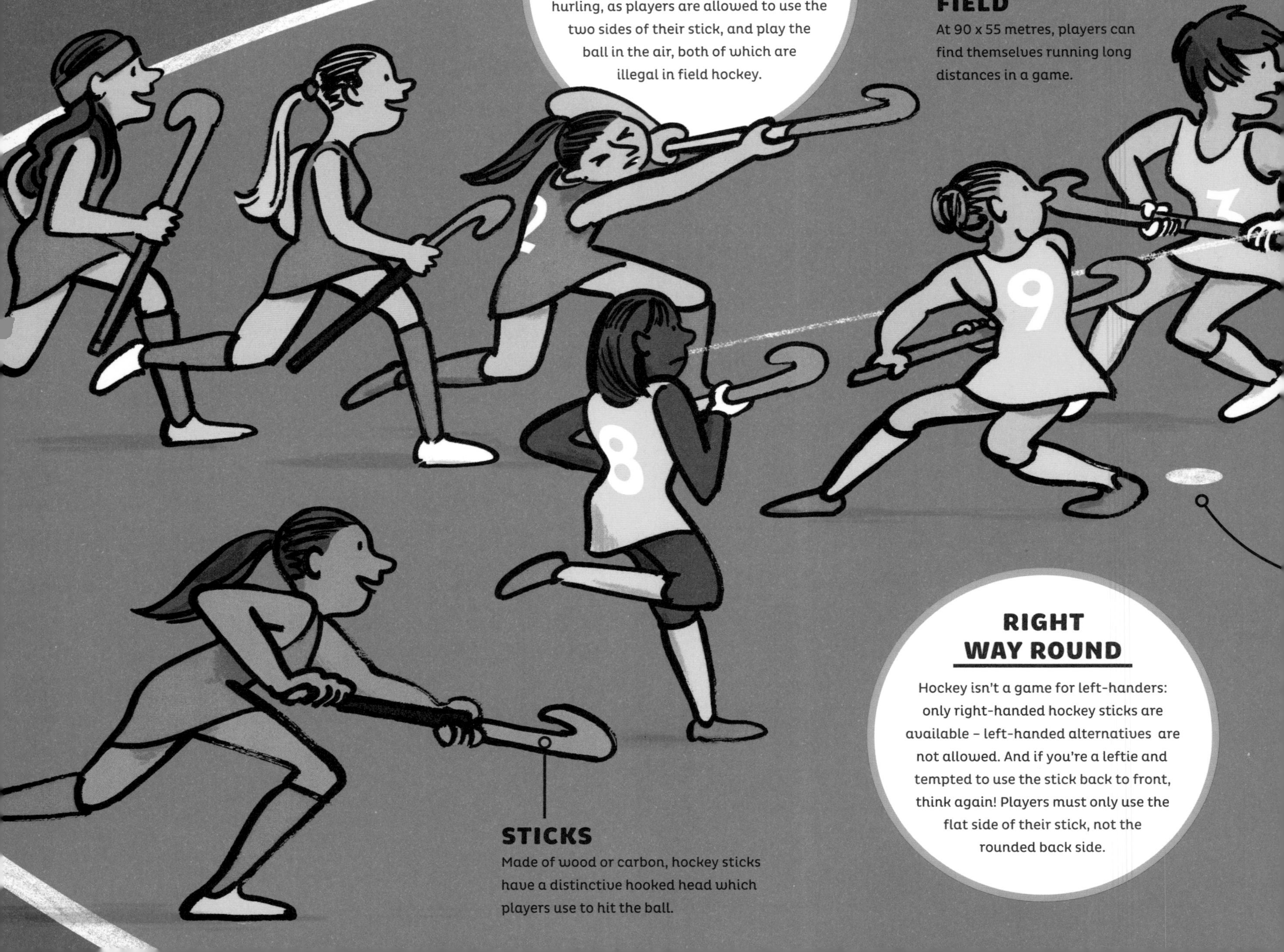

FIELD

At 90 x 55 metres, players can find themselves running long distances in a game.

RIGHT WAY ROUND

Hockey isn't a game for left-handers: only right-handed hockey sticks are available – left-handed alternatives are not allowed. And if you're a leftie and tempted to use the stick back to front, think again! Players must only use the flat side of their stick, not the rounded back side.

STICKS

Made of wood or carbon, hockey sticks have a distinctive hooked head which players use to hit the ball.

THE PITCH

SHOOTING CIRCLE Players must shoot within this area.

PENALTY CORNERS are taken here.

HALF WAY LINE

23 METRE LINE

23 METRE LINE

BALL
This plastic ball (which can have a cork core), is small in diameter at 7 centimetres, but heavy in weight at 155 grams, making it fast-moving on the pitch.

GOALKEEPER
Wears equipment to protect face, legs and chest. And they need it... Hockey balls can travel over 100 km/h!

PENALTY SPOT
Penalty shots are taken from here.

LAW AND ORDER

The referee is known as the umpire in field hockey. They are armed with three cards to punish rule infringements:

GREEN: warns the player

YELLOW: temporary suspension from the game for a minimum of five minutes

RED: permanent exclusion from the game.

FACTS OF THE MATTER

- Stick and ball games similar to hockey were played in a number of ancient civilisations. Another more recent version, played in 19th century Scotland, went by the name of '**SHINTY**'!
- Hockey is the **THIRD-MOST WATCHED** sport in the world, after football and cricket.
- Men's hockey has the **FASTEST SWING SPEED** of any sport, often reaching speeds of more than **160KM/H**. That is faster than a golfer swings his club or baseball player swings his bat.
- Hockey was spread throughout the British Empire by the British army and is extremely popular in **INDIA**, **PAKISTAN** and **AUSTRALIA** as a result.
- There are four main positions in hockey, and the average player can **FLICK THE BALL** between 80–110km/h.
- **LEFT HANDED?** Tough luck! There is no such thing as a left-handed hockey stick. Left-handed players must simply learn to use a right-handed stick.
- The Indian men's team has won the **OLYMPIC GOLD MEDAL** on eight separate occasions – at least four more times than any other nation.
- Hockey players are extremely fit, often travelling more than **8 KILOMETRES** in a single game.

RULES

» Matches are 70 minutes long, split into two halves of 35 minutes each.

» Goals must be scored within the shooting circle, meaning no long-shots are allowed.

» The goalkeeper is the only one who can touch the ball with their hands.

» Fouls are awarded for various rule infringements such as obstruction or dangerous use of the stick. For fouls around the goal area, a short corner – or penalty corner – is awarded.

» A penalty stroke is awarded for major infringements inside the shooting circle. The attacking player then gets a free shot against the goalkeeper from the penalty spot.

» Most scoring chances in hockey games come from penalty corners.

» Unlike almost every other team sport, hockey players are not allowed to shield the ball with their body.

» Long corners are awarded if the ball hits a defending player and then crosses the end line.

BASKETBALL

A game of humble beginnings, basketball is now played by more than 25 million people throughout the United States.

And many more are fans of one of this fast-paced, end-to-end team sport. Matches are usually thrilling spectacles, with scores regularly running into the hundreds of points. Two teams of five players try and score points by bouncing or passing a ball around a hard court and putting it through a hoop.

The idea came from a Canadian P.E. teacher called James Naismith in 1891. He wanted to invent an indoor sport to keep his students from being bored when they could not play sports outside in bad winter weather.

While many of Naismith's fundamental rules are still in place, over time the game has become increasingly sophisticated, quicker and more physically demanding.

RULES

» Five players from each team are on court during play. Each team also has seven substitutes they can rotate at any time.

» Players 'dribble' the ball by bouncing it on the court as they run.

» A 'travelling' violation is called if players run with the ball without bouncing it.

» Professional matches are split into four periods of 12 minutes each, and an extra five minutes is played if the scores are level after this time.

» Teams have just 24 seconds to make a shot after getting the ball. If they fail to do so, they lose possession to the other team.

» Once a team is in the attacking half of the court, they cannot go back over the half-way line.

» Points are scored every time the ball goes through the hoop. Different plays are worth a different number of points.

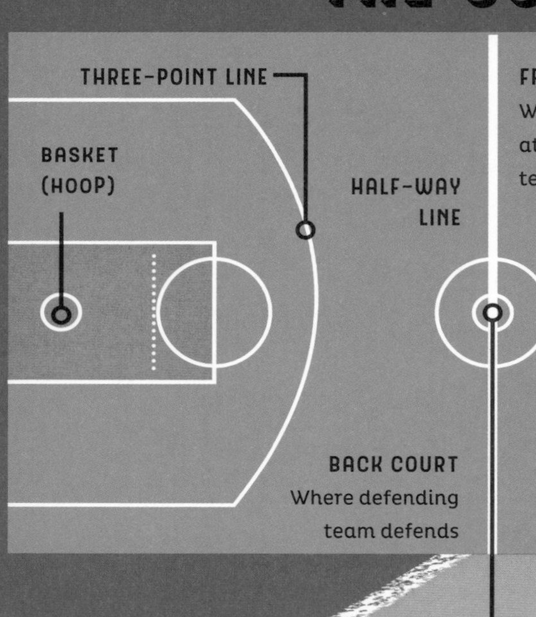

REFEREE
The rule-enforcer wears a distinctive kit of black and white stripes and is usually assisted by two umpires.

WHEELY GOOD

Wheelchair basketball is played by athletes with disabilities and is just as ferocious and thrilling as the able-bodied game.

This form of basketball places great emphasis on the arms, and athletes need incredible upper-body strength to power up and down the court, as well as impeccable technique when it comes to shooting.

Such is its popularity, able-bodied athletes often play the game too.

SLAM DUNK!

To make this crowd-pleasing shot, a player jumps high and puts the ball straight through the hoop.

BACK-BOARD

Players use this to bounce the ball off, into the hoop. It was invented to stop spectators from interfering with shots, as the hoop was originally nailed to the viewing balcony!

HOOP

The hoop stands 3.05m from the ground. Corey 'Thunder' Law threw the longest-ever successful shot at a distance of 33.5m.

BALL

Dimpled for grip, men's are 75–76 centimetres, while the women's are smaller. Originally brown, today's balls are orange.

THE COURT

Court sizes can vary, but in the NBA it is 29 metres long and 15 metres wide – twice the original size!

FREE THROW LINE

Free throws, awarded for various infringements, are taken from here (4.6 metres from the hoop) and are worth one point.

THREE POINT ARC

Baskets scored from outside this line are worth three points. From inside they are worth two.

FACTS OF THE MATTER

- The original hoop used was a **FRUIT BASKET!** Games would be halted after every point for a janitor to retrieve the ball from the fruit basket. Eventually people saw sense and removed the bottom!
- Basketball was once played with a football ball, which was not easy to dribble. As a result, **DRIBBLING** did not become a major part of the game until the ball changed in 1950.
- Teams were made up of **NINE PLAYERS** until 1897 because there were nine players on a baseball team.
- The team was reduced to five because teams of **AMERICAN FOOTBALL** players, which used to be made up of 10 players (now 11) would come into the gym when it was **RAINING** and it was easier to split them into two teams of five.
- America's NBA players are among the **BEST-PAID** sportsmen anywhere on the planet. In 2016, LeBron James earned **$77.2 MILLION** (£61.6 million).
- A lot of basketball players are extremely **TALL**. The tallest-ever professionals are former stars Gheorghe Muresan and Manute Bol – who both stood at a towering 2 metres 31 centimetres.
- The **BOSTON CELTICS** have won 17 NBA Championships – the most of any team.
- The women's counterpart of the NBA, called the **WNBA**, was formed in 1997.

AMERICAN FOOTBALL

America's most-watched sport combines speed, strategy, teamwork... and aggression!

As its name suggests, American football originated in the United States, although it was influenced by games such as rugby and football. The similarities are clear, but the complex rule changes made in 1880 by the 'Father of American Football', Walter Camp, make it unique.

While the first American football game was played 11 years before, at a college match in 1869 between New Jersey (now the Princeton Tigers) and Rutgers Queenstown, Camp's ideas form the basis of the game seen in America's National Football League (NFL) today.

The aim of the game is to score points by taking the ball into the other team's end zone, or through the posts. Two teams of 11 players work an oval ball up the pitch towards their opponents' end zone, by throwing the ball to a teammate, or running with it until tackled... Ooph!

RULES

» American football is based around 'downs'.

» These are essentially chances. Each team has four chances to gain 10 yards by either running with the ball or throwing it to a teammate.

» If the team gains 10 yards within four 'downs', they earn four more chances to gain another 10 yards.

» If they don't gain 10 yards, they lose possession. Teams often kick the ball (a punt) on the fourth 'down' to get the ball as far from their end zone as possible.

» 'Downs' are started at the line of scrimmage – an imaginary line separating the two teams; something Walter Camp introduced.

» The centre throws or hands the ball back to a player – almost always the quarterback. This is called 'the snap'. They hand the ball off to a teammate to run or throw it to someone further up the field.

» Penalties are awarded for various violations, such as offside, pushing in the back or obstruction.

» Teams are made up of 11 players.

» A match is split into four 15-minute quarters.

BALL

This oval, laced ball is made from cowhide or rubber, and is 28 centimetres long.

MATCH OFFICIALS

Seven officials operate at the same time. They throw yellow flags onto the pitch to indicate fouls.

YARD MARKERS

White markings on the pitch help players, officials and fans keep track of how far the ball has travelled.

FIELD

The field is 110 metres long and 48.5 metres wide.

THE SUPER BOWL

This is the championship game of the NFL between the two best teams of the season – always on a Sunday.

It is the most-watched television event in the whole of the United States, attracting more than 100 million viewers in the country.

The cost to advertise on television during the event is estimated at $5 million for a 30-second slot!

END ZONE

The end zone, where touchdowns are scored, is 9.1 metres deep.

TOUCHDOWN!

When a player takes the ball into the other side's end zone, their team receives six points. In fact, the ball doesn't have to 'touch down'. Peyton Manning broke the single season passing touchdown record in 2013, throwing 55 touchdowns.

A TYPICAL FORMATION

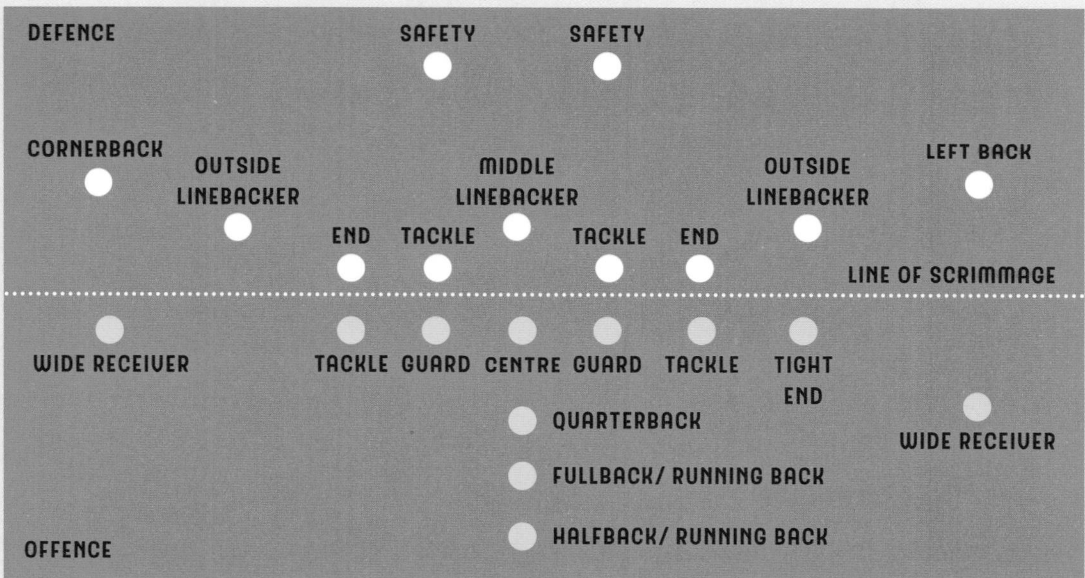

FIELD GOALS & CONVERSIONS

Kicking the ball through the posts after a touchdown is worth an extra point, while taking a field goal kick during play is worth three extra points.

GOALPOSTS

The ball must be kicked between these posts to score points.

FACTS OF THE MATTER

- The sport is often referred to as '**GRIDIRON FOOTBALL**' or 'gridiron', a reference to how the playing field once looked.
- Games often last around **THREE HOURS**, but the ball is typically in play for only **11 MINUTES** of that time!
- **DEION SANDERS** played baseball **AND** American football professionally. He is the only player ever to hit a home run and score a touchdown in the same week.
- During World War II, NFL teams lost players to military service. So, in the 1943 season, the Philadelphia Eagles and the Pittsburgh Steelers merged to form the **PENNSYLVANIA STEAGLES**.
- **CHEERLEADERS** often perform at the games, but six NFL teams don't employ them: the Bears, the Browns, the Bills, the Steelers, the Giants and the Packers.
- The Miami Dolphins are the only team ever to remain **UNBEATEN** for a whole season.
- Although there are only 11 players on the pitch at one time, teams are often made up of around **50 PLAYERS** who can be switched between downs.
- Teams will employ players for specialised positions, such as the kicker. **THE KICKER** usually only comes onto the pitch to kick field goals or punt the ball.

KIT

MOUTH GUARD

Helps protect the player's teeth and jaw - an essential piece of kit for players who engage in lots of tackles!

HELMET

Introduced in 1939, this is made of hard plastic and includes a chin strap and protective mask.

SHOULDER PADS

These have a hard shell with shock-absorbing foam underneath.

SHOES

Spikes underneath, called 'cleats', grip the grass.

RUGBY

Rugby is a fierce, full-contact sport.

There are several different versions of the game, but rugby union is by far the most popular game, with almost 2.5 million registered players – some of the fittest athletes in the world – in more than 120 countries.

Two teams of 15 players handle an oval ball and aim to score points by touching the ball down (a 'try') in the opposition's 'try zone' or, by kicking the ball through their posts.

The game was said to have been invented by school pupil William Webb Ellis, who apparently picked up the ball during a game of football in 1823 and ran with it in his hands. This story has been widely discredited, but has gone down in rugby folklore nonetheless. The Rugby World Cup trophy is even named after him!

POSITIONS

FULL BACK
ROLE: Receives deep kicks, catches high balls

NUMBER 8
ROLE: Back of scrum, strong ball-carrier

WINGER
ROLE: Finishes attacks and scores tries, fast

FLANKER
ROLE: Excellent all-rounder, lots of energy!

CENTRE
ROLE: Strong runner with an eye for a try

LOCK
ROLE: Second row, scrum powerhouse

FLY HALF
ROLE: Good attacker, often the penalty kicker

HOOKER
ROLE: front row, coordinates the scrum

SCRUM HALF
ROLE: Link between the forwards and the backs

PROP
ROLE: front row, strong!

ALL IN A NAME

The sport is named after Rugby School, where William Webb Ellis was a pupil. The game took a while before the rules were refined... in 1839, when the school had a visit from Queen Adelaide, the two teams were School House (75) versus The Rest (225)!

SCRUM

A scrum is used to restart play after a minor offence. The forwards from both sides lock together and try to win possession of the ball.

PITCH

The pitch can be up to 100 metres long and 70 metres wide.

RULES

» Games are 80 minutes long, divided into two 40-minute halves.

» Players can run with the ball, kick it and pass it. Passes must be sideways or backwards – never forwards!

» Each team tries to tackle the player holding the ball to the ground.

» A try (five points) is scored if a player reaches the opposition's goal line and touches the ball down.

» That team then gets a chance to kick the ball between the posts for a conversion (two points).

» Play is restarted after a minor foul with a scrum, when eight players from each team lock horns and push to win possession of the ball under their feet.

» If the ball goes over the side line, play is restarted with a lineout.

» During a penalty kick, the team can either try for a goal, which is worth three points, or kick the ball out of play.

ANOTHER LEAGUE

Rugby League is a popular version of rugby, particularly in the north of England and Australia. Differences between the games include:

- Teams consist of 13 players and 10 substitutes.
- Teams are given six tackles to try and score. If they are tackled six times before scoring, possession is given to the other team, who then get six chances to score.
- A try is worth four points rather than five. Conversions are worth two.

FACTS OF THE MATTER

- Rugby balls were not always oval. They were originally plum-shaped due to the shape of the **PIGS' BLADDERS** they used to be made from.
- The old balls had to be **BLOWN UP BY HAND**. In the mid-1800s, Richard Lindon, a rugby-ball maker, had his wife help blowing them up. She fell ill as a result and eventually **DIED**.
- In 1906, Gerald Hamilton scored a drop goal for South Africa against England from 77.7 yards (71 metres). It remains the **LONGEST-EVER** successful drop goal.
- Although it is now the highest-scoring play, a **'TRY'** originally had **NO POINTS** value. It only allowed the attacking team an attempt to kick the ball at the goal.
- Rugby union has only been an Olympic sport once, in 1924. The USA won it, making them the **REIGNING OLYMPIC RUGBY CHAMPIONS**.
- **RUGBY SEVENS** – a seven-a-side version of the game – is now an Olympic sport.
- Rugby was an **AMATEUR SPORT** until it turned professional in 1995.
- **PROFESSIONAL** first-team players earn a yearly salary of **£70,000** on average.
- The **WHISTLE** used for the opening match of every World Cup is the same one used back in 1905 for a match between England and New Zealand.

VOLLEYBALL

Almost every country on the planet plays volleyball.

Its basic rules, which have become even simpler as the game has evolved, make it easy for people to take part. As a result, it is practised and watched all over the world – from the huge number of indoor courts throughout Europe to the luscious beaches of South America, Australia and Africa. It was introduced as an Olympic sport in Japan, at the Tokyo games in 1964.

Originally called 'mintonette', the first-ever match can be traced back as far as 1895. William G. Morgan, a physical education director at the YMCA in Holyoke, Massachusetts, created volleyball by trying to combine four sports: basketball, baseball, tennis and handball!

Many of his original rules are still in place: the game is played by two teams of six who hit a ball – usually with their hands or arms – over a net. If the ball hits the floor within the boundaries of the court or leaves the court, a point is won.

RULES

» Each team has six players.

» The game is started with an overarm serve.

» Teams can touch the ball three times on their side of the net.

» The first two touches are normally used to 'set' the play.

» The third is the 'spike', used to hit the ball over the net – usually with great power.

» No player can touch the ball twice in succession.

» The other team tries to block the spike and return the ball.

» Points are won if the ball hits the ground, leaves the court, or for a bad serve.

» Whoever wins the point serves next time.

» The first team to 25 points wins the set, as long as they are two points ahead of the other team.

» 'Best-of-five' sets wins the whole match.

» If a last set is played, it only goes to 15 points.

BEACH FOR THE STARS

An adaptation of the original sport, beach volleyball is played on a smaller-sized court on sand, with just two players on each team. It has enjoyed a rapid increase in popularity since it was made an Olympic sport at the games in Atlanta, Georgia, in 1996.

In some parts of the world, the most famous volleyball stars prefer this format. It is even played on the ice-cold beaches of Brighton, on England's southeast coast!

KIT

Women wear a T-shirt and shorts, while men wear sleeveless tops and long trunks... making beach volleyball the only Olympic sport with rules stopping players from wearing too much!

FIRST REFEREE

Standing on a raised side platform, the referee controls play and always has the final say on decisions.

SERVE

The server must stand behind the 'end line' at the back of the court.

THE COURT

	Attack area	Attack area	
Left back	Left forward	Right forward	Right back
Centre back	Centre forward	Centre forward	Centre back
Right back	Right forward	Left forward	Left back

Net

Serving area

FACTS OF THE MATTER

- Volleyball founder, William G. Morgan, thought the game an **EASY ALTERNATIVE** to basketball for weaker athletes at the YMCA where he worked.
- Modern-day competitors might disagree – a spike can reach **120KM/H**, faster than the UK speed limit!
- A player jumps **300 TIMES** in an average game.
- **PRIOR TO 1999**, points could only be scored by the team that was serving. Back then, if the other team won, they only won the right to serve.
- Matches could go on for hours, so in 1999, the rules changed: a point could be won on every turn, making the game shorter and more **EXCITING FOR TV**.
- Players **ROTATE** around the court each time the serve is won, so that everyone gets a turn in each position.
- Players can use **ANY PART** of their body to hit the ball.
- Rookie players earn just £7,000 a season – far less than other sports – however, the world's best players can earn more than **£100,000 A YEAR**.

BALL

A volleyball has an inflated rubber inside, with 18-20 leather panels on the outside.

DIG: When a player creates a playable ball from an opponent's attack.

GOOFY: A player's wrong-footed jump.

KONG: A one-handed block – often played in response to being caught off-guard.

PANCAKE: When a player places their hand flat on the ground, and the ball bounces off it.

NET

A volleyball net is comparatively high, at 2.43 metres for men and 2.24 metres for women.

THE LIBERO

A specialist defensive player. Each team is allowed only one.

POSITION: Back row

SPECIALITY: Defence, passing and 'digging out' spikes

OTHER SKILLS: Lightning speed, sharp reflexes, aggression

INTRODUCED: 1998

The ball must land inside or on these 5-centimetre-thick lines, otherwise it is 'out'.

NETBALL

Netball is a non-contact – but hotly contested – team sport.

Although invented by the English, netball is most popular in New Zealand and is played mainly by women. It is based on early basketball, but there are two main differences between both sports. Netball teams have seven players instead of five, and players are not allowed to run with the ball. Players pass the ball around the court and score goals by putting it through a raised hoop. Players can only move in certain parts of the court, so teamwork and strong passing skills are vital.

BALL

Made of leather or rubber, a netball is comparatively light at around 450 grams.

GOALPOST

Attackers score one point every time the ball goes through the net, 3.05 metres from the ground.

GOAL KEEPER

The goal keeper tries to stop the opposition from scoring.

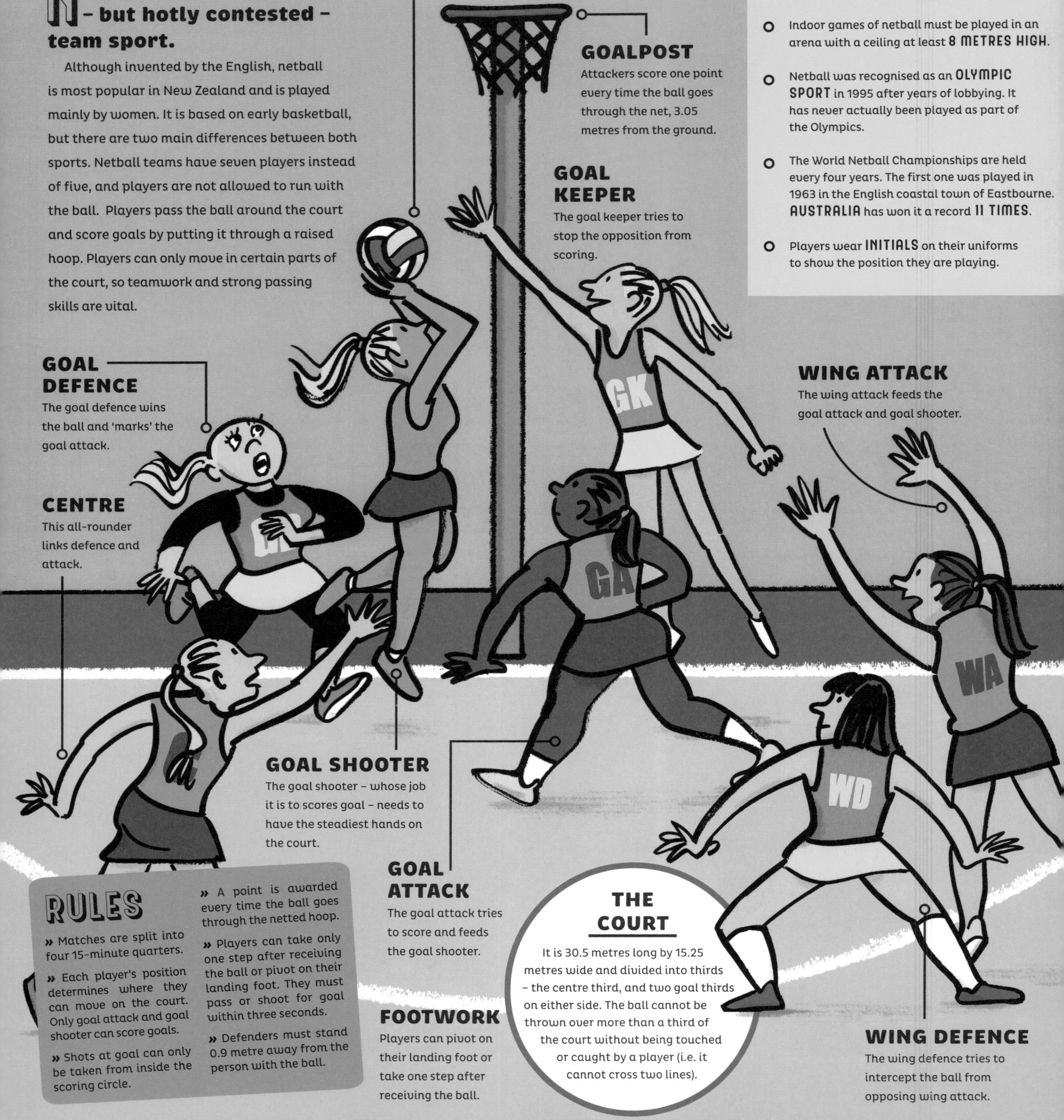

GOAL DEFENCE

The goal defence wins the ball and 'marks' the goal attack.

CENTRE

This all-rounder links defence and attack.

WING ATTACK

The wing attack feeds the goal attack and goal shooter.

GOAL SHOOTER

The goal shooter – whose job it is to scores goal – needs to have the steadiest hands on the court.

GOAL ATTACK

The goal attack tries to score and feeds the goal shooter.

FOOTWORK

Players can pivot on their landing foot or take one step after receiving the ball.

WING DEFENCE

The wing defence tries to intercept the ball from opposing wing attack.

FACTS OF THE MATTER

- Although it started in England, netball is most popular in **NEW ZEALAND**, where around 80,000 people play the game.
- Indoor games of netball must be played in an arena with a ceiling at least **8 METRES HIGH**.
- Netball was recognised as an **OLYMPIC SPORT** in 1995 after years of lobbying. It has never actually been played as part of the Olympics.
- The World Netball Championships are held every four years. The first one was played in 1963 in the English coastal town of Eastbourne. **AUSTRALIA** has won it a record **11 TIMES**.
- Players wear **INITIALS** on their uniforms to show the position they are playing.

RULES

» Matches are split into four 15-minute quarters.

» Each player's position determines where they can move on the court. Only goal attack and goal shooter can score goals.

» Shots at goal can only be taken from inside the scoring circle.

» A point is awarded every time the ball goes through the netted hoop.

» Players can take only one step after receiving the ball or pivot on their landing foot. They must pass or shoot for goal within three seconds.

» Defenders must stand 0.9 metre away from the person with the ball.

THE COURT

It is 30.5 metres long by 15.25 metres wide and divided into thirds – the centre third, and two goal thirds on either side. The ball cannot be thrown over more than a third of the court without being touched or caught by a player (i.e. it cannot cross two lines).

HANDBALL

Handball combines the skills of football, basketball and water polo.

Two teams of seven players – one goalkeeper and six outfielders – move a ball around a court with their hands and try to score goals by throwing it into the opposition goal.

The game as we know it today originated in northern Europe in the late 19th century. However, some believe women in ancient Rome were among the first to play it.

THE CIRCLE RUNNER

Also known as a pivot or line player.

POSITION: Offensive, but stands with their back to the opposition goal

SPECIALITY: To try to get in between the defenders and create space for a shot

SKILLS: Physically tough and aggressive

FACTS OF THE MATTER

- Handball is normally played on an indoor court, but **BEACH HANDBALL** has become increasingly popular in recent years. It is played on a much smaller pitch.
- The coach, as well as team members, can receive a **TWO-MINUTE SUSPENSION** from the match. A player takes the coach's time.
- The **FIRST-EVER** international handball game was between Germany and Belgium in 1925.
- Handball is generally considered to be the **SECOND-FASTEST** team sport in the world, after ice hockey.
- The U.S. astronauts who orbited the moon on **APOLLO 10** in 1969 were all keen handballers.

GOAL

It is 2 metres high and 3 metres wide.

BALL

The size of the ball, its weight and softness differs between the men and women's game. In the men's game it is 19 centimetres in diameter and weighs between 425-475 grams. The women's ball is 18cm and weighs 325-400 grams.

REFEREES

There are two referees in handball They stand diagonally aligned so they can watch one side each.

GOAL AREA

Only the goalkeeper is allowed in this area.

THE PITCH

The court is bigger than a netball court, at 40 metres long and 20 metres wide.

RULES

» A standard game is 60 minutes, divided into two halves of 30 minutes each.

» Goals must be scored from outside the goal area or while diving into it.

» When in possession of the ball, players can dribble by bouncing the ball or take up to three steps for three seconds at a time without dribbling.

» The ball cannot be passed back to the goalkeeper at any point.

» Free throws are awarded for minor infringements from where it took place.

» A 'seven-metre throw' is awarded if a clear scoring chance is unfairly blocked. A player then has a free shot at the goal from only seven metres. It usually results in a goal.

LACROSSE

Lacrosse, the 'fastest game on two feet', is a contact team sport, which showcases incredible finesse and brute strength. It was originally played by Native Americans as far back as AD 1100 and early games were epic affairs, contested by hundreds of tribesmen on each side. Nowadays, it is popular in American and Canadian colleges, and its profile continues to rise all over the world.

Lacrosse players handle a small rubber ball with a long stick called a 'crosse', which has a net on the end to control the ball. The aim is to move the ball around a pitch and try to score goals past the opposition goalkeeper, while defenders try to stop opposing players.

The game is played by men and women, although the men's game is considered far rougher! Body checks (barging) and stick slashes are commonplace and players need to be extremely fit to cope with the physical demands and sheer amount of running involved in the game.

RULES

» Lacrosse teams are made up of 10 players on each side – four defenders (including the goalkeeper), three attackers and three midfielders.

» Men's lacrosse games are divided into four quarters of 15 minutes each. Women's matches are two halves of 30 minutes, while high school and college games differ.

» Matches are started with a face-off – the ball sits on the ground between two players who contest it after the referee blows a whistle.

» Players can body check their opponents when they are within 4.5 metres of them. This is essentially a barge from the front between the waist and shoulders.

» The winner is the team that scores the most goals. If scores are level, the game enters a final 15-minute sudden death. The next goal wins, but if there is no score after 15 minutes, a tie is called.

BALL

The small, hard ball can be thrown around at speeds of more than 100 km/h, meaning the players have to wear protective goggles.

OFFENSIVE HALF

Three players must be in the offensive half at all times.

KIT

GLOVES

Designed to protect hands and wrists from the ball and body checks. Players can cut out the palm to help with gripping and controlling their crosse.

HELMET

Worn by all players to provide protection for the head. It is compulsory in the men's game, but optional in the less-physical women's version.

THE CROSSE

The stick used to handle the ball and usually made from hollow metal. It has a mesh on the end known as 'the pocket', which is used to carry and catch the ball. It measures around a metre in length, although four players (normally defensive enforcers) from each team can deploy a long crosse (1.3-1.8 metres).

FACTS OF THE MATTER

- The Native American **IROQUOIS PEOPLE** were some of the first to play the game. They inhabited the northeast coast of America, where the sport remains hugely popular today.
- In 1763, an American tribe called **THE OJIBWE** staged a game of lacrosse to distract British soldiers, who had occupied Fort Michilimackinac. The tactic allowed them to gain entrance and claim control of the fort.
- In fact, Native American tribes used the sport as a means to **PREPARE** young men **FOR WAR**.
- In 2014, a man called **ZACK DORN** hit the fastest-ever recorded lacrosse shot at a whopping 51 metres per second. But Zack wasn't a player... he was **A FAN**!
- Unfortunately for Zack, his record was beaten by lacrosse star **PATRICK LUEHRSEN** (53.6 metres per second) the following year.
- During the 1930s, the Canadians invented **'BOX LACROSSE'**, a version of the sport, with six players per team, played on a covered ice hockey rink.
- The best players play in America's **MAJOR LEAGUE**. This was started in 1999, and despite showcasing the globe's top talent, it remains only semi-professional.
- Lacrosse has only been part of the official **OLYMPIC PROGRAMME** twice: in 1904 and 1908, when it was a men-only competition.

GOAL

The netted goal is small and square: 1.83 metres high and wide.

THE CREASE

Opponents are not allowed to step inside this 5.5 metre-wide area around the goal, but can reach in with their stick to pick up the ball.

THE FIELD

Players charge at speed up and down the 100 x 55 metre field.

REFEREE

The referee is sometimes helped by an umpire and a field judge but has the final say on all decisions.

POSITIONS

GOALTENDER

ROLE: To stop shots and direct the defence

DEFENCEMEN

ROLE: To stop attackers from scoring

ATTACKMEN

ROLE: To feed fellow attackers and to score goals.

THE FIELD

WING AREA

DEFENCE AREA

ATTACK AREA

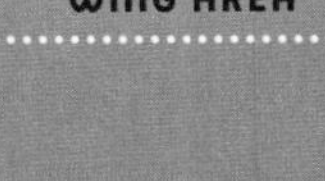

PENALTY BOX
Players are sent here for varying amounts of time as punishment for infringements

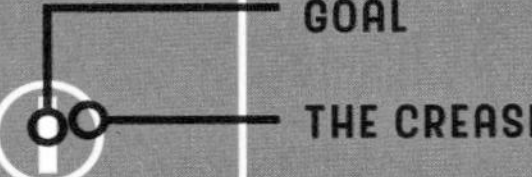

ICE HOCKEY

Ice hockey is fast, furious and physical.

One of sport's roughest and most exhilarating games, it places massive demands on its players. Brutal matches take place on an ice rink and require skill, speed, agility and, perhaps most importantly, extreme grit. Body checks are an integral part of the sport, and fights between rival players are not a rare sight.

Two teams compete to score goals by working a small rubber puck around the ice with a stick and past the opposing goaltender. Moving the puck quickly and accurately is key and players need impeccable skating technique. It is one of North America's most loved sports and has a huge following in certain parts of Europe, where some believe it originated. While its exact origins are largely unknown, it was influenced by older stick-and-ball games such as field hockey that have European roots. However, the rules which make up the sport as we know it today were invented in Canada and the United States.

RULES

» Teams are made of up to 22 skaters, with six allowed on the ice at any one time – a goaltender, two defenders and three attackers.

» Games start with a puck being dropped between two opposing players, who contest to win possession in a 'face-off'.

» Games are divided into three periods of 20 minutes, with a sudden death followed by a penalty shootout, if scores are level.

» Offside occurs when a player travels over the blue line before the puck.

» 'Icing' occurs when a player hits the puck past the central and end red lines. This rule is to stop long passing.

» If offside or icing is called the game is restarted with a face-off from one of the eight face-off spots on the rink.

» Penalty shots are awarded if a player is obstructed before they can shoot. They get a free shot against the goaltender.

PENALTIES & POWERPLAY

Players serve time-penalties inside a perspex box on the edge of the rink. The penalty time varies from two minutes for a minor violation, such as tripping or slashing, to 10 minutes for 'intent to injure another player'. The opposition team then has a man advantage and enters the 'powerplay', while the defending team is on 'penalty kill'.

The penalised player can re-enter the ice before the penalty time is over if the other side scores.

OFFICIALS
The two referees and two linesmen wear black-and-white uniforms.

SKATES
Skaters move across the ice in bladed boots.

PUCK
Made of vulcanised rubber, the wide, flat puck weighs in at a heavy 170 grams, or thereabouts.

JARGON

FIVE-HOLE: Nickname for the space between the goaltender's legs. This is one of the five open areas where an outfield player can score.

CHANGING ON THE FLY: When players are substituted without stopping play – a rule unique to ice hockey.

ENFORCER: An intimidating presence on the ice. The enforcer's job is to intimidate opponents to make them think twice about taking cheap shots at any of his teammates.

PROTECTIVE EQUIPMENT
Players wear helmets, body armour, gloves and pads.

GOALTENDER
The last line of defence wears much bigger pads and has a bigger stick.

FACTS OF THE MATTER

- The game's rules were set by the National Hockey Association (NHA), who formed in Montreal, Canada, in 1910. **THE NATIONAL HOCKEY LEAGUE** (NHL) replaced the NHA in 1917. The league now includes 23 American teams and seven from Canada.
- Until 1930, only **BACKWARDS PASSES** were allowed in ice hockey.
- The gruelling regular season in the NHL is 82 games long and players can often play up to **THREE GAMES A WEEK**. Then, once the regular season ends, the best teams compete in playoffs for the Stanley Cup. The winners will have played more than 100 games.
- The average attendance for a game in the NHL is **17,487 SUPPORTERS**.
- In 1919, the Stanley Cup was not awarded to anyone, as the Montreal Canadiens were struck down with **SPANISH FLU**, which was raging at the time.
- Canada has won **13 GOLD MEDALS** in ice hockey at the Winter Olympics. Russia are next best with seven.
- Bobby Hull struck the **FASTEST SLAPSHOT** on record, at 190 km/h!
- In the early days, ice hockey pucks were made from **FROZEN COW DUNG!** Today's rubber versions are still frozen before games to stop them from bouncing.

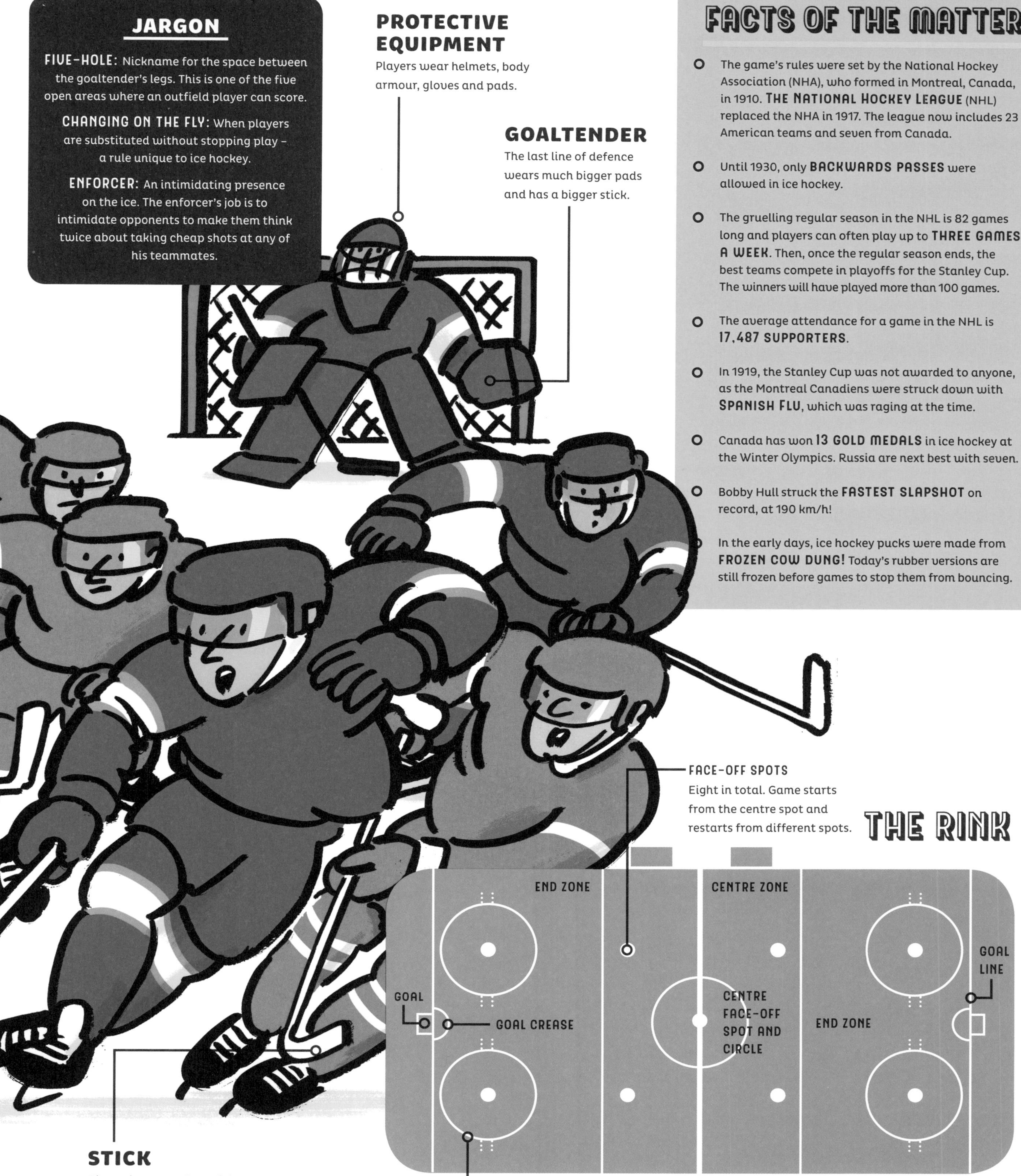

CRICKET

Steeped in tradition, cricket can lay claim to being the oldest bat-and-ball game.

It requires concentration, coordination and precise timing. The premise is built around two teams trying to score runs. One team bats to try to score as many runs as possible, while the other team attempts to get them out by bowling and fielding.

Referred to as 'creckett' in the sport's earliest-known reference, the game dates back to 16th-century England. At that time, it was only really played by children and did not become popular with adults until the following century. But by the 1700s, cricket had become the national sport of England and spread to other parts of the world via the British Empire. It remains particularly popular in the Caribbean, India, South Africa and Australia.

JARGON

GOOGLY: A delivery by a spin bowler that turns in the opposite direction. Australians normally call it a 'wrong'un'.

DOLLY CATCH: An easy catch for a fielder. Drop a 'dolly' at your peril!

HOWZAT?: Word shouted by bowler or fielding team to appeal that the batsman is out.

COW SHOT: The batsman slogs the ball from the leg side – normally with their eyes closed!

LBW: If the ball strikes the batsman's leg in front of the wicket, they are given out LBW (leg before wicket).

KIT

Players wear all white in Test matches but more colourful kits in shorter versions of the game.

CREASE

If the batsman steps outside these chalked lines around the wicket, the opposition can get him 'out'.

BOWLER

Bowlers try to bowl the batsman out, and stop them scoring runs, with difficult deliveries.

UMPIRE

The umpire, who makes decisions and enforces the rules, can be assisted by video technology.

RULES

» Cricket is played by two teams of 11 players – who take turns to bat and field.

» The batting team attempts to score runs, while the other bowls try and get the batters out and restrict the scoring of runs.

» It is played on an oval field with a long pitch (20 metres) in the centre. A set of three wooden stumps (the wickets) are at each end of the pitch.

» A bowler bowls a set of six balls. This is called an 'over'. Once the bowler has bowled six times, another bowler comes on and bowls from the other end of the pitch.

» The batsman hits the ball to score runs, which can be scored by running between the wickets or hitting the ball over the boundary of the pitch.

» There is a batsman at either end – both of which can run after a hit.

» There are ten different ways to get the batter out – the most popular being caught, bowled, LBW, run out and stumped.

» Each time a bowler gets a batter out, it is called 'a wicket'.

BATSMAN

The batsman receives deliveries from the bowler and tries to score runs. There are always two batsmen on the pitch – one at each end. West Indian batsman Brian Lara scored 400 not out against England in 2004, giving him the highest individual score in Test cricket history.

BOUNDARY

The batsmen needn't run if the ball is hit as far as the boundary rope around the edge of the pitch. Four runs are scored if the ball reaches the boundary after hitting the ground and six if it is cleared entirely. Batsman Chris Gayle is the only player to have hit a six off the first ball of a Test match.

WICKET KEEPER

Stands behind the batsman and receives the ball from the bowler. Can get the batsman out by striking the wicket with the ball if the batsman steps outside the crease.

WICKETS

Batters run between the two sets of stumps – or wickets – at each end of the pitch to score runs. But if the ball strikes the wicket, of even if it is accidentally hit with the bat, the batter is out.

FIELDERS

Fielders try to stop the batsmen from scoring runs, and can get them out by catching a hit ball before it touches the ground. There are various fielding positions, often with strange-sounding names, such as this one: 'silly mid on'.

FACTS OF THE MATTER

- Cricket matches are played in different formats, from **TEST MATCHES**, which will last for a number of days, to **LIMITED OVER** formats, which last for just a few hours.
- Teams combine a mixture of **SPECIALIST** batsman and bowlers – often six batsmen and five bowlers. One (normally a batsman) is also named as the wicket keeper. One or two will be all-rounders.
- In 2003, a delivery from Indian bowler Shoaib Akhtar was clocked at **44.8 METRES PER SECOND** – the fastest-ever recorded in cricket history.
- Cricket is not all about fast bowling. Teams also deploy **SPIN BOWLERS**, who rely on the ability to move the ball by spinning off the surface of the pitch.
- Former **SRI LANKAN SPINNER** Muttiah Muralitharan holds the record for most Test wickets. He took 800 in his career. The second-best is also a spinner – Australian Shane Warne, with 708.
- **WEATHER** plays an important part in the game, with matches being suspended due to rain or bad light.
- When a batsman scores 100 runs in a game, it is called **A CENTURY** and is considered a big achievement, whilst a bowler taking five wickets in an innings (a five-for) is also highly acclaimed.
- The cricket **WORLD CUP**, a limited overs tournament played by international teams, takes place every four years. Australia have won it a record five times.

KIT

BALL

The ball is extremely hard and made from cork, string and leather. Bowlers often polish one side to make it 'swing' in the air.

HELMETS

These are fitted with metal faceguards, but were rarely worn until the 1970s.

PADS AND GLOVES

Batsman wear pads to protect their legs, while gloves protect the hands.

BAT

Bats are made from wood and have a rubber grip on the handle.

RACKET

SPORTS

TENNIS

Tennis is the most popular racket sport. It is intense and fast, while gruelling matches can go on for hours.

The modern game originated in England in the 19th century, although earlier forms of tennis were played in France as far back as the 1200s, when it was known as 'jeu de paulme' or 'game of the palm' as players used their hands instead of rackets. Wooden rackets were introduced when the laws of the modern game were compiled in the 1890s. And the rules have barely changed since.

Tennis is played between either two (singles) or four (doubles) players on a rectangular court, who hit a ball over a net with a stringed racket. The aim is to force your opponent into errors so they cannot hit the ball over the net or keep it within the lines of the court.

Tennis's biggest stars play in professional tournaments, the biggest of which are the annual four 'Grand Slams' – Australian Open, French Open, Wimbledon and American Open.

RULES

» Players try to win points by hitting the ball over the net so that the other player is unable to return it.

» The overall aim is to win games and sets.

» Points are started with a serve. The server must serve each point from alternate sides of their own baseline and into the 'service box' diagonally opposite.

» The first player to score four points in a row wins the game. Zero points is called 'love', one is '15', two is '30' and three is '40'. If both players reach 40, this is known as 'deuce', and one player must then win two points in a row to win the game.

» The set is awarded to the first player to win six games by a margin of two. If both players win six games, the set is decided by a tiebreaker.

» The deciding set of a match cannot be won by a tiebreaker. Instead, players go on playing until the set is won by two clear games.

» Matches are the best of three sets (first player to win two sets) for women or best of five sets (first to three) for men.

COURT TYPES

GRASS

Tennis's original playing surface; now the only Grand Slam played on grass is Wimbledon.

CLAY

A mixture of crushed shale and stone or brick, as used at the French Open.

HARDCOURT

Made of acrylic or asphalt; the US Open and Australian Open are played on hardcourt.

LINE JUDGES

Up to nine assistants help the umpire to rule whether the ball was in or out.

RACKETS

Players use this to hit the ball. Modern rackets are made from lightweight graphite or titanium.

UMPIRE

The chair umpire officiate the game and rules on whether a ball is 'in' or 'out', as well as foot faults and service faults.

HAWK-EYE

Players can challenge calls they believe are incorrect. Hawk-Eye technology then decides whether the ball was in or out.

KIT

THEN

Early players in Victorian times wore their everyday clothes on court, sporting laced-up corsets with high-collars, long-sleeved blouses and floor-length bustle skirts.

NOW

Nowadays players' kit allows much more freedom of movement, and while any colour clothing is permitted for most competitions, Wimbledon insists on all-white kit.

FACTS OF THE MATTER

- English king Henry VIII was a tennis enthusiast. His second wife, Anne Boleyn, was playing tennis when she was arrested prior to being **EXECUTED**!
- Serves were originally underarm – a lob rather than today's **OVERARM SMASH**. In those days, the net was much higher – similar to a badminton net.
- Men wore long trousers until World War II. **BRAME HILLYARD** was the first man to appear at Wimbledon in shorts in 1930.
- Women's skirts have become shorter over time to allow for better movement. At Wimbledon in 1949, 'Gussie' Moran's outfit included lace-trimmed **KNICKERS** and caused outrage.
- Male players received more prize money than women until recently, when **EQUAL PAY** was introduced.
- American tennis star Jimmy Van Alen complained long matches were like Chinese water torture and invented the tiebreaker. These then became known as '**SUDDEN DEATH**' or 'lightning death'.
- In 2010, a match at Wimbledon between America's John Isner and France's Nicolas Mahut lasted for **11 HOURS** and **FIVE MINUTES**, and was played over three days. The final set finished 70-68 to Isner.
- Australian Sam Groth hit the fastest-ever serve in 2012 – at **263 KM/H**. Germany's Sabine Lisicki holds the record for a female player (210.8 km/h)

ACE

A serve that the other player can not get their racket to is called an ace. One of the most crowd-pleasing tennis shots, the fastest ace ever recorded in a competitive match, clocked at 250 km/h, was served by Andy Roddick. Ivo Karlović has the most career aces with 12,302.

BALL

Normally covered in yellow felt, it is 6.7 centimetres in diameter, made from vulcanised rubber and filled with air.

BALLBOYS AND BALLGIRLS

They retrieve balls on court and return them to players.

TRAMLINES

These oblongs add 1.4 metres width to become part of the in-play court for doubles matches.

NET

The net is 1.07 metres high at the posts and 0.91 metre in the centre.

BASELINE

SERVICE BOXES

The server aims to deliver the ball into these on the opposite side from where they stand.

THE COURT

TABLE TENNIS

'Ping-Pong' might just be the most fun and accessible sport to play in this book.

It is an indoor game based on the outdoor version of tennis, which can be played almost anywhere – from tournament tables at the Olympic Games to your very own kitchen table.

Although anybody can play table tennis, to compete at the top level a player needs a quick-thinking mind, fast hands and excellent reflexes.

It is played between either two (singles) or four (doubles) players, who use a small bat (sometimes called a paddle) to hit a ball over a net back and forth.

Power and spin is crucial in table tennis, with players trying to outsmart their opponents by using smash shots and other spins that move in the air and kick off the table.

FACTS OF THE MATTER

- The average top-level game lasts for around 30 minutes and the best players often smash the ball at speeds exceeding **160 KM/H**.
- The game has gone by various names, including 'indoor tennis', 'gossima', 'flim flam' and '**WHIFF-WAFF**' until finally 'table tennis' became the official name in the 1920s.
- The sport was banned in the Soviet Union in the 1930s as it was believed to harm the **EYES**.
- Research has shown table tennis to be the best sport for the **BRAIN**. It is understood to activate more parts of the brain than any other.
- The sport originated in England during the late 1800s, where it was played by the upper-class as an after-dinner **PARLOUR GAME**.

BAT

Bats are made of wood and covered in rubber – some are smooth (for power) and others are dimpled to help with spin.

BALL

The ball is made of a plastic-like material and filled with air... and it can travel fast: the record number of back-and-forth shots stands at 173 in 60 seconds!

SERVE

A serve must bounce on the server's side first then over the net on the opponent's side.

NET

The net is 15.25 centimetres high.

TABLE

Made of wood, it is 2.74 metres long, 1.53 metres wide, and 76 centimetres high.

RULES

» Each point starts with a serve. The server tosses the ball at least 15 centimetres into the air and must strike it so the ball hits their own side of the table before landing on the receiver's side.

» A point is won if the ball bounces twice on the opponent's side or bounces once and then hits the floor.

» A point is awarded to the opponent if the ball is hit into the net, hit twice with the bat in the same shot or the ball is struck by anything other than the bat.

» The first player to reach 11 points is awarded the game and games must be won by two clear points.

» Table tennis matches are played to the best of three or five games.

SQUASH

Squash is an exhausting and relentless racket-and-ball sport.

Like tennis, players hit a ball back and forth using a stringed racket. However, instead of hitting it over a net, squash is played indoors against a wall. The game is named after the soft ball used in the sport, which is light and easily 'squashable'. While squash doesn't receive as much media coverage as many other sports, it is enjoyed by millions as a hobby and there are thousands of elite-level players.

OUT LINE

Shots hit above this line are out.

SERVICE LINE

Serves must land between here and the out line.

FACTS OF THE MATTER

- The **TITANIC** ship, which sank on its way from England to America in 1912, had a squash court on board. Professional player Fred Wright went down with the ship and died.
- Squash players are incredibly fit and even recreational players can burn around **1,000 CALORIES** in a single match.
- Prince Philip played squash while his wife, Queen Elizabeth II, was in labour for 30 hours giving birth to **PRINCE CHARLES** in 1948!
- The game developed in the 1830s and today there are just under **50,000** squash courts in the world, while **188 COUNTRIES** have at least one court.
- The rubber ball warms up, **BOUNCES** more and gets **FASTER** as the game progresses.

BALL

Different colour dots indicate the bounciness of the ball. In professional competitions, a double yellow ball (slow bounce) ball is used.

THE BOARD

Shots below this line are out.

RACKET

Graphite, with synthetic strings, squash racket's can be no longer than 68.5 centimetres.

SHORT LINE

Serves must land behind this line on the opponent's side of the court.

GOGGLES

Players wear goggles to protect their eyes.

SERVICE BOX

Competitors must keep one foot in here when serving.

» Squash is played in an enclosed court between either two (singles) or four (doubles) players.

» The aim is to keep hitting the ball against the front wall until your opponent cannot return it.

» Points are started with a serve onto the front wall between the service line and out line. The ball must land behind the short line on the opponent's side.

» For the rest of the point (rally) players must hit the wall above the board and below the out line.

» The rally is lost and a point awarded if a player: hits the ball into the floor or outside the lines, lets the ball bounce twice, or hit them.

» Points can only be scored by the player who is serving.

» Matches are made up of five games, and a game is won with nine points.

BADMINTON

This could well be the game for you if you are new to racket sports.

Badminton is easy to play, heaps of fun and even novices can become capable players in a short space of time. Instead of using a ball like in other racket sports, players hit a 'shuttlecock' back and forth over a high net and trade shots to try and force each other into errors. Formal matches are played indoors on a rectangular court, while there are probably casual games being played in back gardens and beaches all over the world right now. In fact, it is estimated that badminton is played by more than 14 million people in 160 countries. Indeed, it has been played all over Europe for centuries.

The origins of the game are not entirely clear, but shuttlecock games have been played in parts of Asia for at least 2,000 years. The modern game developed in Britain in the mid-19th century, from earlier shuttlecock sports.

RULES

» The game starts with a coin toss. The winner decides whether to serve or receive first.

» Games are played between two (singles) or four (doubles) players.

» Games are played to 11 or 21 points and must be won by two clear points.

» The player who wins two games claims the match.

» Each point is started with an underarm serve.

» After the serve, players exchange shots back and forth over the net. This is called a rally.

» Whoever wins the rally wins the point. To win the rally, the shuttlecock must land in your opponent's half of the court.

» The rally is lost if the shuttlecock hits the net or lands outside the court.

» The shuttlecock mustn't be 'carried' or allowed to rest on a player's racket.

» A player mustn't reach over the net to hit the shuttlecock.

DIFFERENT STROKES...

There are a number of basic strokes to master if you want to become a badminton pro.

CLEAR SHOT

The shuttlecock is hit in the middle of the racket to get it high in the air and into the opponent's back court. It is mainly a defensive shot used to buy time, but can be tactical if your opponent is at the net.

DRIVE SHOT

A quick and powerful shot which goes directly over the net. A good drive goes just over the net. Or a player may aim to hit their opponent directly so they are unable to return it.

DROP SHOT

A finesse shot used when the opponent is at the back of the court. The aim is to drop the shuttlecock just over the net. Players will often fake hitting a drive before dropping it over the net with a deft touch.

SMASH

The most powerful and attacking shot in badminton. It is basically an angled drive. Best done when the shuttlecock is high in the air, it is normally hit away from the opponent – but sometimes straight at them!

OTHERS

More advanced shots include spins, lifts and net kills. The best players in the world have become masters of every type of shot, using a mixture of amazing wrist speed and a brilliant slight of touch.

SHUTTLECOCK

Feathered to help them fly through the air, shuttlecocks weigh just 5 grams and can take severe damage – so can be changed after every point.

RACKET

The extremely lightweight rackets allow players to flick and smash and are usually made from graphite. At less than 100 grams, they weigh about the same as a pack of cards!

SERVICE COURT

Both the server and receiver must stay within the service court until the server strikes the shuttle.

GRIP

Players can apply drying agents to help keep a good grip on the handle of their racket.

FACTS OF THE MATTER

- Shuttlecock speeds often exceed 90 metres per second. The fastest recorded shot was hit by China's Lee Chong Wei – **113.34 METRES PER SECOND**.
- Shuttlecocks are made using **16 FEATHERS**. Goose feathers are best – especially ones from the left wing.
- Badminton was first played at the 1992 Olympics in Barcelona. More than **1.1 BILLION** people watched the first Olympic match on TV.
- Players from China and Indonesia are considered the best in the world. Competitors from these countries have won **70 PER CENT** of all world events.
- An average of 10 shuttles are used in each top-level match, with players hitting it around **400 TIMES** each in a typical game.
- A version of badminton called 'Ti Zian Ji' used to be played in China. Instead of rackets, they used **FEET**!
- The strings on the racket are normally made from synthetic materials. In the early days of the sport, rackets were stringed with **DRIED STOMACH LINING** from animals such as cows or cats.
- The game was called 'shuttlecock' until 1873, when the Duke of Beaufort held parties at his estate, **BADMINTON HOUSE**, and the name was born there.
- The shortest ever badminton match lasted just **SIX MINUTES**. In an Uber Cup match in 1996, South Korea's Ra Kyung-min beat Julia Mann of England 11-2, 11-1.

OFFICIALS

The umpire is the main judge in any badminton game and sits to the side of the court. They are assisted by a service judge and a line judge.

SERVES

There are four main serves in badminton:

LOW: Played gently over the net and lands at the front of the opponent's half of the court.

HIGH: A powerful serve which is played high and falls at the back of the receiver's court.

FLICK: The most common serve in badminton is played up, but not as high as the high serve.

DRIVE: Played flat and fast towards the back of the court.

NET

The net is 1.55 metres high at the posts and 1.52 metres in the middle.

SMASH SHOT

This overarm shot is the most powerful in badminton. Shuttlecocks have been recorded at speeds of 493 km/h – faster than a train!

COURT

Games are played on a wooden court, measuring 13.4 metres long and 5.2 metres wide for a singles game.

SHOES

Light rubber shoes give the players extra agility on the court.

A T H L
103
085

47
105
135
ETICS

SPRINTING

Sprinting sees the fastest people on the planet race one another.

Perhaps the most exciting and exhilarating of all athletic sports, sprint races are contested over various distances – most commonly 100 metres, 200 metres and 400 metres. In indoor events, some races are as short as 60 metres. Lightning-quick 100-metre sprinters reach speeds of over 9 metres per second – races at the highest level are often completed in under 10 seconds.

The 100 metres is almost always the highlight of the modern Olympics. An audience of more than 35 million tuned into watch the final at the 2016 Games in Rio de Janeiro, Brazil.

And history placed just as much importance on the event. The inaugural Olympic Games in Athens, Greece, in 1896 featured the first-ever race over 100 metres – a shorter version of the hugely prestigious 'stadion' sprinting race, which took place in ancient Greece over a distance of around 180 metres.

RULES

» The rules of sprinting are incredibly simple. The winner is the first person to cross the finish line.

» Sprinters start the race crouched down in 'blocks' and can only leave once the race starter announces the following commands: 'On your marks', 'Set,' and then fires a starting gun.

» If a racer goes before the gun sounds, a false start is called and they can be disqualified from the race.

» Sprinters are assigned a lane and must stay there for the duration of the race. Failure to stay in your own lane can also result in disqualification. The middle lanes are generally favoured by athletes.

HURDLE POWER

Hurdling is an Olympic track event where, instead of sprinting flat out, racers must jump over ten hurdles before reaching the finish line. The hurdles are between 68 centimetres and 107 centimetres in height, depending on the age and gender of the runners.

Hurdle races are run over 100 metres, 110 metres or 400 metres, and the hurdles are spaced differently depending on the distance. Racers will often deploy a set stride pattern so that they are leading with the same leg each time they jump over a hurdle. The athlete keeps their body as low as possible as they clear the hurdles. Knocking over hurdles won't get the runner disqualified, but it will seriously affect the athlete's time.

UPPER BODY STRENGTH

This is extremely important for sprinters as they drive with their arms to pick up speed throughout the race.

STARTER

The starter fires the starting gun to indicate the start of the race.

SHOES

Spiked running shoes help the sprinters grip the track.

STRIDES

Most sprinters will average between 40 and 45 steps in a typical 100-metre race.

RELAY GOOD

- In a relay race, a team of four sprinters take turns to run a leg each and pass a baton to their teammate once they have finished their leg.
- The handover of the baton must take place within a certain part of the track and often prove tricky to do at such high speeds.
- There are two types of relay race – 4 x 100m and 4 x 400m.

FACTS OF THE MATTER

- Jamaican sprinter Usain Bolt is the **FASTEST HUMAN** on the planet. He holds the world record for the 100 metres (9.58 sec) and 200 metres (19.19 sec).
- He was clocked running at **12.5 METRES PER SECOND** in 2009 .
- The 100 metres and 400 metres have been held at every Olympics since the first modern Games in 1896 – but only for men. **WOMEN** could not run in the 100 metres until 1928 and the 400 metres until 1964.
- On a 400-metre running track, the 100-metre race is run on the **HOME STRAIGHT**. Usually the start is set on an extension, to make it a straight-line race.
- The United States has won **GOLD**, **SILVER** and **BRONZE** in the men's 200 metres at the Olympics on six occasions – 1904, 1932, 1952, 1956, 1984 and 2004.
- Record sprint times are helped by **HOT WEATHER** and a good tailwind – the temperature reduces drag from the air, while the **TAILWIND** propels the runner forward.
- But if the **WIND SPEED** is measured at more than two metres per second, sprinters aren't eligible for records. However, the race results still stand.
- Although sprinting is one of the most physically-demanding events in athletics, a 100-metre runner burns an average of only **SIX CALORIES** in the race.

LONG-DISTANCE RUNNING

Long-distance running is the ultimate test of stamina and endurance.

Racing over long distances also requires acute tactical planning as well as impressive mental and physical strength. Professionally, races are run over various set distances – anywhere from 800 metres to more than 96 kilometres. Away from the professional circuit, long-distance running has enjoyed a rapid rise in popularity among keen amateur runners. Many people run regularly to keep fit and even compete in races alongside professional athletes.

In sport, a variety of races are run on tracks, inside stadiums and cross-country. Perhaps the most gruelling of all of them is the marathon. The race is 42.1 kilometres long – the same distance run by Greek soldier, Pheidippides, when he delivered a message to Athens from a battlefield near the town of Marathon in 490 BC.

ULTRA RUNNERS

If a 42.1 -kilometre marathon is simply not long enough, you could always try your hand – or your feet! – at 'ultra-long-distance running'. These races can last for days, measure thousands of kilometres in distance and often take place in extreme conditions.

In 2009-2010, French 'ultramarathoner' Serge Girard ran 27,011 kilometres non-stop in just 365 days. That is almost 75 kilometres a day, every day, for a whole year! His run spanned FIVE continents, taking in no fewer than 25 different countries!

TRACK

- The track is 400 metres long, and runners complete laps of the track to make up a longer distance. For example, a 10,000-metre race consists of 25 full laps.
- Runners in long-distance races can go in any lane. So, to run the shortest distance possible, they move into the inside lane as soon as they can.
- Track shoes are fitted with spikes for grip.

STEEPLECHASE

The 3,000-metre steeplechase is one of the most demanding long-distance events. It is named after the steeplechase in horseracing, and instead of fences, racers must clear 28 hurdles, which have water pits on the other side. Unlike the 110-metre hurdles, steeplechase hurdles remain firmly upright if the runner steps on it on their way over.

FACTS OF THE MATTER

- In pre-industrial times, **FOOT MESSENGERS** would run huge distances to deliver messages. There are mentions of this in the Bible.
- Racers from **KENYA**, **MOROCCO** and **ETHIOPIA** have dominated this sport since the 1980s.
- Ethiopian **KENENISA BEKELE** has held the world record in the men's 5,000-metre since in 2004. He ran it in an impressive 12 minutes and 37.5 seconds.
- Brit **PAULA RADCLIFFE** has held the women's marathon world record since 2003, when she finished the London Marathon in 2 hours, 15 minutes and 25 seconds.
- A study carried out by the University of Durham concluded that runners who wear **RED CLOTHING** are more likely to win long-distance races. It is said that red signals dominance over other runners.
- Long-distance **WALKING EVENTS** are also a prominent part of most athletics events. They are run over 20 kilometres and 50 kilometres for men. Women compete over the 20-kilometre distance. Racers must keep one foot on the ground at all times.
- The 2013 **NEW YORK MARATHON** saw a whopping **50,304** runners finish the race. That is the largest number of people ever to cross the finish line in a single race.

  Such is the popularity of long-distance running that it is estimated that **44.6 MILLION** pairs of running shoes were sold in the United States in 2012.

RUNNING SHOES

These are important for a long-distance runner, to absorb the shock of constantly pounding the road or track.

RULES

» The rules for long-distance races could not be simpler: the first person over the finish line wins.

» On the track, a long-distance race can be run over 800 metres, 1,500 metres, 5,000 metres or 10,000 metres.

» The 'steeplechase' is also run on the track. It is normally 2,000 metres or 3,000 metres, with hurdles and water obstacles.

» Races over 800 metres and 1,500 metres are technically classed as middle-distance. In these races, the start is staggered. Runners then try to get into the inside lane, which is considered the best position.

» Racers start in a line in long-distance races.

» The marathon is a road race. But during the Olympics and other athletics events, runners often finish on the track.

» Cross-country races are run by individuals and teams. They take place outside in natural terrain, often over hills, and can be over any distance.

THE JUMPS

All four jumping events in athletics combine explosive power and speed.

In the long jump and triple jump, athletes compete to jump the furthest distance, while high jumpers and pole vaulters attempt to clear the highest distance.

Jumping is one of the oldest track and field events, with the long jump practised as far back as the ancient Greek times. All the jumping events have evolved over time, though.

For example, athletes used to take a short run up in the long jump or even launch start from a standing position. Nowadays, athletes rely as much on their sprinting speed as they do on their ability to jump.

Events take place on a field inside a stadium at competitions such as the Olympics and the World Championships.

POLE VAULT

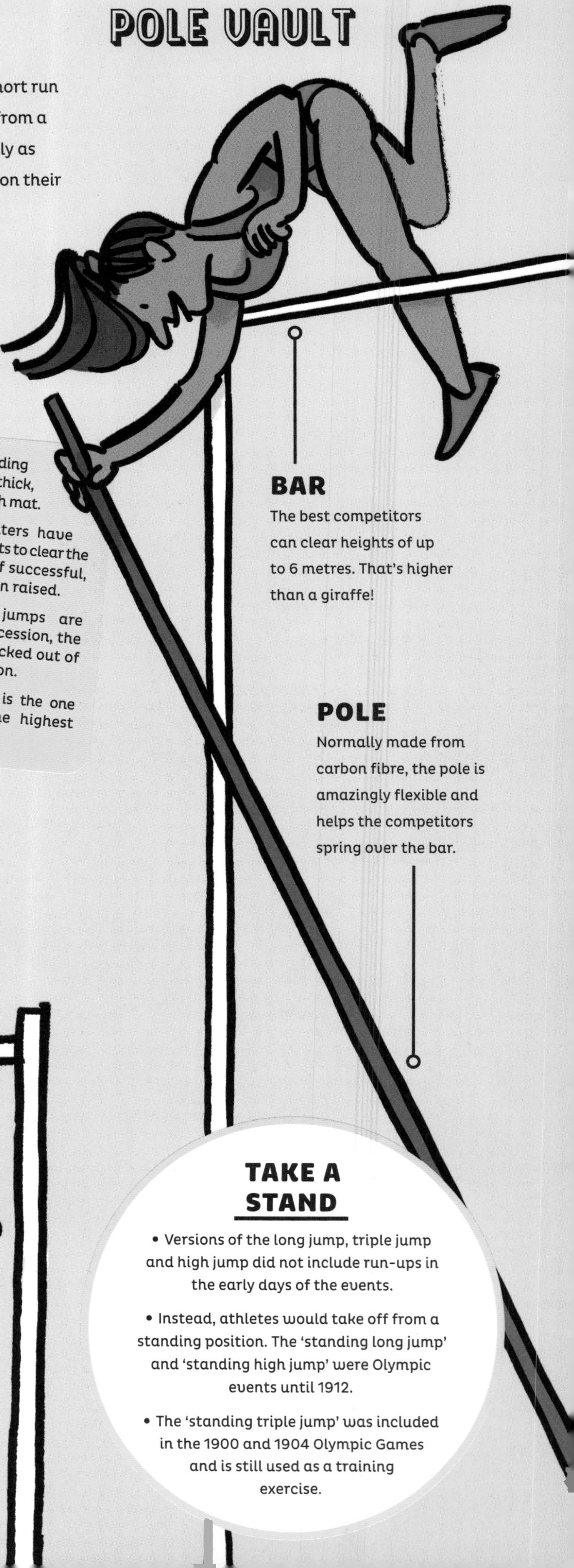

RULES

» Jumpers use a long, flexible pole to help them clear a high bar.

» A jump is started with a sprint before the pole is planted into the 'box' and the jumper swings up.

» When they reach the top, athletes push themselves off the pole and try to arch their bodies over the bar before landing onto a thick, padded crash mat.

» Pole vaulters have three attempts to clear the height and, if successful, the bar is then raised.

» If three jumps are missed in succession, the athlete is knocked out of the competition.

» The winner is the one who clears the highest jump.

BAR

The best competitors can clear heights of up to 6 metres. That's higher than a giraffe!

POLE

Normally made from carbon fibre, the pole is amazingly flexible and helps the competitors spring over the bar.

HIGH JUMP

BAR

Placed between two posts, jumpers must clear the bar without knocking it off.

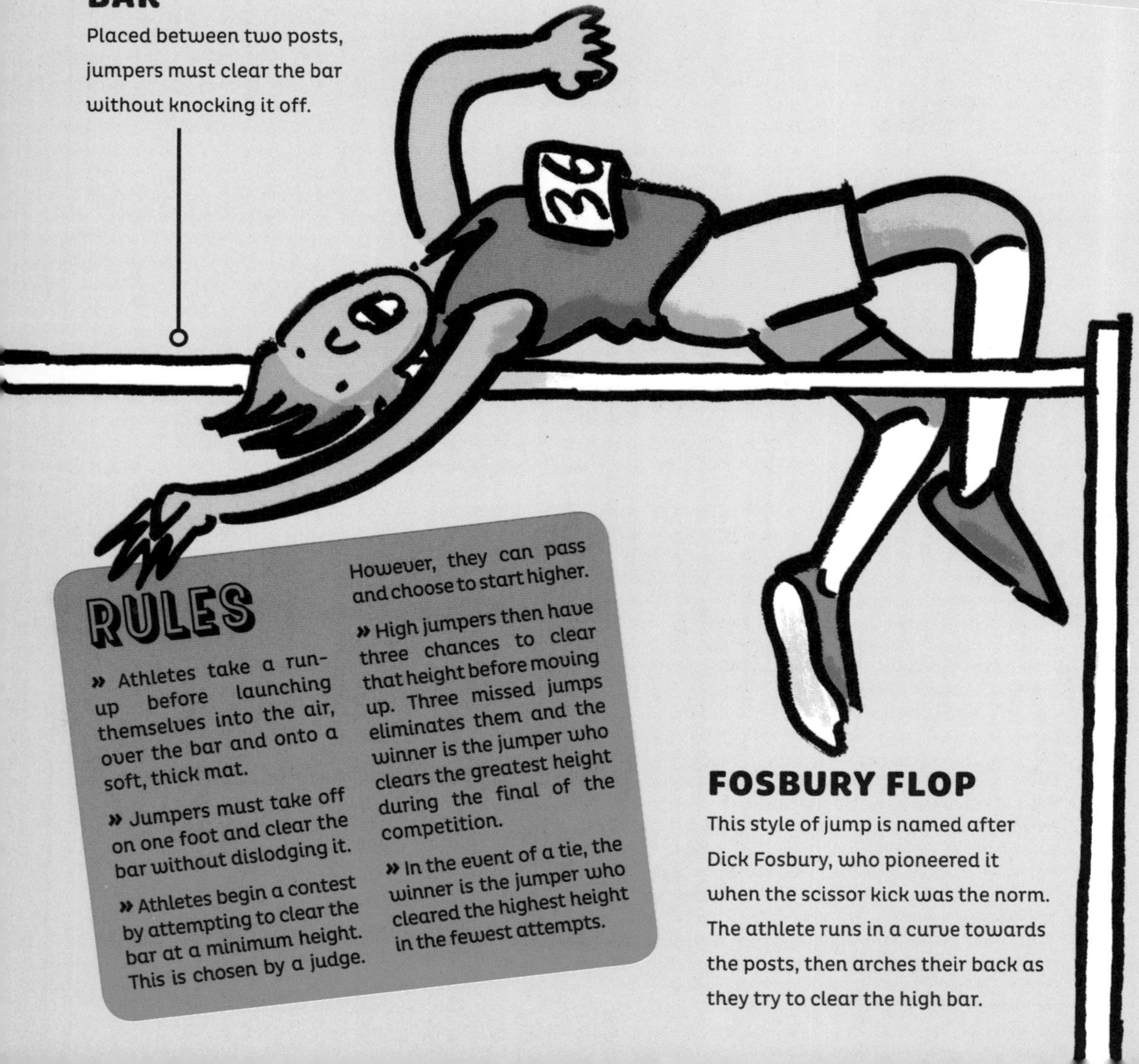

RULES

» Athletes take a run-up before launching themselves into the air, over the bar and onto a soft, thick mat.

» Jumpers must take off on one foot and clear the bar without dislodging it.

» Athletes begin a contest by attempting to clear the bar at a minimum height. This is chosen by a judge. However, they can pass and choose to start higher.

» High jumpers then have three chances to clear that height before moving up. Three missed jumps eliminates them and the winner is the jumper who clears the greatest height during the final of the competition.

» In the event of a tie, the winner is the jumper who cleared the highest height in the fewest attempts.

FOSBURY FLOP

This style of jump is named after Dick Fosbury, who pioneered it when the scissor kick was the norm. The athlete runs in a curve towards the posts, then arches their back as they try to clear the high bar.

TAKE A STAND

• Versions of the long jump, triple jump and high jump did not include run-ups in the early days of the events.

• Instead, athletes would take off from a standing position. The 'standing long jump' and 'standing high jump' were Olympic events until 1912.

• The 'standing triple jump' was included in the 1900 and 1904 Olympic Games and is still used as a training exercise.

TRIPLE JUMP

RULES

» The triple jump starts in the same way as the long jump, on the same sort of track, but the takeoff board is further forward.

» Athletes hit the board and hop back onto that same foot before skipping onto the other foot and then propelling themselves into the sand.

» As in the long jump, the distance is measured from the takeoff board to the nearest mark in the sand. Triple jump distances are usually much longer.

FLAG

A white flag is raised for a legal jump and a red flag for a foul.

SHOES

Most jumpers in all categories use spiked shoes, a lot like running shoes.

HOP

Jumpers take off from one foot before landing on the same one.

SKIP

They then skip on to their other foot.

JUMP

The final step is to propel the athlete into the sand pit.

FACTS OF THE MATTER

- Top 100-metre and 200-metre runners often also make excellent long jumpers. At the 1984, 1988 and 1992 Olympics, American legend **CARL LEWIS** won Olympic gold in both the 100 metres and long jump. In 1984, he added the 200 metres to his medal haul!
- The triple jump is understood to have originated from the ancient children's game of **HOPSCOTCH**.
- Before the Fosbury flop, most high jumpers would high jump using other methods, such as the straddle, Western roll, Eastern cut-off and **SCISSOR KICK**.
- Pole vaulting is thought to have originated with the ancient Greeks, who vaulted over **BULLS IN FIELDS**!
- It's understood that the long jump was used to train warriors in ancient Greece for **WAR**, to prepare them to jump streams and even ravines.
- The length of a long jump sand pit must be **2.75 METRES LONG** and no more than 3 metres wide.
- Legendary Ukrainian pole vaulter **SERGEY BUBKA** held the world pole vault record (6.14 metres) for 20 years between 1994 and 2014, when he was finally beaten by Frenchman Renaud Lavillenie in 2014.
- The **LONGEST HOP** recorded in a triple jump was by American jumper Kenny Harrison at 7.02 metres. That means his hop alone would have been enough to win a medal in long jump at the 2012 Olympics!

LONG JUMP

RULES

» The jump is started with a sprint down a runway, which has the same surface as a running track.

» Athletes then jump as far as they can from a wooden board, known as the 'takeoff board', and into a pit of sand.

» The leading foot must land on the board behind the foul line or a foul is called and the jump is classed as invalid, with no distance recorded.

» Jumps are measured from the takeoff board to the mark in the sand that is nearest to the board.

» Competitors have a set number of attempts, normally three. The best athletes are then awarded three more attempts and the winner is decided by whoever achieves the longest jump overall.

RUNWAY

The runway is at least 40 metres long. Competitors pick up as much speed as possible running down it, before launching themselves into the sandpit.

TAKEOFF BOARD

The takeoff board is one metre from the end of the runway. Jumpers must not land with their foot over the board.

TUCK

The most common technique in long jump sees jumpers bring their knees up to their chest while in the air before kicking into the sand pit.

THROWING

Throwing events feature some of the strongest competitors in athletics.

All four events – javelin, discus, hammer and shot put – are based on one simple rule: who can throw their object the furthest. As well as power, throwers possess speed, along with exceptional mental toughness.

Throwing is one of the oldest forms of sporting competition: it featured in the ancient Olympic Games, as well as other traditional sporting gatherings, such as the Highland Games.

Modern day athletes are so finely-tuned, they can throw their objects huge distances... so much so that modern-day javelins have been adapted to reduce the distance they can be thrown!

THE JAVELIN

This tapered spear, which in centuries before would be used as a weapon, can travel at speed of more than 100 km/h.

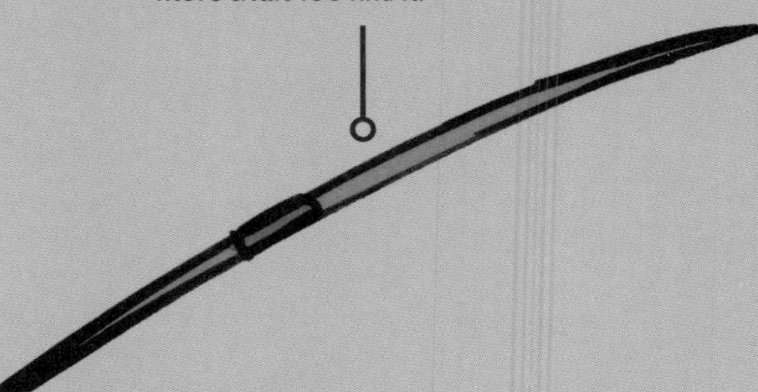

RULES

» Athletes start by sprinting down a runway before hurling a spear – known as the javelin – as far as possible.

» The thrower must stay within the throwing area and not step over the foul line otherwise a foul is called and the throw does not count.

» The metal head of the javelin must land first and within a fan-shaped area known as the 'sector'.

JAVELIN

RUNWAY

The competitor uses the runway, which is 30–33.8 metres long, to pick up momentum before launching the javelin.

FOUL LINE

The thrower must not cross this curved line until the javelin has landed.

HOLD THE PHONE

With the rise of mobile phones comes a new sport. In 2000, mobile phone throwing was invented in Finland. Participants throw their phones and are judged on both distance and technique. The type of phone used can vary, but it must weigh more than 200 grams.

RULES

» The discus is thrown from inside a small chalk circle and the aim is to send it as far as possible.

» The thrower spins around to build up speed and momentum – normally one and a half times – before releasing the discus.

» A foul is called if the discus is dropped, the thrower steps outside the circle or the discus lands outside of the sector lines.

» The throw is measured from the nearest mark left by the discus.

CHALK

Athletes chalk their hands to help grip the discus.

DISCUS

THE DISCUS

The round discus is relatively heavy at 2 kilograms.

THROWING CIRCLE

The discus throwing circle – 2.5 metres in diameter – is usually combined with the hammer circle.

HAMMER

RULES

» Athletes launch the hammer from inside a throwing circle, which is bigger than for the discus.

» The hammer is a heavy ball which is attached to a long piece of steel wire.

» As in the discus, throwers gather speed by spinning the hammer before throwing it as far as they can.

» To be a legal throw, athletes must release the hammer within 90 seconds. They must also stay within the circle.

HAMMER

With a solid iron head and steel wire, hammers come in at an impressive 7 kilograms for the men and 4 kilograms for the women.

SPINNING

Most hammer throwers use a three- or-four turn technique. Right-handed throwers turn to the left and spin in an anti-clockwise direction.

THROWING CIRCLE

The hammer's throwing circle – 2.135 metres in diameter – lies within a netted enclosure to protect bystanders.

SAFETY NET

This is one of the most dangerous sports – especially for the officials! The safety net is there to stop the hammer if it is released in the wrong direction.

FACTS OF THE MATTER

- The men's hammer throw has been part of the **OLYMPIC GAMES** since the 1900 games held in Paris. However, women did not take part until many years later – at the 2000 games in Sydney.
- In 1986, javelins were **RE-DESIGNED** so they could not be thrown too far. This was due to the ever-increasing lengths of throws. Athletes began to regularly throw further than **100 METRES** and it was decided the old javelins could no longer be used safely within the confines of a stadium!
- The hammer throw can be traced back to the late 18th century, at the **HIGHLAND GAMES**, which is still held today to celebrate Scottish and Celtic culture.
- In the first-ever modern Olympic Games in 1896, American shot-putter **ROBERT GARRETT** won gold in the discus despite never having thrown one before.
- Javelins throwers often throw the javelin at speeds of around 100 km/h – as fast as a car on the **MOTORWAY**!
- Discus throwing was a hugely **PRESTIGIOUS** event in the ancient Olympic Games. Athletes took part to show off their precision, coordination and strength.
- Javelin throwers in ancient Greece used to compete **ON HORSEBACK**.
- Early hammer throwing contests between **CELTIC WARRIORS** involved throwing a wheel from a chariot. That was later replaced by a boulder and a drawing from the 16th-century shows King Henry VIII throwing a blacksmith's hammer.

THREESY DOES IT

In all throwing events, each athlete has three attempts to throw their object as far as they can. The ones with the best distances then go into the final, where each competitor is given three more attempts. The thrower with the longest recorded throw in the final is then declared the winner of the event.

SHOT PUT

SHOT

The heavy shot, made of solid iron or brass, weighs between 4 and 8 kilograms.

THE DELIVERY

With the ball held at the base of the fingers (not the palm), the thrower punches the shot away from the neck.

0163

RULES

» Shot put is as much about pushing as throwing.

» The athlete faces the back of the throwing circle before twisting to face the front and launching a heavy metal ball from their neck and shoulder.

» By extending their arm swiftly, the ball is pushed up into the air.

» A foul is called if the athlete takes a step outside the circle before the shot has landed or they take longer than 60 seconds to complete the throw.

» Some throwers spin before their throw to give themselves momentum.

LEG WORK

The competitor extends one leg backwards towards the toe board before starting to spin.

THROWING CIRCLE

The shot throwing circle measures 2.135 metres in diameter.

GYMN

ASTICS

FLOOR EXERCISES

This show-stopping event is one of gymnastics' most popular.

Combining dance and acrobatics, competitors aim to impress a team of judges by performing routines set to music. While the routines can range in style and difficulty, they must perform some prescribed athletics moves, including rolls, leaps, turns, and jaw-dropping 'tumbles'.

Competitors must be precise in their movements, and try to make use of the entire floor space available. The best – and highest-scoring – routines showcase strength, agility and finesse, along with grace and individual personality.

FACTS OF THE MATTER

- Floor exercise has been an Olympic event for men since the **1936 GAMES**, while women did not compete at the Olympics until 1952.
- Unlike the women's floor gynmastics, male routines feature **NO MUSIC**.
- Today, gymnasts must be at least 16 or older to compete in the Olympics but this was not always the case. Before 1997, some gymnasts were competing as young as **AGE 14**.
- **TRAMPOLINING** is another Olympic sport that could fall into the gymnastics category. NASA scientists discovered that it is 68% more effective than jogging at building fitness.
- Simone Biles is America's most decorated gymnast with a combined **19 MEDALS** at the Olympic Games and World Championships

RULES

» Individual floor exercises last 90 seconds for women gymnasts and 60 seconds for men.

» They are performed on a floor area measuring 12 x 12 metres.

» A gymnast's routine is scored by a panel of judges, who base their score on difficulty, artistry, demonstration of the required elements and the overall quality of the performance.

» Some competitions feature team events. A team's routine can last up to two minutes and 30 seconds.

BACK TO BASICS

There are six basic moves for any amateur floor gymnast to perfect – the forward roll, backward roll, handstand, bridge, back bend and cartwheel.

MUSIC

The competitor and their coach choose the music before the event. Getting the piece right is very important: it must reflect the gymnast's personality and create bursts of energy so the gymnast can showcase their skills.

LEOTARDS

Gymnasts wear leotards to help with flexibility. They are named after the French acrobat, Jules Léotard, who popularised them in the mid-19th century.

POSTURE

Gymnasts must keep their toes pointed when performing leaps.

JUDGES

Scores are awarded for difficulty, artistry, inclusion of set moves and overall impression.

FLOOR

The floor is sprung to help with jumping. In the Olympics, the mat is 12-metres square.

BOUNDARY LINE

This marks the edge of the floor.

RHYTHMIC

Rhythmic gymnasts combine floor exercise with ballet and dance.

Individuals, or groups of five or more gymnasts, can perform freestyle, or make use one of five pieces of hand apparatus in a routine that covers the entire floor.

Each routine lasts two minutes and 30 seconds, and is marked by a panel of judges, who score the gymnast's performance based on skill and execution of leaps, balances, pirouettes and the handling of apparatus.

JUDGES

There are three sets of judges in rhythmic gymnastics – compared with two in other gymnastic events.

RIBBON

Often used in individual events, the ribbon must be kept in motion for the entire routine, while the gymnasts use it to create elegant shapes and patterns.

FACTS OF THE MATTER

- If apparatus **BREAK** or even **GET STUCK** in the ceiling during routines, the group or gymnast must simply continue their routine.
- Strict rules around outfits state rhythmic gymnasts must wear a leotard. Despite being influenced by ballet, the official rule book states: 'The look of **BALLET TUTU** is forbidden!'
- Rhythmic gymnastics is one of just two Olympic sports in which **ONLY WOMEN** can compete. The other is synchronised swimming.
- Individual rhythmic events were introduced at the **LOS ANGELES GAMES** in 1984. The team competition was introduced in 1996 (Atlanta).
- A lot of the world's top gymnasts began their training as young as **THREE OR FOUR YEARS OLD**.

APPARATUS

There are five approved pieces of apparatus: the rope, hoop, ball, clubs and ribbon.

BALL

The 0.2-metre rubber ball can be thrown, balanced or rolled... but never held by a gymnast.

CLUBS

Judge and crowd-pleasing tricks and catches are performed with these bowling-pin like clubs. They weigh a minimum of 150 grams, so missing a catch could easily lead to someone losing a tooth!

HOOP

The wooden or plastic hoop can be tossed and caught.

ROPE

The rope can be wrapped around the body, thrown and caught, or leapt through while the gymnast holds it in both hands.

CAN YOU HANDLE IT?

Each piece of apparatus has a different set of rules that controls how each one is used during a routine.

ARTISTIC

This is considered to be the most difficult sport in the world.

There are five main categories in artistic gymnastics: pommel horse, rings, bars, the beam and the vault. These demanding and varied apparatus each require a different set of skills. Some events are only contested by men and some only by women, while some events are individual, and others, team.

Routines are scored by two panels of judges – one judging the execution of a routine and the other the difficulty. All events are scored the same way and the gymnast with the highest number of points on each apparatus wins the event. To be successful, gymnasts need immense strength, fitness, precision and daring to carry out their ambitious, eye-catching routines.

THE RINGS

RULES

» This male-only event showcases strength and balance like no other gymnastics event.

» Gymnasts suspend themselves from the rings and routines normally include a series of swings and holds.

» The rings themselves must not swing to and fro.

» At least one static strength move is required, such as the 'iron cross', in which the gymnast holds themself, arms straight, in the air. It requires extreme upper-body strength.

» Routines end with a precise dismount.

RINGS
The rings require enormous upper-body strength. They hang on a wire cable 5.75 metres off the floor.

BALANCE BEAM

RULES

» Contested by women only, gymnasts are given 90 seconds to wow the judges with a choreographed routine on the beam.

» Routines are made up of leaps, jumps and acrobatics.

» The beam is very thin so that gymnasts require incredible balance. Judges also mark them on their flexibility, grace, poise and demonstration of strength.

» Routines must take in the entire length of the beam and include various moves from both seated and standing positions.

BEAM
The thin padded beam measures just 10 centimetres wide.

THE UNEVEN BARS

THE BARS
The upper bar is 250 centimetres high, and the lower bar is 170 centimetres.

RULES

» Only women are allowed to compete in the uneven bars during the Olympics.

» Running mounts and springboards are allowed.

» A routine must include: flight from high to low bar and from low to high bar; at least two different grips of the bar; a circle around the bar; a turn on the bar, e.g. during a handstand; and a dismount.

» If a gymnast falls from the bars, she has 30 seconds to remount; this can include adjusting grips and rechalking her hands.

» Unlike in the men's high bar, the gymnast may not be lifted up to the bar by the coach, except after a fall during the routine.

» If, however, the coach sees the gymnast is about to fall, they are allowed to catch her or break her fall. Coaches often step in during 'high-risk' moves.

SET THE BAR

Male gymnasts compete on the parallel bars and the high bar. On the parallel bars, they perform a series of swings and balances, and even handstands! Spectators of a top-notch high bar routine will witness daring twists, somersaults and a stunning final dismount.

POMMEL HORSE

ONE, TWO

Gymnasts perform single and double leg moves as they try to use the whole of the 'table'.

RULES

» The routine is done on an artificial horse – only by male gymnasts.

» Gymnasts balance on their hands and swing their legs in a circular motion.

» To increase the difficulty of a routine, it will normally include more daring moves rather than just going around in circles. This could be anything from straddling their legs (flairs) to performing handstands on the horse.

» A routine ends when the gymnast dismounts, normally by swinging onto the mat or pushing themselves from a handstand position, with feet landing firmly.

» Judges favour routines that are smooth and show the gymnast using all parts of the pommel horse.

HORSE

The pommel horse is 1.6 metres long and 115 centimetres high – closer, in reality, to the size of a pony than a horse!

BORN ENTERTAINERS

Some gymnasts have used their performance skills to get into showbiz. American John Orozco has dabbled in acting and appeared in three episodes of hit US TV drama *Law & Order*, while Olympic gold medallist Louis Smith won the UK show *Strictly Come Dancing* in 2012.

THE VAULT

UP AND OVER

The aim of the run-up and takeoff is to send the gymnast as high as possible over the vault.

THE TABLE

In 2001, 'the table' replaced the 'vaulting horse' for safety reasons.

RUNWAY

The gymnast can start their run-up anywhere along the 25-metre long runway.

RULES

» The vault starts with a sprint run-up, which varies in distance depending on the gymnast's height, strength and sprint speed.

» Gymnasts then jump onto a springboard and onto the 'vaulting table'. They then propel themselves in the air over the horse.

» Moves are executed in mid-air such as tucks, pikes and somersaults, before landing on to a mat with both feet being planted firmly on the floor.

» Both men and women can take part in this event.

FACTS OF THE MATTER

- The **POMMEL HORSE** was designed by the ancient Greeks as a means to practise mounting and dismounting a real horse.
- The most common method for a vault is the **YURCHENKO TECHNIQUE**, which means gymnasts have their hands on the runway while their feet land on the springboard – effectively doing a full somersault before taking off on the springboard.
- The word gymnastics comes from the ancient Greek word 'gymno' meaning '**PLACE TO BE NAKED**', as that's how the ancient Greeks performed gymnastics!
- A number of gymnasts are experts in a couple of gymnastic events. Briton **MAX WHITLOCK** won gold medals in both the floor exercise and pommel horse at the 2016 Olympics in Brazil.
- Russian Larisa Latynina has won **18 OLYMPIC MEDALS** – nine golds, five silver and four bronze – making her the most successful gymnast (male or female) in Olympic history.
- The first official gymnastics club was set up 1811 by German Friedrich Ludwig Jahn. He was known as '**TURNVATER**', which means 'father of gymnastics'.
- Japanese Shun Fujimoto broke his **KNEECAP** during the floor exercise at the 1976 Olympic Games in Montreal, but went on to score highly in both the pommel horse and rings to help his country to glory.
- Some track and field events, such as the **POLE VAULT**, were once thought of as gymnastic events due to the grace showcased by its athletes.

WATER

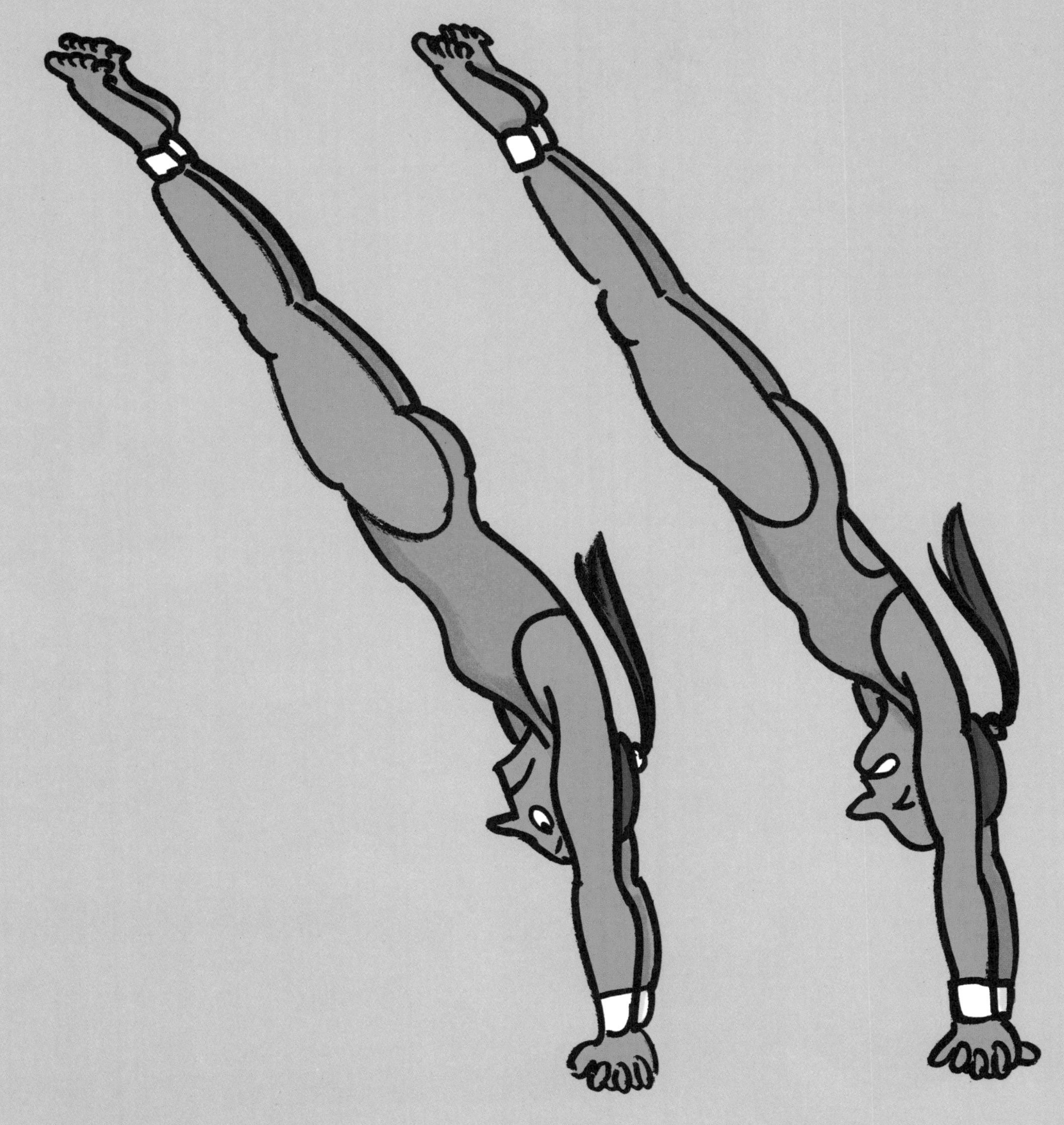

SPORTS

SWIMMING

Swimming is one of the world's most popular recreational sports.

With millions of swimmers all over the globe, swimming has been a prominent hobby since the pre-historic times, with drawings from ancient Egypt suggesting that people have been swimming for more than 10,000 years. Competitive racing was introduced in the 1830s and now takes place in indoor pools, natural open water, lakes and rivers.

The variety of races is mind-boggling – with races for different strokes, over various distances, for individuals or relay teams – but all of them have the same aim: to move through water using the legs and arms as fast as possible.

The challenges of the sport, which requires strength and explosive speed for shorter races as well as exceptional stamina when competing in long-distance events, leads all swimmers to be incredibly fit, whichever their chosen event.

STARTER'S ORDERS

A race starts with the words 'take your mark', before a button is pushed to start the race with a loud noise.

If a swimmer starts the race before hearing the starting sound, a false start is called and the swimmer is disqualified. A false start rope is dropped down to stop other swimmers who might not hear the false start from carrying on swimming.

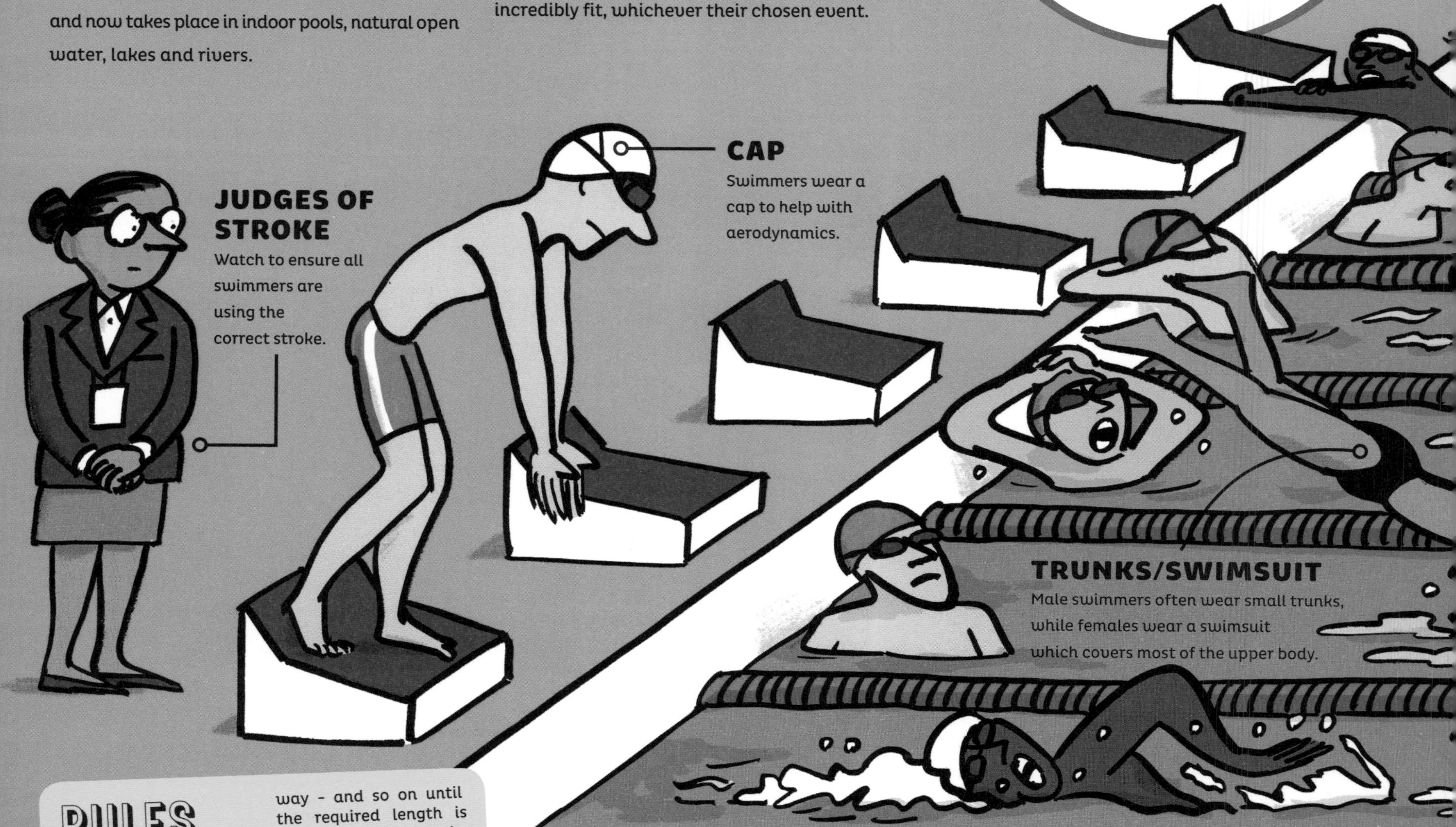

JUDGES OF STROKE

Watch to ensure all swimmers are using the correct stroke.

CAP

Swimmers wear a cap to help with aerodynamics.

TRUNKS/SWIMSUIT

Male swimmers often wear small trunks, while females wear a swimsuit which covers most of the upper body.

RULES

» Races are started by diving into the water and swam using a variety of different strokes – freestyle, breaststroke, butterfly or backstroke.

» Each swimmer is assigned a lane for a race and is required to stay in their own lane for the duration or face disqualification.

» In races longer than 50 metres, swimmers swim a length before touching a pad at the end of the pool and turning around to swim back the other way - and so on until the required length is completed. For example, in a 200-metre race, a swimmer will swim four lengths in total.

» In a relay, four swimmers take turns to race a length each.

» The individual medley is different: swimmers are required to swim one length of each stroke in a 200-metre race.

» The medley can also be run as part of a relay team of four. Each swimmer will then swim one length each of one of the strokes.

DIFFERENT STROKES FOR DIFFERENT FOLKS

There are four main strokes in swimming. All swimmers must use the same stroke in a competition race, although 'medley' events incorporate various – sometimes all – strokes.

FREESTYLE

Swimmers are able to choose any stroke to use in these races - but front crawl is practically always used. This the fastest of all the strokes. Most of the speed is generated through alternatively rotating the arms while quickly kicking the legs in a 'flutter' motion.

THE POOL

STARTING BLOCKS

FALSE START ROPE

BACKSTROKE TURNING ROPE

FACTS OF THE MATTER

- An Olympic size swimming pool (50 metres long) is around **TWICE THE SIZE** of the average pool you might find in your local gym, and can hold between 700,000–850,000 gallons of water.
- Perhaps there is a reason why swimming is so popular: after all, the ocean covers more than **70 PER CENT** of the entire planet.
- American swimmer Michael Phelps is the most successful Olympian of all time – with an incredible **TWENTY-THREE** gold medals: at least 14 more than any other athlete in the history of the Olympics.
- Professional swimmers are some of the most dedicated and hard-working sports people – often training for **FIVE HOURS A DAY**, up to seven days a week.
- The first swimming clubs were introduced in England in the 1830s. **MAIDSTONE SWIMMING CLUB**, established in Kent, is understood to be the first-ever swimming club. It was opened to bring people inside from the unsafe River Medway, where swimmers would often drown.
- The world's largest swimming pool resides in **ALGARROBO, CHILE**. It is 1,013 metres long.
- Swimming has been part of the Olympics since **1896**, but women's events were not introduced until 1912.
- Swimming the English Channel has become a popular challenge among enthusiasts. **CAPTAIN MATTHEW WEBB** was the first person to do it in 1875. In 1926, **GERTRUDE EDERLE** became the first woman to do it – and she did it faster than any man had at that time.

GOGGLES

Goggles keep the water and chlorine out of a swimmers' eyes.

BACKSTROKE

The only stroke performed on a swimmer's back requires them to bring their arms alternatively over their head, and use flutter kicks to propel their body through the water.

BREASTSTROKE

Like the front crawl, the breaststroke is performed on the swimmer's front. They move their arms forwards in a circular pattern, and do a similar motion with their legs. While generally considered the slowest stroke, it is extremely popular with casual swimmers.

BUTTERFLY

Perhaps the hardest stroke to perform, in butterfly the swimmer lifts both arms out of the water at the same time to propel themselves forward. As well as requiring precise timing and coordination, it is extremely physically demanding.

DIVING

Dare-devil divers compete in one of the most eye-catching spectacles in sport.

They are strong, graceful and flexible, and execute their bold moves from platforms as high as 10 metres above the water.

A diver begins by launching off a diving board using their feet, or sometimes from a handstand position. Other events involve springboards, which allow a diver to propel themselves even higher in to the air.

As they plunge downwards, divers perform tucks, rolls, somersaults, twists and other bold manoeuvres before entering the water as smoothly as possible.

It has been competitive sport since the mid-1800s, with the first-ever recorded competition taking place in 1871 off the London Bridge across the river Thames! Diving can be done as an individual sport, while a synchronized version is performed by a team of two.

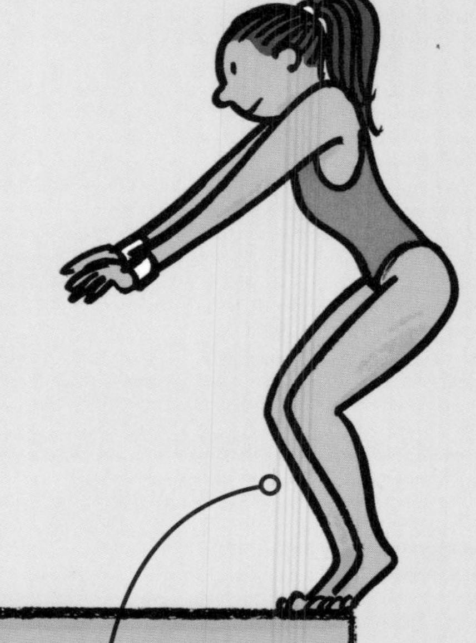

STRONG START

Dives can be started forwards, backwards, or with a handstand. Divers launch themselves from the board or platform. These normally have a high difficulty rating.

CLIFF-HANGER

Cliff diving is a more extreme version of the sport. Cliff dives take place all over the world on natural cliff faces from dizzying heights of between 23-28 metres for men and 18-23 metres for women competitors.

The fundamentals of the sport are the same, with divers performing ambitious routines. However, divers enter the water feet first due to the danger of entering head-first from such great heights.

This adrenaline sport has origins that can be traced back to the late 1100s, when Hawaiian warriors used to perform cliff dives to show off their bravery.

IN FLIGHT

Divers are 'in flight' after taking off from the board. This is where they perform their moves.

IN A TWIST

On their journey down towards the pool, divers perform a number of twists and spins in the air.

JUDGES

A panel of judges score each dive. There are a different number of judges depending on the competition. In the Olympics, individual dives are scored by seven and synchronized dives are scored by 11.

SPLASH DOWN

Water is sprayed across the pool to soften the impact for a diver when entering the water. Judges look out for a clean entry, and penalise divers for splash.

FACTS OF THE MATTER

- A number of divers used to be dancers and gymnasts due to the similar skills required in each of the sports. The main difference? Divers perform their routines while falling from **HUGE HEIGHTS**!
- Not sure exactly how high 10 metres is? Well, the average **ELEPHANT** stood on its back feet is around 5 metres high. Now just imagine two of them stood on top of each other!
- A diving pool is approximately 5 metres deep – more than **TWICE AS DEEP** as the deep end in your average swimming pool.
- At the 1988 Olympic Games in Seoul, American diver **GREG LOUGANIS** hit his head on the platform during his dive in the early rounds of the competition… but recovered to take the gold medal!
- Men's diving events became part of the Olympics back in 1904 – when it was known as **'FANCY DIVING'**. Women joined the Olympic programme in 1912, while synchronized diving was not an official Olympic sport until 2000.
- When men's diving made its Olympic debut in 1904 it was a **'DISTANCE' EVENT**. The diver who remained underwater for the longest time (distance) before resurfacing was declared the winner.
- Divers enter the water at a speed of around **65 KM/H** when diving from the 10-metre platform.
- The USA have dominated the diving events ever since it was introduced at the Olympics. After the 2016 games in Rio, they held a total of **138 MEDALS**. Next best is China with 69.

RULES

» Individual dives at major events are scored by a set of seven judges, who mark a diver between 0 (completely failed) to 10 (excellent).

» Judges can score a maximum of three points each for the takeoff, flight and entry in to the water, and another point for how well the dive was executed.

» Each dive has a pre-determined score of difficulty.

» The top score and the bottom score are ignored and the remaining five scores are added together then multiplied by the difficulty rating to give the final score of the dive.

» In synchronized diving, scoring is done the same way but by a panel of up to 11 judges.

» Divers must submit a list of the dives they intend to execute before the start of a competition. They must then perform those dives only or be scored a zero.

» The diver – or team of two in synchronized – with the highest score at the end of the competition is declared the winner.

SURFING

In many ways, surfing transcends sport – to some it is a way of life.

Surfers are finely-tuned athletes, but they place equal importance on being part of a subculture that has influenced music, fashion and art.

And its appeal is easy to see. Mostly taking place in the ocean, surfing is practised in some of the most naturally beautiful and scenic places on earth. Surfers travel far and wide in search of the biggest thrill – riding the biggest waves they possibly can.

The ancient Polynesians were the first people spotted surfing the seas in the late 1700s. Nowadays, the sport involves riding waves while standing on a surfboard and gliding across the water until the wave breaks.

SURFING THE WEB

The word surfing has been hijacked by other parts of our culture. People 'surf' the internet. The first recorded use of 'surfing the internet' was in 1992, not long after the World Wide Web was created in 1990.

WIND SURFING

Windsurfing combines the laid-back culture of surfing with the strict rules of sailing. A windsurfer's board is similar to a surfboard but with a sail that catches the wind to help windsurfers reach speeds of up to 90 km/h.

Windsurfing boards come in various designs – some are good for speed, others are designed for tricks, but in the Olympics, all competitors must use the same type.

However, there are a variety of different events such as racing and freestyle, which showcase speed, agility and a whole host of tricks. It is a relatively new sport, having emerged – also as a recreational activity – in the late 20th century.

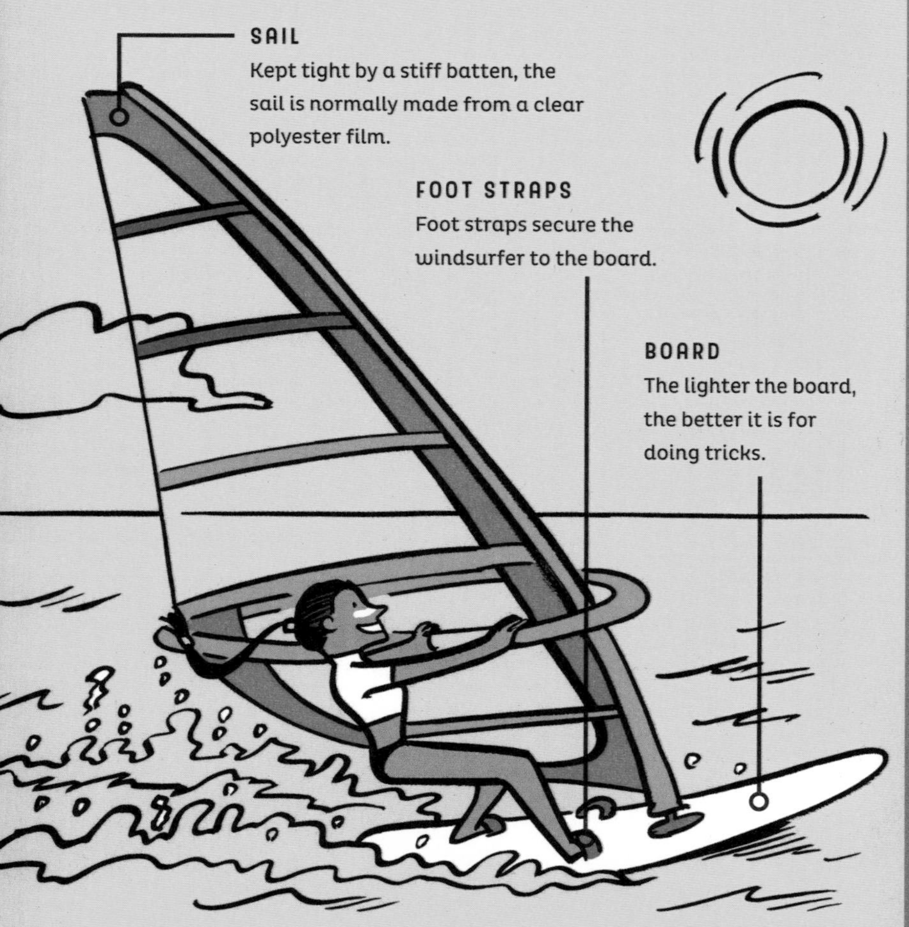

RULES

» In competitive surfing, surfers perform routines and are marked by a panel of judges.

» Two or four surfers will usually compete at the same time.

» Points are awarded based on the difficulty of the wave being surfed (the bigger the better), as well as how they are surfing it. More points are awarded for getting close to or on the crest of the wave.

» Points are also awarded for tricks and the surfer with the best score wins the competition.

FACTS OF THE MATTER

- British explorer Captain James Cook was the first person to give an account of surfing, when he saw it being practised in **HAWAII** in **1778**.
- The normal stance for a surfer is with the left foot forward, but some prefer to ride with their right foot at the front of the board. This stance is known as **'GOOFY'**.
- Surfing has never been an Olympic sport but is being introduced for the **FIRST TIME EVER** in the 2020 Games in Tokyo, Japan.
- **GARY SAAVEDRA**, a surfer from Panama, holds the record for the longest-ever surf ride. He surfed an artificial wave created by a powerboat for a whopping 3 hours and 55 minutes in 2011.
- American Garrett McNamara holds the world record for riding the **LARGEST WAVE**. In Portugal in 2011, the wave he surfed was a whopping 23.7 metres.
- Huntington Beach in California hosts a surfing competition for **DOGS!** It is held every year to raise money for animal welfare charities and organisations.
- Fancy a job in surfing? Well, you can study a degree in **SURF SCIENCE AND TECHNOLOGY** at Plymouth University in England. The course was introduced in 1999.
- While the ocean is the most popular – and most practical – place to surf. At certain times, some rivers create a backflow and produce waves that are big enough to surf. These are called **TIDAL BORES**.

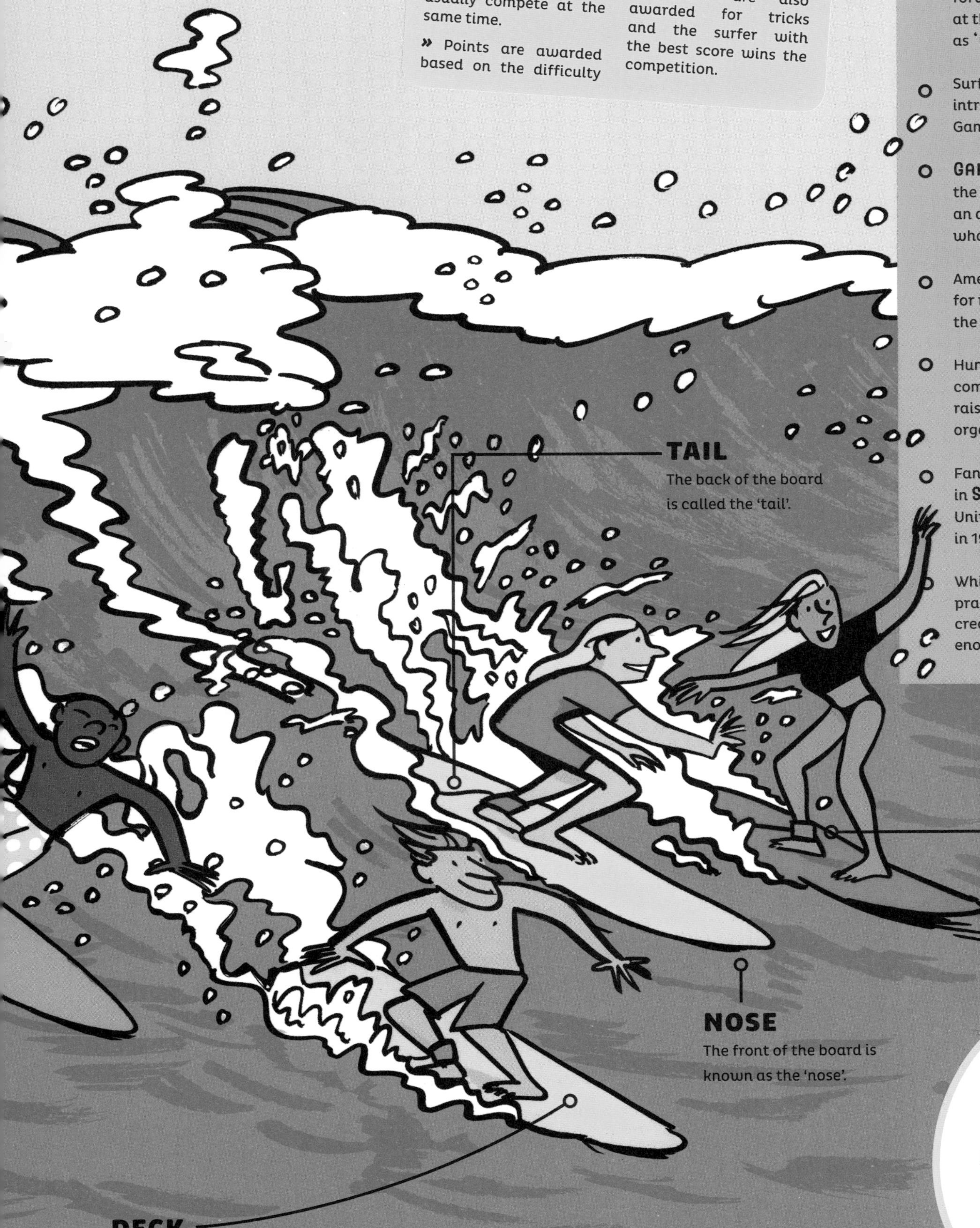

TAIL
The back of the board is called the 'tail'.

LEASH
The surfer wears a leash around their wrist or ankle so the board does not float away when they fall off.

NOSE
The front of the board is known as the 'nose'.

DECK
The top of the surfboard is known as the 'deck'.

BOARD
Surfers can choose to ride a longboard (up to 3.7 metres long) or a shortboard (around 1.5 metres). They are normally made from polystyrene or fibreglass.

BODY BOARDING

Bodyboarding is similar to surfing, but the surfer rides waves on a bodyboard while lying on their belly or on a dropped knee. The smaller board used is often referred to as a 'boogieboard'. It is rectangular and varies in size depending on the the surfer's height and weight.

CANOEING

As well as being a thrilling sport, canoeing and kayaking are wonderful ways to explore the world.

Both are extremely similar but use different boats and paddles. There are two main events at major competitions – the slalom and the sprint. The slalom takes place in an artificial course, which produces choppy white water. Competitors navigate the course and must travel through gates which are placed throughout.

Sprints take place on a calmer, flatter course, but are extremely fast paced and see canoers or kayakers go head-to-head with one another.

FACTS OF THE MATTER

- Canoes and kayaks have proved useful during **MILITARY COMBAT** in the past. During World War II, British special forces used them to conduct raids. Even today they are used by US Marines and the British Commandos.
- In 1932, German canoeist Oskar Speck paddled from his homeland all the way to Cyprus. His 80,000-kilometre journey took him **SEVEN YEARS** to complete!
- Germany have won a total of **70 MEDALS** in canoeing and kayaking at the Olympics since it was first introduced in 1936, which is at least 19 more than any other nation!
- The word kayak means **'HUNTER'S BOAT'**. That is because they were invented by the Inuit and the Aleut for hunting.
- Original kayaks were made from **ANIMAL SKIN** – often a seal skin – which was stretched over wood or whale bone.

GATES
Competitors must go through all the gates in a slalom race.

JUDGES
The judges watch on to ensure racers go through all the gates correctly.

CANOE
The paddler kneels down in their canoe.

HAZARDS
Many hazards are scattered around in a slalom race.

PADDLES
A kayak paddle has two blades and a canoe paddle just the one.

RULES

» There are a number of different events, all which have a designated letter and number to outline the type of boat and number of competitors. For example, 'C1' is a singles canoe event and a 'K2' indicates a kayak doubles.

» In a flat race (sprint), the first canoe or kayak over the finish line is the winner. Sprints can be 200, 500 or 1,000 metres.

» The slalom is different. Competitors race against the clock individually and have two chances to complete the course as quickly as possible, with the best time declared the winner.

WATER POLO

There is nothing quite like water polo!

The sport cobines aspects of basketball and rugby, but – as its name would suggest – in the water!

This fast-paced team sport is action-packed, ultra-competitive and extremely physical. Water polo payers require four basic skills – swimming, treading water for long periods, accurate passing and clinical shooting.

It was one of the first sports introduced in the Olympics and was invented in Scotland in the late 19th century by swimming coach and journalist William Wilson. Nowadays it is played everywhere from Europe and America, to Brazil, China, Canada and Australia.

FACTS OF THE MATTER

- In 1900, water polo became the first-ever **TEAM SPORT** in the Olympic Games.
- When water polo was first invented, it had huge similarities with **RUGBY**. Teams scored goals by touching the ball down in the defending team's part of the pool – much like a try – instead of throwing it in the goal like in the modern game.
- **PRINCE WILLIAM** is a keen water polo player. He represented the Scottish National Universities team when he was studying at the University of St Andrews in Scotland – coincidentally the natural home of the sport.
- A good **GOALKEEPER** will only let in around 30 per cent of the shots they face. They are considered the most important player in a water polo team as they can face around 30 shots every single game.
- Early versions of the game in America allowed holding, sinking and **DUNKING** your opponent!

GOAL
It is 3 metres wide and 90 centimetres high.

BALL
The ball is made from waterproof material, and is bigger in the men's game than it is in the women's.

POOL
The size of the pool can either be 20 x 10 metres or 30 x 20 metres and must be at least 1.8 metres deep throughout.

CAPS
The two teams must wear caps of different colour, while goalkeepers on either side always wear red.

RULES

» Each team consists of one goalkeeper and six outfield players. The outfield players are split into offensive and defensive positions.

» Games are divided into four periods of eight minutes and players must be on the move for the entire duration.

» A team must not be in possession of the ball for more than 30 seconds without taking a shot at goal. If they fail to get a shot off in that time, possession is surrendered to the opposition.

» Teams move the ball by throwing it to teammates and try to throw it past the opposition goalkeeper and into the goal.

» The team with the most goals at the end of the game is declared the winner. In the event of a tie, a shootout takes place.

ROWING

Rowing is one of the world's oldest competitive sports.

With origins that stem from ancient Egypt, it was one of the original events in the first-ever modern Olympic Games held in 1896, and today, there are 14 different rowing races at the Games, which showcase a vast array of powerful rowers.

Their aim is simple: to row their boat - known as a shell - using oars and to be the first one to cross the finish line.

Racers can compete on their own (in the individual sculls) or as part of a crew, which range from two to nine members. As part of a crew, it is absolutely vital that each member works in tandem, meaning tactics and strategy are just as important as immense strength and power.

FACTS OF THE MATTER

- In the 1928 Olympics in Amsterdam, rower Henry Pearce stopped mid-race in the quarter-final of the individual sculls to allow a family of **DUCKS** to pass in front of his boat... And he still went on to win the gold medal!
- The United States are the most successful nation in rowing at the Olympics with **33 GOLD MEDALS**. Great Britain is not far behind with 31 golds.
- In 1829, the universities of **OXFORD** and **CAMBRIDGE** competed in a boat race that has become tradition, and is held every year on the river Thames in London.
- The **MOST SUCCESSFUL** rowing Olympian is Romanian Elisabeta Lipă who has won five gold medals, two silver and one bronze.
- If the **COX** is deemed underweight, they have to carry a sandbag with them.

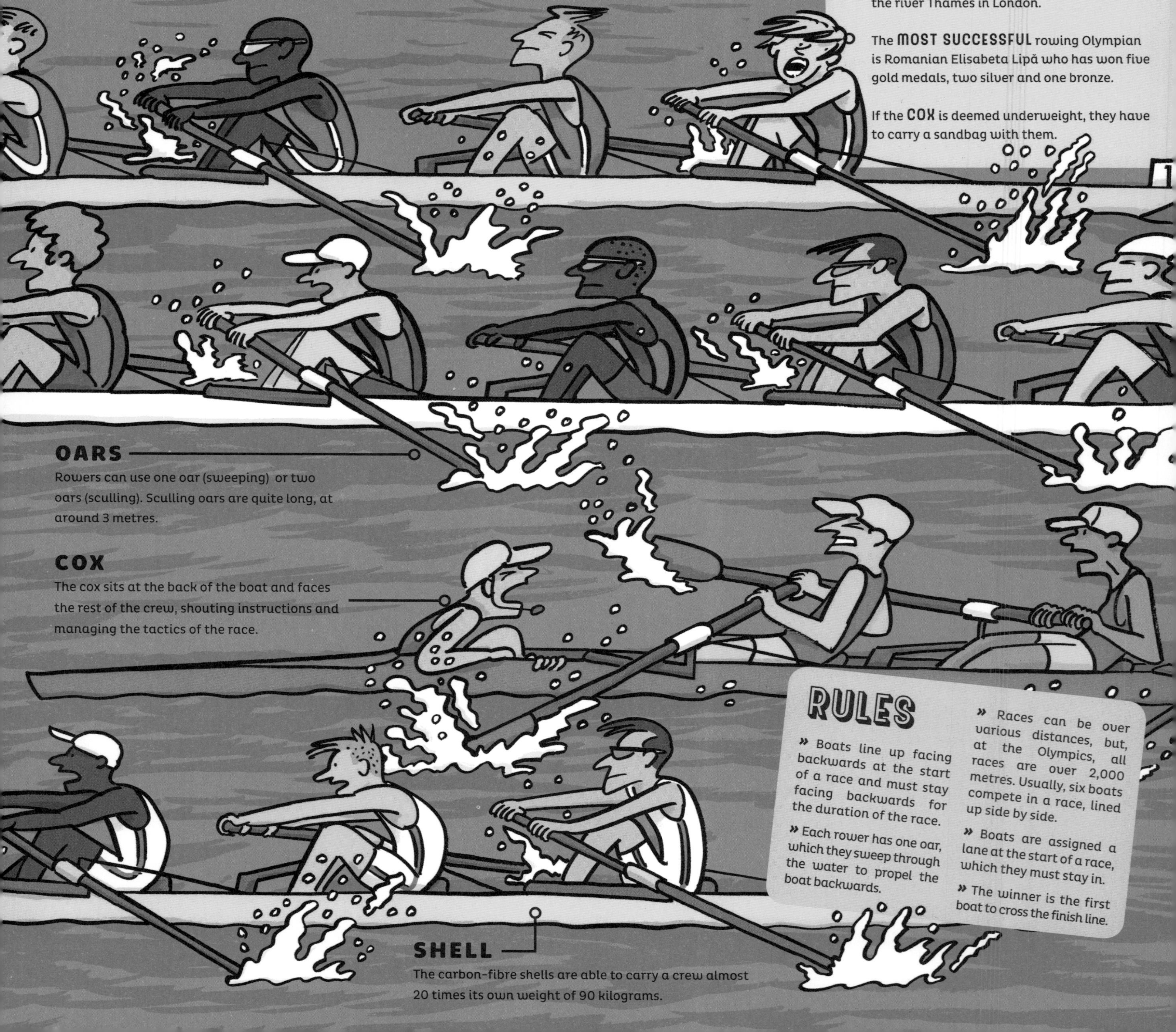

OARS

Rowers can use one oar (sweeping) or two oars (sculling). Sculling oars are quite long, at around 3 metres.

COX

The cox sits at the back of the boat and faces the rest of the crew, shouting instructions and managing the tactics of the race.

RULES

» Boats line up facing backwards at the start of a race and must stay facing backwards for the duration of the race.

» Each rower has one oar, which they sweep through the water to propel the boat backwards.

» Races can be over various distances, but, at the Olympics, all races are over 2,000 metres. Usually, six boats compete in a race, lined up side by side.

» Boats are assigned a lane at the start of a race, which they must stay in.

» The winner is the first boat to cross the finish line.

SHELL

The carbon-fibre shells are able to carry a crew almost 20 times its own weight of 90 kilograms.

SAILING

Sailing is a gruelling test of skill, mental strength and endurance.

Races can take place over huge distances in open seas, or closer to the coastline in special marked-out courses.

Events can be team, or individual, and a whole host of boats can be used – with laser yachts perhaps the most popular in the major competitions, and larger boats preferred for ocean races to help navigate the rough seas.

Sailors who race in the ocean rely on the natural elements, using just the wind to move through the water, and often braving the most brutal of conditions.

FACTS OF THE MATTER

- Many sailors have sailed around the entire world. France has a prestigious history of solo **CIRCUMNAVIGATIONS**, and the current record is held by Thomas Coville, with a time of 49 days, 3 hours, 7 minutes, and 38 seconds.
- The **YOUNGEST** person to complete a single-handed round-the-world trip is Laura Dekker from New Zealand. She was just 16 when she did it in July 2010!
- Paul Larsen holds the **SPEED SAILING** record. The Australian reached a speed of 65.45 knots (121.2 km/h) in his Vestas Sailrocket 2 in November 2012.
- **HYDROFOIL** boats can travel even faster. They have wing-like foils under the hull and help to achieve speeds that are twice the wind-speed.
- There are two categories of sailing in the Olympics: **FLEET** racing (in which several boats compete) and **MATCH** racing (one-on-one contests).

RULES

» Each race will have a course marked out by floating buoys and the first boat to cross the finishing line is the winner.

» Crashes and collisions do happen, although sailors must try and avoid this happening.

» Sailors are penalised for rule infringements and other yachts can raise a red flag to appeal if they believe another sailor has broken the rules.

» Etiquette is a huge part of sailing. If a competitor appears to be in danger, sailors are obliged to help even if it costs them in the race.

MOTOR

SPORTS

FORMULA 1

Formula 1 is the pinnacle of all motor racing sports.

'Formula' racing refers to using a car which is open-wheeled and single-seated. There are various other forms of Formula racing such as Formula 2 and Formula 3, but none can compete with the glitz, glamour and wealth of its more popular and richer counterpart, which features the world's most impressive cars and highly-skilled drivers.

Teams pump millions of pounds into making their cars faster, more reliable and technically advanced to try and win the biggest prize in Formula 1 – the World Championship. The cars regularly hit speeds in excess of 324 km/h on the track, making it an exhilarating spectacle for its millions of fans.

Since the first Formula 1 race, held in France in 1906, it has continued to evolve and push the boundaries like no other sport.

RULES

» Races are contested by drivers, who all represent a team. Each team has two drivers.

» The driver who completes the required number of laps around the circuit first wins the race.

» Drivers are awarded points based on where they finish in the race. The driver with the most points at the end of the season wins the World Championship.

» The team whose drivers have the most points is awarded to the 'Constructors Championship'.

» Races take place over three days and involve practise, qualifying and the final race.

» The fastest drivers during 'Qualifying' are lined up at the front of the 'grid' at the start of the race.

» Drivers can stop in the pits throughout the race to re-fuel, change tyres or repair damage.

JET SET MONACO

The Monaco Grand Prix is probably the most prestigious race of the entire F1 calendar. Set in the streets of the tiny, beautiful principality, the race itself is not always that exciting due to its narrow track.

Instead, the most jaw-dropping spectacle is the array of celebrities and super-rich attendees, who flock to Monaco every year to experience the race in this gorgeous setting – many watching from the comfort of one of the superyachts that litter the sea around the track. Some of the yachts on show cost more than £60 million... or a cool £100,000 if you fancy hiring one for a week!

HELMET

This essential headwear protects the driver's head in a collision or if debris spraying up from the track. It is incredibly tough and tested to withstand temperatures as hot as 800 degrees C.

STEERING WHEEL

This is nothing like your average steering wheel! A Formula 1 wheel costs around £20,000 and has a lot of control buttons.

MECHANICS

wait in the pit stops to carry out repairs, tyre changes and refuelling.

TRACK

Each track is made from its own distinctive surface. Some (like the Monaco Grand Prix) are public roads, while others are made especially for racing.

POINTS WIN PRIZES

Ten teams enter two cars each into the World Championship (20 drivers in total). Drivers are awarded points if they finish in the top 10 of a race, as such:

1ST: 25 POINTS
2ND: 18 POINTS
3RD: 15 POINTS
4TH: 12 POINTS
5TH: 10 POINTS
6TH: 8 POINTS
7TH: 6 POINTS
8TH: 4 POINTS
9TH: 2 POINTS
10TH: 1 POINT

WINGS

These push the car down and help it to grip the track, to help driver car take corners at high speeds.

SUSPENSION

Made of carbon fibre, the car's suspension system translates the power of the engine and the downforce from the wings into speed.

TYRES

Different types of tyre are used depending on the track surface, temperature and the weather.

FACTS OF THE MATTER

- The average cost of a Formula 1 car is **£6.8 MILLION**. Hundreds of millions more are spent on developing the car throughout the season.
- Approximately **80,000 COMPONENTS** are needed to build a car.
- An **ENGINE** in a Formula 1 car will usually last for only two hours before blowing up. Domestic car engines can last for around 20 years.
- Juan Pablo Montoya holds the record for the **FASTEST LAP** ever recorded in F1. During pre-qualifying for the 2004 Italian Grand Prix, the Colombian driver smashed the course record with a whopping average speed of 262.2 km/h. On the same track a year later, he recorded a speed of 372.6 km/h.
- Legendary German driver **MICHAEL SCHUMACHER** has won an incredible seven World Championships, including five in a row between 2000-2004.
- **GREAT BRITAIN** is the most successful nation in the history of Formula 1, with 16 world titles from 10 different drivers. Lewis Hamilton is the most decorated Brit, winning on four separate occasions.
- The average driver will lose around 4 kilograms of weight over the duration of a race, despite being sat down. Drivers have a bottle of drinking water installed in the car for **HYDRATION**.
- The shortest-ever F1 career lasted just **800 METRES**! In 1993, Marco Apicella was involved in a multi-car pile-up just after the start of the race and had to retire.

RALLY DRIVING

Rally drivers might be the most daring, highly-skilled racers in all of motorsport.

Races are held all over the world, where drivers can face treacherous conditions at high speeds on bumpy dirt tracks, deserts, and even ice! The unpredictable nature of rally driving makes it an incredible spectator sport and fans flock in their droves to watch.

The sport has grown in popularity since the first-ever race – held in Monte Carlo – in 1922, while the World Rally Championship – the sport's biggest prize – has been held every year since 1973.

FACTS OF THE MATTER

- Rally cars are built to deal with **EXTREME** conditions, but all must be road-legal, too.
- Once the race starts, any **REPAIRS** must be carried out by the driver and co-driver – and no one else.
- The **FRENCH** invented rally driving and have dominated the sport in recent years – Sébastien Loeb won every world title between 2004 and 2012, and fellow Frenchman Sébastien Ogier won the top prize between 2013 and 2016.
- **VOLKSWAGEN** and **CITROEN** are the two most successful teams.
- The World Rally Championship is broadcast in more than 18 countries worldwide to an audience of around **800 MILLION PEOPLE**.

CO-DRIVER

Before the race, the co-driver tests the course and takes pacenotes, which he uses to navigate the driver through the race. Often, he is focussing on his notes so hard, he can't look out the window, and relies on feeling the turns instead to know where he is on the course!

TYRES

The tyres are changed specifically to help with the conditions. For example, in snow or ice, tyres will require more grip.

SPOILER

The spoiler at the back helps with aerodynamics, making the car go faster.

RULES

» Unlike other motorsports, cars do not race head-to-head on a circuit, but against a clock. The race is divided into special stages (checkpoints) and the aim is to reach each one in the quickest time.

» Whoever completes the whole course in the fastest time wins the race.

» There are also untimed transport stages that the cars must navigate to reach the start of each timed stage.

» Before each race, each car does two practise runs on the course: the first is to take notes; and the second is for the co-driver to read them back to the driver. This is called 'reconnaissance'.

» Points are awarded to the top-ten fastest finishers. The driver with the most points at the end of the season wins the World Championship.

» Drivers race as part of a team – normally two cars per team – and the team with the most points at the end of the season wins the Constructors' Championship.

TRANSMISSION

Most rally cars are fitted with a six-speed gearbox.

ENGINE

The engine is usually fitted with a turbocharger, which sucks in air to make it more powerful.

MOTORCYCLE RACING

Few sports are as dangerous as racing motorbikes.

There are many forms of motorbike racing, but Moto Grand Prix (GP) remains its premier class and most popular. The purpose-built bikes are often prototypes and manufacturers use them to push the boundaries and try out new innovations... Meaning the riders hurtle around the track at speeds of more than 325 km/h on just two wheels!

HELMET

The most important piece of safety equipment is fitted with a visor and protects the rider's head.

TYRES

Can be up to 15 centimetres wide to help the bike grip the track.

ENGINE

The engines range anywhere between 125 cc and 1,000 cc in Moto GP, and between 800cc and 1,200 cc in Superbike.

SUITS

Leather suits protect the rider's body, and come with knee pads, as riders often scrape their knee on the track as they lean over to take corners.

FACTS OF THE MATTER

- Moto GP bikes are not allowed on public roads. They can only race on **SPECIAL CIRCUITS**.
- The first motorcycle race can be traced back to **1897**. It was held at Sheen House in Richmond, London, over a distance of 1.6 kilometres.
- **KAWASAKI** is one of the world's leading manufacturers of motorcycles. They also make spaceships and only began making motorbikes in 1962 to promote their brand.
- A bike in a Moto GP race will average a speed of around **160 KM/H** in a race.
- **DUCATI** are the most successful manufacturer of superbikes – they have won the World Championships more than any other team.

SUPERBIKES

Superbike racing is another popular from of motorcycle racing. Superbikes are road bikes that have been highly modified to make them more powerful than the ones you might see on the road. The sport is not as popular among fans as Moto GP... But is loved by the manufactures, as it helps to promote and sell their products!

RULES

» At the start of a race, riders line up on the grid depending on how well they did in qualifying laps. As in Formula 1, the fastest qualifiers start at the front of the grid.

» Racers complete a pre-determined number of laps around the circuit and the one to complete the set number of laps first wins the race.

» Motorbikes are made by different manufacturers, but the bikes in each category must conform to strict guidelines, such as engine type, weight and fuel load.

» The size of a Moto GP engine is 1,000 cc. There are two other forms of Grand Prix racing, which use smaller engines – Moto 2 (600 cc) and Moto 3 (250 cc).

MOTOCROSS

Off-road motocross racing challenges its riders with jumps, drops and other obstacles.

Racers use specially-designed motorcycles to deal with the unpredictable terrain.

The sport has been around in one form or another since the early 1900s, evolving from motorcycle time trials (known as scrambles) that were held in the UK, and the machines have evolved as the sport has become more advanced. They are designed to deal with grass, gravel or mud courses, and cope with the demands put on them by the riders, who take the jumps at great speeds to be the first over the finishing line.

TEAR-OFFS

Plastic layers on the riders' goggles can be torn off through the race as they get dirty, revealing a clean piece of plastic that gives the riders clear vision.

BODY ARMOUR

The riders wear armour with a chest plate, neck brace and knee and elbow protectors.

TYRES

Bumpy tyres help the bike grip the track.

SUSPENSION

The bikes' suspension is critical to protect the rider –and the bike! – on landing.

FACTS OF THE MATTER

- Freestyle Motocross (FMX) and Big Air (or Best Trick) are spin-offs from Motocross (MX) involving **JUMPS AND STUNTS** to impress judges.
- **SUPERMOTO** features motocross bikes racing on traditional tracks.
- Edison Dye, the 'Father of American Motocross', introduced the sport there in the **1960S**.
- Motorbike stuntman Robbie Maddison holds the record for the **LONGEST JUMP** on a motocross bike. He launched his bike 98.1 metres from a ramp over an American football field in 2009.
- Motocross is **CHEAP** to participate in compared to other motorsports – an MX dirt bike can cost a few thousand dollars, whereas a Formula 1 car can cost millions.

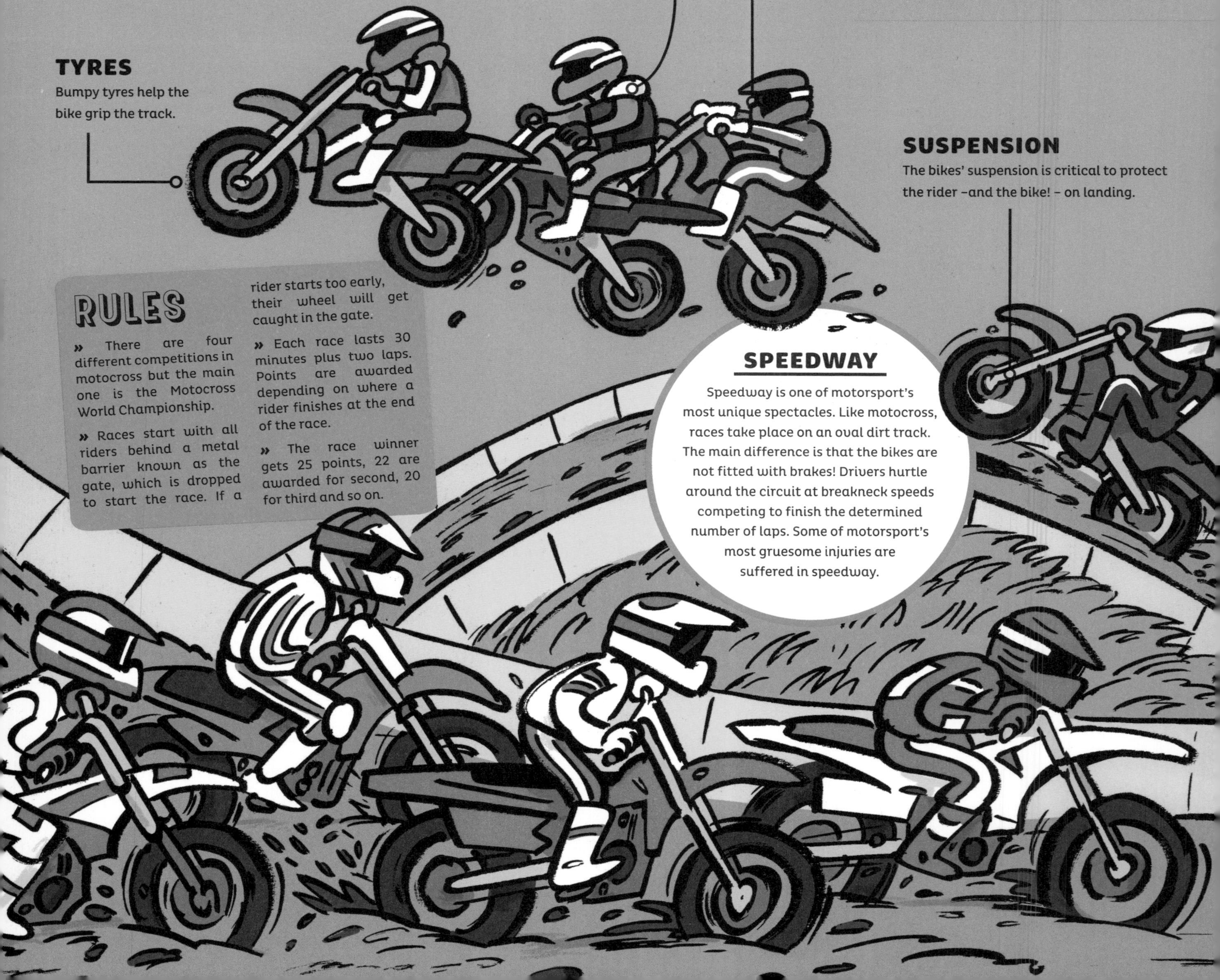

RULES

» There are four different competitions in motocross but the main one is the Motocross World Championship.

» Races start with all riders behind a metal barrier known as the gate, which is dropped to start the race. If a rider starts too early, their wheel will get caught in the gate.

» Each race lasts 30 minutes plus two laps. Points are awarded depending on where a rider finishes at the end of the race.

» The race winner gets 25 points, 22 are awarded for second, 20 for third and so on.

SPEEDWAY

Speedway is one of motorsport's most unique spectacles. Like motocross, races take place on an oval dirt track. The main difference is that the bikes are not fitted with brakes! Drivers hurtle around the circuit at breakneck speeds competing to finish the determined number of laps. Some of motorsport's most gruesome injuries are suffered in speedway.

POWERBOAT RACING

Adrenaline-fuelled and super-fast, powerboat racing is one of the world's most unique sights. Combining both watersport and motorsport, races can be offshore or inshore, with boats exceeding speeds of more than 250 km/h.

The sport originated in Great Britain in the early 20th century, but quickly made its way across the pond and over to America. The first-ever race was from the east coast of England to Calais in France in 1904, but races are often much shorter now, using track-like circuits to make it more interesting for supporters.

FACTS OF THE MATTER

- The first **POWERBOAT RACE** was in 1904, but the sport unofficially began in 1863 when Frenchman Jean Lenoir put a petrol engine on his small boat.
- Australian Kenneth Warby took the **WATER SPEED RECORD** with his hydroplane in 1978, Spirit of Australia, reaching a speedy 510 km/h.
- The Venture Offshore Cup is considered to be the **TOUGHEST** powerboat race on the planet.
- In 2013 competitors in the **VENTURE CUP** raced 965 kilometres, from Cowes in the UK to Monte Carlo in Monaco.
- **ACCIDENTS** used to be common, because the wooden boats couldn't cope with high speeds, but today's carbon fibre boats are much safer.

BOAT
Up to 14 metres long, class 1 powerboats, must weigh a minimum of 4,950 kilograms.

HULL
The carbon fibre and Kevlar hulls have evolved to skim across the water, making the boast even faster.

COCKPIT
The cockpit has an airbag and harness to keep the driver safe, while the steering wheel and throttle are often designed to detach in a crash.

RULES

- In offshore powerboat racing, boats do not physically race against each other, but against the clock. Whoever finishes the course in the shortest time is the winner.
- The annual Class 1 World Powerboat Championship is considered the most competitive race in powerboating (offshore or inshore).
- Inshore racing sees boats race head-to-head on a circuit marked out in the water.
- The Formula 1 Powerboat World Championship (inshore) has been held every year since 1981 and is contested by around 20 racers.
- In the F1 World Championship, racers are awarded points based on where they finish in a race and accumulate points throughout the season. Each race is 45 minutes long.

TARGET SPORTS

GOLF

Golf is one of the simplest sports to learn – yet it might just be the hardest to master.

Golfers require incredible patience, skill and impeccable technique, something which is honed over years. Even the world's best golfers still take regular lessons!

While many countries claim to have invented the sport, the modern game originated in 15th-century Scotland – and the original rules have barely changed since then. Golfers use a variety of different clubs to hit a small ball around a marked course, and into a series of holes, using as few shots (or 'strokes') as possible. Meanwhile, they must try to avoid hazards, such as sand bunkers, rivers and lakes – and if they hit the ball 'out-of-bounds', they will be penalised and have to retake the shot... Meaning that golfers require both physical and mental endurance!

RULES

» There are nine or 18 holes in a round of golf, all measured in yards.

» Each hole is started by the golfer hitting the ball off a tee.

» Players mustn't touch the ball during play, except on the putting green, where they are allowed to clean it.

» Holes have a rating depending upon how many shots it should take for a golfer to play it. This is known as 'par'.

» Most holes have a 'par four' rating, while each course has some par three and par five holes.

» Getting around in one shot fewer than par is called a birdie; two shots under par is called an eagle; and three under par is known as an albatross.

» One shot over par is called a bogey and two over is a double bogey.

» Tournaments are usually four rounds, with the bottom players cut after the first two rounds.

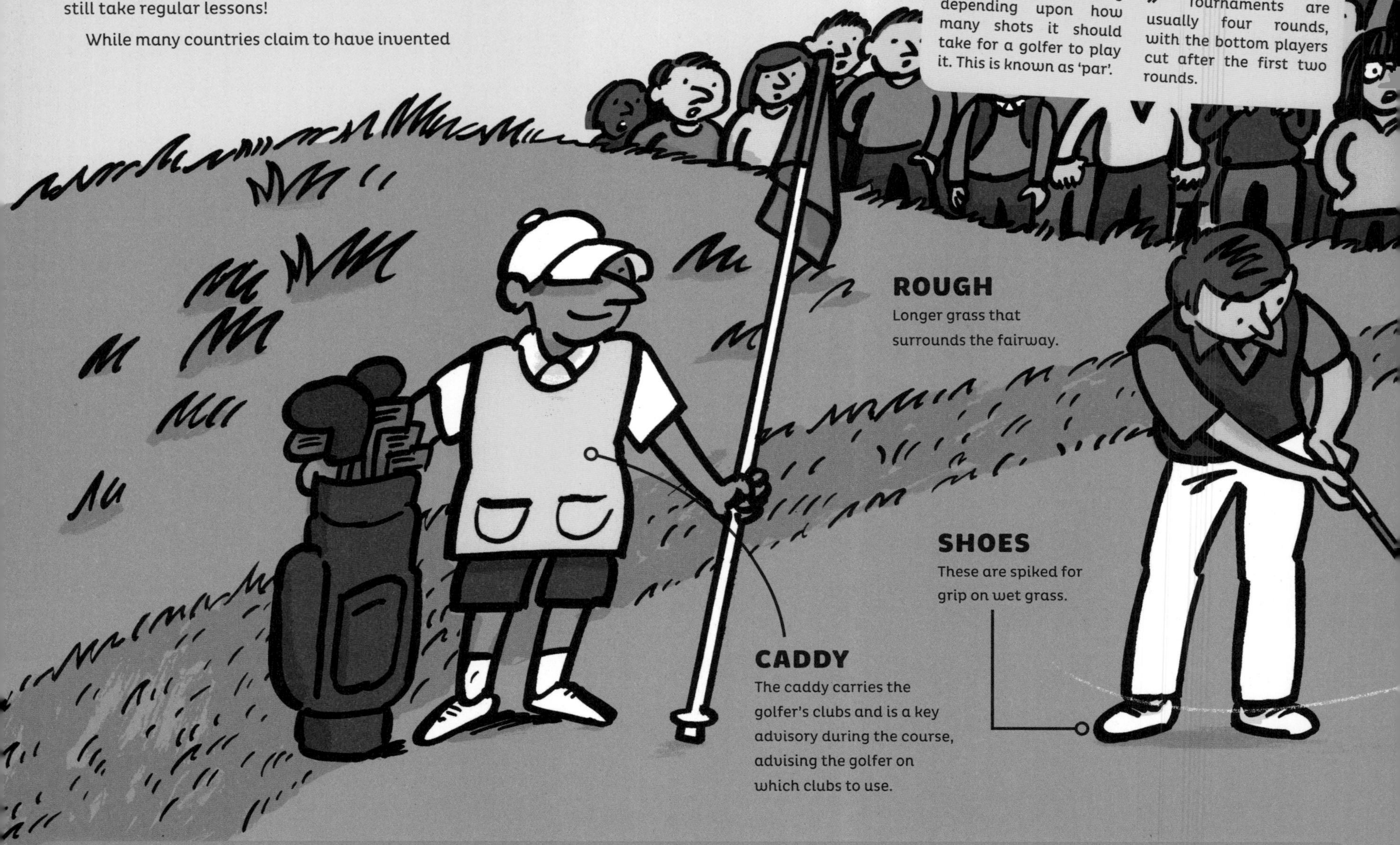

ROUGH
Longer grass that surrounds the fairway.

SHOES
These are spiked for grip on wet grass.

CADDY
The caddy carries the golfer's clubs and is a key advisory during the course, advising the golfer on which clubs to use.

JOIN THE CLUB

Golfers are allowed a maximum of 14 clubs in their bag, although most golfers usually carry just 12: three woods (a driver, a 3-wood and a 5-wood), eight irons (3-9 iron and a pitching wedge), plus a putter. The numbers on the clubs refer to the angle of the head, which determines the direction and distance of the shot.

IRONS
Normally used to approach the green, its medal head (or blade) is thin.

WEDGE
These specialist irons usually have a shorter shaft and are used for accurate short-distance lobs onto the green or out of a hazard.

WOODS
Used off the tee and for long-distances, 'woods' are often, in fact, made of metal.

PUTTER
Designed for short, low-speed strokes, this club is used on the green to sink the ball.

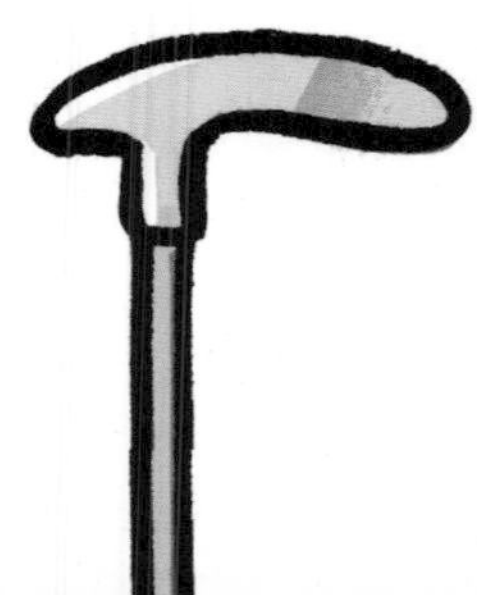

FACTS OF THE MATTER

- The term **BIRDIE** was coined by American AB Smith. After playing a good stroke back in 1899, he shouted, **'THAT WAS A BIRD OF A SHOT!'**
- The first written record of golf came from King of Scots **JAMES II IN 1457**. He banned golf as he felt it distracted his military from more important activities, such as archery.
- The pinnacle of golf is to win a **MAJOR TOURNAMENT**. There are four of them – the British Open, the Masters, the US Open and the PGA Championship.
- American legend Jack Nicklaus won an incredible **18 MAJORS** in his career – more than any other golfer in the history of the sport.
- The most famous team tournament in the world is the **RYDER CUP**, held every two years, with group teams from Europe and America going head-to-head.
- Russian astronaut, Mikhail Tyurin, became the first person to **HIT A BALL IN SPACE** in 2006.
- A **'HOLE-IN-ONE'** is one of the rarest things in golf, with the ball going in the hole on the first shot. But in 1971, 25-year-old John Hudson holed **TWO IN A ROW**. The probability of which is said to be lower than being struck by lightning.
- Mary Queen of Scots called her golf assistants cadets, which later became **'CADDIES'**.

BALL

A golf ball is covered in dimples – 336 to be exact! – to help it fly through the air.

GREEN

Each hole is measured in yards from the tee box to the putting green.

HOLE

Holes are just 10.8 centimetres wide, demanding extreme accuracy from players.

IN THE SWING

A professional golfer's swing can be more than 160 km/h – and the hotter the day, the further the ball can travel!

THE COURSE

WATER
Golfers are penalised if they hit the ball in these hazards.

GREEN

TEE
This small piece of wood or plastic raises a golf ball off the grass.

BUNKERS
Hazards – pits full of sand.

FAIRWAY
Short grass.

FRINGE

BUNKER

TEE BOX
This area is where the first shot is taken from. For longer-distance shots, this is called a drive.

ROUGH

FLAG
The flag shows golfers where the hole is.

SHOOTING

Shooting is a test of accuracy and nerve. with competitions that are often decided by the smallest of margins.

It is a sport which is steeped in history, having emerged in Great Britain in the 1850s to encourage volunteers into the military. The Americans were quick to embrace the sport – after becoming concerned by poor marksmanship during the Civil War, and now it is one of America's most beloved pastimes. There are a number of different competitions at the elite level, each using different guns but all showcasing competitors with exemplary technique.

Shooters have been demonstrating their skills at the Olympics ever since the first modern Games in Athens in 1896, and it has been a part of every Olympic Games - except two - ever since.

FACTS OF THE MATTER

- **LIVE PIGEONS** were used as moving targets at the 1900 Olympic Games in Paris. They were replaced after those games with clay pigeons.
- Shooting at the Olympics has been dominated by the **AMERICANS**. They have won a total of **111 MEDALS** – 54 of them gold. No other nation can get anywhere near them in terms of golds. China are next best, with 22.
- The average pistol will normally weigh less than 1 kilogram – that is lighter than a **BAG OF SUGAR**. However, they can require more than 5 kilograms of force to pull the trigger.
- The **OLDEST** ever Olympic champion is a shooter. At the Stockholm Games in 1912, Oscar Swahn was part of the Swedish team that won the Gold medal at the tender age of **64**!
- Hungary's Karoly Takacs defied the odds when he won golds in 1948 and 1952, after teaching himself to shoot with his **LEFT HAND** after injuring his right.

PISTOL

PISTOL
These handguns are operated with just one hand, and can vary in size and fire rate.

LASERS
Nowadays special laser pistols are used in major competitions.

TAKING AIM
There are four separate pistol events at the Olympics, which vary in distance and style. Some events involve shooting a target from the same position, while others require shooters to move and take aim at the target from different angles. Shooters aim at a tiny target and can be marked on both accuracy and speed.

SHOTGUN

SHOTGUN
A 12 gauge shotgun is normally used in shotgun events.

SHOTS
The shotgun is similar to a rifle but they have bullets which contain a number of smaller bullets that project once they have exited the gun. These are known as shots.

TRAPS
The main shotgun events are clay pigeon and skeet. In these events, targets (called traps) are fired out of a machine and shooters must react quickly to try and hit them as they fly through the air.

RING OF FIRE
Accuracy and a steady hand is imperative. In the Olympics, targets in rifle and pistol shooting have ten rings. More points are awarded for shooting closer to the middle of the target.

RULES

» Shooters are marked on accuracy or speed depending on the competition.

» In most events, competitors shoot at targets and points are awarded based on how close each shot is to the centre of the target.

» The distance a shooter stands from the target varies in each event and there are 15 different events in total at the Olympics

» Competitors are eliminated throughout a competition, with eight shooters usually left to contest the final.

» Whoever accumulates the highest score in the final round is crowned as the winner.

RIFLE

GOGGLES
These protect the shooter's eyes

BARREL
A rifle is a long gun with a rifled barrel. An air rifle is used for the 10-metre rifle event and the long rifle for the 50-metre.

DARTS

You don't have to be the fittest sportsperson in the world to play darts. After all, the game originated in English pubs! But that's not to say it doesn't require incredible skill: mental toughness and perfect hand-eye co-ordination is key for darts players at any level.

Matches are contested by two players, who throw darts at a board to score points as quickly as possible. Each section is worth a different number of points, with the smallest areas providing the biggest rewards.

Many spend years perfecting their throwing technique but nowadays the rewards are handsome. Interest in the game has risen dramatically since the late 1970s and top players can now earn millions of pounds in prize money.

FACTS OF THE MATTER

- There are two main governing bodies in darts, the Professional Darts Corporation (**PDC**) and the British Darts Organisation (**BDO**).
- The PDC is the world's most popular darts competition. It is held at London's Alexandra Palace and attracts thousands of fans – many of whom turn up in **FANCY DRESS**!
- All players have nicknames. Englishman Phil '**THE POWER**' Taylor is the greatest ever darts player and is a record 16-time world champion.
- A 'nine-dart finish' or the '**PERFECT LEG**' involves winning a leg using just nine darts. This is the fewest number of darts that a player can throw to check out from 501 and is incredibly rare.
- The first televised nine-darter was thrown by **JOHN LOWE** in 1984 and he received £102,000 prize money for the incredible feat. Phil Taylor has thrown a record 11 perfect legs on TV.

DARTS

Made from different types of metal, the grip helps players to hold the darts while the flight helps it through the air.

SHIRTS

Darts players are known for wearing colourful shirts during matches.

BOARD

The darts board is hung so the centre of the bullseye is 173 centimetres from the floor.

OCHE

The thrower must stand behind this line, which is 236 centimetres from the dartboard.

KNOW THE SCORE

The value shown on the outside edge indicates the number of points scored if the dart lands in that area.

The score is doubled by landing the dart in the outside ring and trebled if it lands in the inner ring.

Fifty points are awarded for hitting the circle right in the middle – known as the bullseye – and 25 are given for hitting the 'outer bull'.

The highest score that can be achieved with three darts is 180, which is done by hitting the treble 20 three times in one turn.

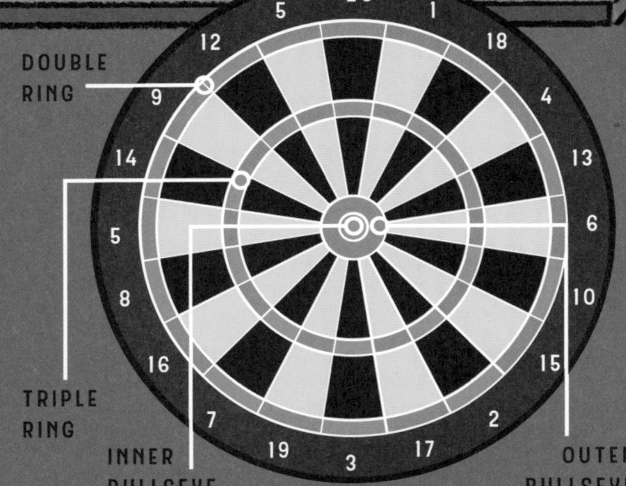

RULES

» Matches are divided into legs and sets. A player needs to win three legs to win the set.

» Each player starts a leg with a score of 501 and the aim is to get that down to 0 as quickly as possible.

» Reaching 0 is known as checking out. The final dart – or the check-out – must land in the double. So, if a player is left with 40, they must hit the double 20 to check out and win the leg.

» If a player's score goes below zero, they 'go bust' and their score resets to what it was before they went bust at the start of the next turn.

ARCHERY

People have been shooting bows from arrows for thousands of years.

Possibly as far back as 20,000 BC, archery has been used to hunt animals and as a weapon of war. While the use of archers declined rapidly after guns were invented, it remains a popular sport to this day.

In the sport, archers propel the arrow towards a target, scoring points based on their accuracy.

It requires a steady hand, an eagle-eye and takes years of practise to perfect.

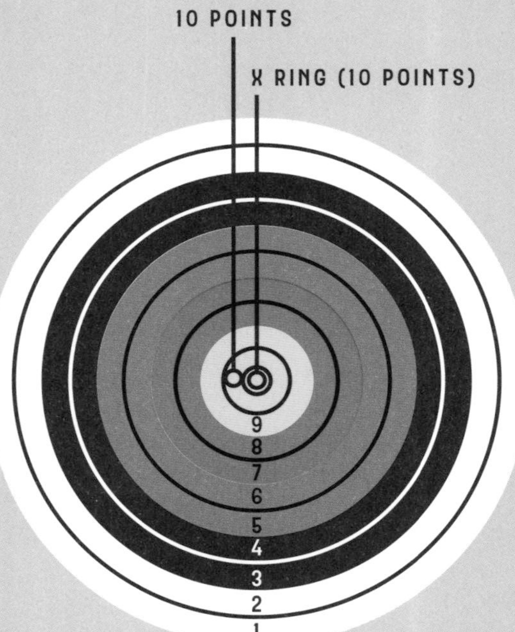

FACTS OF THE MATTER

- An archer can be referred to – albeit rarely – as a **'TAXOPHILITE'**. The word comes from the Greek for 'lover of the bow'.
- The English military were, historically, skilled archers. Their longbowmen killed almost 2,000 French soldiers during the **BATTLE OF CRÉCY** in 1346 – losing just 50 of their own men.
- A number of British monarchs **BANNED** other sports so men would concentrate on perfecting their archery skills for military combat.
- Arrows in top-level competition can reach speeds of around **240 KM/H**!
- The central circle of a target measures just 12.2 centimetres across – from the archer's position 70 metres away, it looks no bigger than a **DRAWING PIN**.

HOTSPOT

The centre of the target is worth 10 points.

SIGHT

This helps the archer line up their shot.

BOW

This is made from wood or carbon fibre.

ARROW

Usually made from aluminium, the arrows are held in a pouch called a quiver.

RULES

» Archers stand 70 metres from the target.

» Scoring is simple. Archers score points based on where the bow lands on the target. The highest single score is 10 – for an arrow that lands right in the centre of the target.

» In competitions, three or six arrows (known as rounds) are fired to make up what is known as a turn or end. Each arrow is added up at the end of each turn and the archer with the highest score is the winner.

» In team events, each individual score is added up to give the team's total.

» Before shooting a round, archers will be given a signal and must release the arrow within a certain time limit.

TENPIN BOWLING

Enjoyed by people of all ages and walks of life, tenpin bowling is both a popular hobby and a hugely competitive sport. It involves rolling a heavy ball down a wooden lane and trying to score points by knocking down pins.

Known simply as 'bowling' in most countries, the sport has been around for thousands of years – a bowling ball and pins were discovered in the grave of an Egyptian child, believed to have been buried as far back as 3,400 BC.

Modern bowling may have taken influence from there and other forms of the game, which were played in Europe. While they share similarities with the modern game, the way we play bowling now was invented by the Americans. That is also where most of the world's best players come from. They are highly-skilled and the top bowlers are able to manipulate the ball expertly, using swerves and curls to strike the pins with 'pin-point' accuracy!

FACTS OF THE MATTER

- Bowling is the **NUMBER ONE SPORT** in America for participation levels.
- In America, the sport is worth around **$6 BILLION**.
- A place with bowling lanes is known as a **BOWLING ALLEY**. The world's biggest bowling alley, Inazawa Grand Bowling Centre, has a whopping 116 lanes!
- The highest score possible in a game of bowling, 300, is achieved by bowling **TEN STRIKES** in a row, and two more in the bonus rolls.
- To bowl a strike, the bowler will usually aim to hit the edge of the **HEAD PIN**, meaning the ball will only hit four pins directly, and the back rows are toppled by the front pins falling over.

GUTTER

Gutters run down either side of the lane. A misplaced shot will go down the gutter... and score zero points!

BALL

The bowling ball has three finger holes and varies in weight depending on the needs of the bowler. The maximum weight is 7.25 kilograms.

PINS

The pins are arranged in a triangle. The one at the front is called the head pin.

LANE

Made of varnished wood, the lane measures 18.29 metres from the foul line to the head pin and is 1.05 metres wide.

FOUL LINE

A bowler is deducted points for crossing this line.

SHOES

Bowlers have to wear special shoes to help with grip and protect their feet in case the ball is dropped.

SPLIT AIN'T EASY

When two or more pins are left after the first roll and they are not next to each other, it is known as a split. A split shot is the hardest in bowling – especially the infamous 7-10 split, when the furthest left (7 pin) and the furthest right (10 pin) are the only ones left. To successfully pull off the shot, the bowler must hit one of the pins off the back wall and into the other pin.

RULES

» A game of bowling is divided into 10 frames. The bowler has two rolls per frame to try and knock down all the pins. If all the pins are knocked own in one roll that is called a strike. Knocking down all the pins in two rolls is known as a spare.

» The score is kept by adding up the number of pins knocked down in each frame. However, bonuses are awarded for spares and strikes.

» A strike earns 10 points plus the points for the next two rolls. So, if a player bowls a strike and follows it up with a six and a two, they would score 10+6+2 (18). A spare earns 10 points plus the points for the next roll.

» If a bowler throws a strike or spare in the final frame, they are awarded up to two further bonus rolls.

SNOOKER

Snooker might seem like a simple game... but it takes years to perfect. Most snooker stars started playing the game when they were as young as four years old! The main aim is to hit the white ball (the 'cue ball') with a long cue into other coloured balls so they go in to one of the six pockets on the table. This is known as a pot. Sounds simple enough, right? Wrong!

Balls have to be potted in the correct order and the player must try to maintain a good position with the cue ball in order to help with the following shot.

On top of that, the table is huge and the pockets are tiny. It is the ultimate, unforgiving test of precision where the smallest of errors can have a huge impact on the outcome of a match.

As such, snooker payers must be ice cool, have nerves of steel and be able to withstand relentless pressure. As an individual sport, there is no place to hide.

RULES

» Matches are divided into a pre-determined number of frames. The final of the World Championship, for example, is played to the best of 37 frames (first to 18 wins).

» Players must pot the 15 red balls first. Each time a red is potted they can then try and pot any of the other colours. If successful, the colour is placed back on to the table and they continue until all the reds are down as such: red, colour, red, colour, red , colour.

» Once all the reds are down, players then try and pot the rest of the colours – but in a specific order. Yellow is first, then green, brown, blue, pink and black.

» Each time a player comes to the table, they start what is known as a break. The break is only over when they miss a shot. A century break is when a player scores 100 points during a single visit to the table.

» The maximum points which can be scored in one break is 147. To do that, players must pot all the reds - each one followed by the black - and then all the remaining colours. This is known as a 'maximum' or '147 break'.

» Fouls are called for infringements such as hitting the wrong ball or knocking the cue ball with a part of the body or clothing. Players are given point penalties and – in very rare cases – might have to concede the frame.

THE D

A frame starts with a break. The player who is breaking shoots the cue into the cluster of reds from inside the D.

POCKETS

The table has pockets on each corner and one at the centre of each of the longest side, which are just 86 millimetres wide!

TABLE

The table has wooden legs, and its top is made up of a number of slates pushed together.

POOL

Pool is similar to snooker but is played on a much smaller table. Although, the shots in pool are less difficult, games are fast, frenetic affairs. There are two types of pool – 8 ball and 9 ball. In 8 ball, each player pots their own balls – either spotted or striped – before trying to pot the black (eight) ball. They must not hit their opponents ball and not hit the black before all their balls are potted.

JARGON

'SNOOKER'

When a player leaves his opponent in a situation where they cannot directly hit the ball they need to. They must try and come off the cushion or swerve around the ball which is in the way.

PLANT

When two balls are not touching but are played into one another to make a pot, this is known as a plant.

CANNON

A shot where the cue ball is made to contact more than one ball, it is normally used to help improve position and help with developing breaks.

FACTS OF THE MATTER

- Snooker is understood to have been invented by bored British army officers serving in India in the late 1800s. Sir Neville Chamberlain (not the former prime minister) is known as the **FATHER OF SNOOKER**.
- The World Championship, the pinnacle of snooker, is held every year at the **CRUCIBLE THEATRE** in Sheffield.
- Scottish snooker legend **STEPHEN HENDRY** is the sport's most decorated player with seven world titles.
- Joe Davis earned just **£6 10 SHILLINGS** when he was crowned first-ever world champ back in 1927.
- Snooker has come a long way since those early days: Mark Selby picked up a cheque for **£375,000** after winning the 2017 world championship.
- Snooker is sometimes accused of being boring – but try telling the players that. All of them have **NICKNAMES** or aliases and enter the arena to a rousing theme song.
- '**ROCKET**' Ronnie O'Sullivan made a 147 break in just five minutes and 20 seconds at the world championship in 1997. It remains the fastest-ever maximum break.
- The word 'snooker' was a **SLANG** word used in the military for someone who was inexperienced. The game was Christened snooker after Chamberlain a player a 'snooker' when he missed a pot.

CHALK

Players dust the tip of their cue with chalk to help it grip the balls.

CUE

Used to hit the cue ball, cues vary in size are made from wood.

BAIZE

This green cloth covers the slates and cushions.

CUSHION

Vulcanized rubber cushions surround the edges of the table. Players sometimes opt to play shots off the cushions and use them to escape snookers.

POINTS WIN PRIZES

Each colour ball is worth a different number of points:

RED
1 POINT

YELLOW
2 POINTS

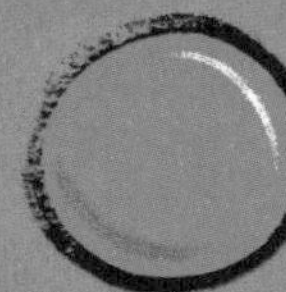

GREEN
3 POINTS

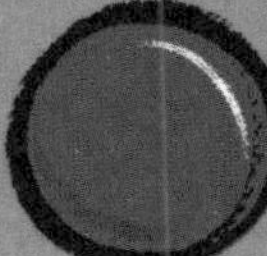

BROWN
4 POINTS

BLUE
5 POINTS

PINK
6 POINTS

BLACK
7 POINTS

COMBAT

SPORTS

BOXING

Boxing is the sport of fighting with fists.

Early boxing matches, or 'bouts', were fought using just bare knuckles, but gloves were made compulsory when the laws (the Queensberry Rules) that still codify modern boxing were laid down in England in 1865.

Although the sport is now a highly-organised, multi-million pound business, it is still brutal and blood-fuelled, with boxers trying to land punches to their opponent's head and body inside the ring.

Boxers are among the fittest and most disciplined athletes around: before a bout, they are put through gruelling training regimes which involve intense exercise and an extremely strict diet. Some boxers even fight in different weight classes, requiring an even more extreme body transformation.

The reward for such sacrifice? How about becoming the champion of the world, or earning millions of pounds?

RULES

» Bouts are fought over a series of rounds. At the top level, there are normally 12 rounds which are three minutes long.

» Boxers try to land punches on their opponent, while blocking and dodging.

» They are not allowed to aim punches below the waist, on the kidneys or at the back of the head.

» Bouts are scored by a set of judges on a 10-point system. Each round is scored by the judges and the winner of each gets 10 points, while the loser gets nine. Close rounds can be scored 10-10, while more dominant rounds (usually if one fighter is knocked down) are scored 10-8.

» At the end of the fight, the points are added up and the boxer with the most points is the winner.

» Fights can also be won by knockout – when the referee will end the fight if they decide a competitor is unfit to continue. A technical knockout occurs if a boxer is knocked to the floor three times in a single round.

HEAVY DUTY

Boxing is divided into different weight categories and boxers will only fight someone of a similar weight to them. For example, a flyweight boxer must weigh no more than 49 kilograms, while a heavyweight could weigh as much as 90 kilograms. Before a professional bout, the two fighters are weighed at a 'weigh-in' to make sure they meet the requirements.

JUDGES
Judges score the fight.

PUNCHES

Fighters become known for their boxing 'style' inside the ring. The three basic styles are: outside fighter, or 'boxer', who showcases fancy footwork and favours quick jabs; the brawler or 'slugger' who lacks finesse, but can endure – and deliver – a heavy blow; and the inside fighter, or 'swarmer', who delivers intense flurries of hooks and uppercuts.

JAB

A quick, straight punch which is thrown from the lead hand. There are two different stances – orthodox and southpaw: the lead hand for an orthodox fighter is the left...

while a southpaw leads with their right.

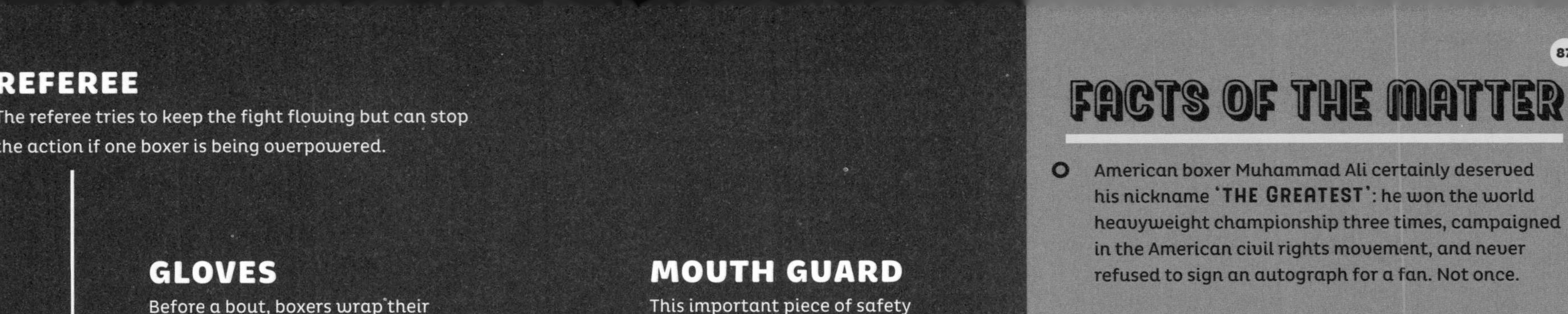

REFEREE

The referee tries to keep the fight flowing but can stop the action if one boxer is being overpowered.

GLOVES

Before a bout, boxers wrap their hands and don leather gloves designed to protect their hands .

MOUTH GUARD

This important piece of safety equipment protects the boxers' teeth.

FACTS OF THE MATTER

- American boxer Muhammad Ali certainly deserved his nickname **'THE GREATEST'**: he won the world heavyweight championship three times, campaigned in the American civil rights movement, and never refused to sign an autograph for a fan. Not once.
- A select number of elite boxers finished their career **WITHOUT LOSING** a single bout. American pair Rocky Marciano and Floyd Mayweather Jr. share the record, both fighting, and winning, all of their 49 bouts.
- Fans often have to pay a one-off fee to watch the fight on television – making some boxers multi-millionaires off the back of one bout. When Floyd Mayweather Jr. took on Manny Pacquiao in 2015, the pair earned a staggering **$180 MILLION** between them.
- Boxing careers can be short and can **END ABRUPTLY** after one heavy defeat.
- Great Britain's Len Wickwar fought no fewer than **463 BOUTS** between 1928 and 1947 (winning 336!).
- Gloves were not just introduced into boxing for safety reasons. It was also thought that they would help boxers to land more punches, increase **KNOCKOUTS** and make the sport more entertaining.
- In 1997, American boxer Mike Tyson was disqualified for biting off part of opponent Evander Holyfield's **EAR**.
- This **AGE-OLD TRADITION** was showcased at the first-ever ancient Olympic Games.

TRUNKS

Trunks normally display the boxer's name or nickname.

BELL

A bell is rung to signal the start and end of a round.

UPPERCUT

One of boxing's most devastating shots, the uppercut is a rising, vertical punch from the rear hand.

CROSS

More powerful than the jab, it is a straight punch thrown with the rear hand. It can also called a 'straight' or 'right'.

HOOK

Extremely powerful, the hook is swung in a semi-circular motion from the rear hand. Boxers usually set the hook shot up with a series of jabs.

WRESTLING

Wrestling dates back 15,000 years! This ancient combat sport requires strength, tactics and fitness, as wrestlers look to beat their opponent by performing throws, holds, clinches and takedowns, while maintaining a superior position. Bouts take place on a mat, and there are various different forms that incorporate distinctive styles and embrace historic traditions.

This accessible sport is available to everyone and actively embraces athletes with disabilities. In American colleges, where the sport is popularly played, the best student wrestlers go on to compete on the world's biggest stage at events like the Olympics.

FACTS OF THE MATTER

- **GRECO-ROMAN** wrestling featured at the first modern Olympic Games in 1896. It was joined by freestyle wrestling in 1904.
- The national sport of Turkey is **OIL WRESTLING**, where wrestlers cover themselves in olive oil before a bout. Historic matches could last for days but a time limit of 40 minutes was introduced in 1975.
- Wrestling was popular among the **ROYAL FAMILIES** of England, Japan and France in the Middle Ages (5th to 15th century).
- English settlers brought wrestling to America in the **15TH CENTURY**, where it went on to become one of the country's most loved sports.
- Up until 2004, wrestling at the Olympics was a **MEN-ONLY** event. At the 2004 Games held in Athens, four women's freestyle events were finally brought in.

PASSIVITY ZONE

New moves cannot be started in this area.

WWE

WWE is a form of professional wrestling which has millions of fans. It combines wrestling along with scripted theatrical performance. Bouts take place in a ring instead of a mat and combine traditional wrestling techniques with striking attacks and spectacular special moves such as jumping from the ropes. While pro wrestling bouts are put on mainly for entertainment, pro wrestlers are incredible athletes, who put their body on the line every single time they enter the ring.

SINGLET

All wrestlers wear all-in-one outfits which are either red or blue. These are known as singlets.

INNER CIRCLE

Most of the wrestling takes place in the inner circle, and there is another circle just outside to mark the edge of the zone where wresting can take place.

MAT

The mat is made of thick rubber and foam.

BOOTS

The boots are usually the same colour as the singlet. They help the athlete grip the mat and protects their ankles.

RULES

» Bouts are scored by judges who award points to wrestlers for various moves. The wrestler with the most points at the end of the bout is declared the winner.

» Wrestlers can also win a bout with by pinning both of their opponent's shoulders to the mat.

» At the Olympics, there are two forms of wrestling – Greco-Roman and freestyle.

» In Greco-Roman wrestling, the legs are off-limits. All throws and holds must be above the waist.

» In freestyle wrestling, wrestlers can grab their opponent's legs and throw them to the floor. This is called a takedown.

» Like many combat sports, wrestling is divided into different weight categories.

UFC

The Ultimate Fighting Championship (UFC) is a ferocious mixed martial arts sport.

It blends different styles of fighting such as Taekwondo, jujitsu and karate, as well as other fighting techniques like boxing and wrestling.

While martial arts originated thousands of years ago, UFC is extremely new. It did not become properly organised until November 1993 and almost went out of existence shortly after.

Nowadays it is big business, retaining a huge, dedicated fan base who flock to UFC fights in droves, while millions more watch from their TV screens.

Like in boxing, preparation is key for UFC fighters. Training regimes in the lead-up to a fight can be extremely demanding. However, its rapid rise in popularity in recent years means fighters can earn vast sums of money for reaching the top of their game.

FACTS OF THE MATTER

- The record for the quickest-ever **KNOCKOUT** in UFC is just seven seconds. This has happened on three separate occasions.
- UFC is a sport for **ALL AGES**. The youngest-ever UFC champion is Jon Jones, who won the light-heavyweight title aged just 23 years, 242 days.
- By contrast, the **OLDEST CHAMPION** is Randy Couture (45 years, 146 days).
- The sport was nearly **BANNED** in the late 1990s. US senator John McCain saw a recorded UFC fight and was so shocked by the violence he led a campaign to try and put a stop to it, which failed – much to the delight of its loyal fan base.
- In fact, research shows that UFC is much **SAFER** than boxing. A study by the University of Alberta in Canada discovered that MMA fighters were far less likely to sustain injuries that would affect them in the long term.

HOW TO WIN

POINTS DECISION

When all rounds are completed, it is up to the judges to decide the winner.

KNOCKOUT

If the fighter is knocked unconscious, their opponent wins by knockout. If the referee decides the fighter cannot continue it is a technical knockout.

SUBMISSION

Fighters can deploy holds and clinches to try and get their opponent to 'tap out'. They do this by visibly tapping their opponent or the mat and can also submit by yelling at the referee.

DISQUALIFICATION

Fighters can also be disqualified for illegal moves such as headbutts or hitting below the waist.

KIT

SHORTS: The shorts are usually tight so that an opponent cannot grab hold of them.

GLOVES: UFC gloves are open-fingered and much smaller and lighter that boxing gloves.

FEET: Fighters take to the ring barefoot.

OCTAGON

The ring is known as an octagon as it has eight sides. There is a cage that surrounds the edges and it measures 70 square metres, 9.1 metres across by 2.7 metres high.

RULES

» Fights vary in terms of length but a 'main event' fight can last for no longer than five rounds which are a maximum of five minutes each.

» Non-main-event bouts are a maximum of three five-minute rounds.

» Fights are scored by a set of judges on a the same 10-point system used in boxing (see page 86). If the fight does not finish before all rounds are completed, the fighter with the most points at the end is declared the winner.

» A fight can also be ended early through various means and, in rare cases, finish as a draw.

» UFC fighters are split into weight categories and only fight somebody of a similar weight to them.

SUMO WRESTLING

Sumo wrestling produces huge stars... in more ways than one!

Being Japan's national sport, top-level wrestlers are worshipped by adoring fans – and they are usually enormous in physical stature.

It has been part of Japanese culture for hundreds of years and people travel there from all over the world to try and become the grand champion.

Bouts take place in a ring between two wrestlers. The main aim is very simple: try to force your opponent out of the ring. Each match is just a single round long, and often lasts just a few breathtaking seconds, as one wrestler uses all their strength and agility to overwhelm their opponent with a torrent of power... and flesh!

FACTS OF THE MATTER

- Unlike boxing, sumo does not include weight divisions. A wrestler can sometimes take on someone who is **TWICE THEIR OWN WEIGHT**... and still stand a chance of winning!
- Japan holds six sumo tournaments each year, in which each wrestler fights **15 BOUTS.** They are 15 days long, and begin and end on a Sunday.
- Wrestlers normally go by just one wrestling name. The best name they can be given is **YOKOZUNA**, meaning 'grand champion'.
- Before entering the ring, wrestlers perform a ceremonial ritual. Wrestlers start by throwing salt into the arena to purify it, then perform a dance, or **'SHIKO'**, to drive away evil spirits.
- Sumo wrestlers must adhere to a strict, **TRADITIONAL LIFESTYLE** and are required to live in training stables. They each start as servants before moving up the ranks.

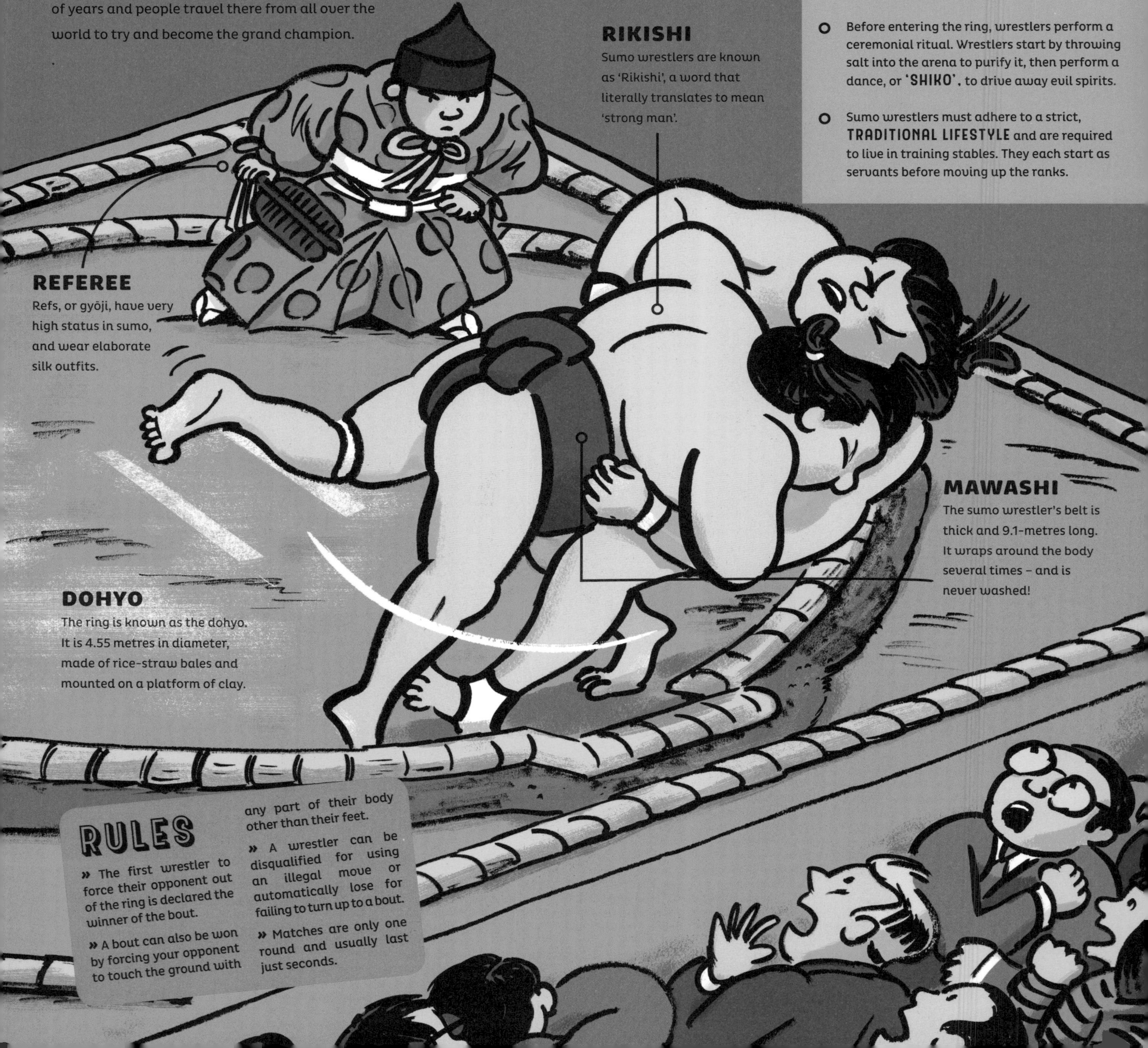

RIKISHI

Sumo wrestlers are known as 'Rikishi', a word that literally translates to mean 'strong man'.

REFEREE

Refs, or gyōji, have very high status in sumo, and wear elaborate silk outfits.

MAWASHI

The sumo wrestler's belt is thick and 9.1-metres long. It wraps around the body several times – and is never washed!

DOHYO

The ring is known as the dohyo. It is 4.55 metres in diameter, made of rice-straw bales and mounted on a platform of clay.

RULES

» The first wrestler to force their opponent out of the ring is declared the winner of the bout.

» A bout can also be won by forcing your opponent to touch the ground with any part of their body other than their feet.

» A wrestler can be disqualified for using an illegal move or automatically lose for failing to turn up to a bout.

» Matches are only one round and usually last just seconds.

KABADDI

Kabaddi is one of sport's rare treasures.

Known as the 'game of the masses', it requires no specialised equipment and is accessible to absolutely anyone.

The game originated in India, is the national sport of Bangladesh, and is loved by millions throughout South Asia.

On the face of it, kabaddi might seem strange to newcomers to the game. But its weird and wonderful rules set it apart from every other sport. The premise is quite straightforward: two teams take it in turns to attack by sending one of their players into the opposition half. Their job is to score points by tagging opponents and then running back to their own side. Sounds simple enough, right? Well, there is a catch. The rules state players are not allowed to breathe while they are attacking!

FACTS OF THE MATTER

- There are actually two different forms of kabaddi. International Rules Kabaddi is played in a **RECTANGULAR** court and is the most popular. Circle-style, as its name would suggest, is played on a **CIRCULAR** pitch.
- The sport has been dominated by **INDIA**. Up to 2016, they have won every single title at the Asian Games and the Kabaddi World Cup.
- The defending team form a close unit by **HOLDING HANDS**. In fact the name kabaddi derives from the Tamil word 'Kai-pidei': to hold hands.
- The **PRO KABADDI LEAGUE** is the biggest competition in India. Only cricket can trump it for viewing figures – in 2014, it was estimated that 435 million people tuned in to watch it.
- Kabaddi has never been featured at the **OLYMPICS**. However, it was demonstrated at the 1936 Games held in Berlin.

RULES

» Teams consist of seven players and each team take turns to send one individual player into the opponent's half. This player is called the raider.

» The raider tries to tag one of the seven members of the other team and then run back to their side. Each player the raider touches counts as one point if they make it safely back to their own side.

» The raider must take one breath before entering the opponent's half by stepping over the mid line and not breathe again until they have returned to their side of the court. To make sure the raider is not breathing they must repeatedly yell the word 'Kabaddi'.

» The attacking team has 30 seconds to complete their raid.

» Defenders on the opposing side try can prevent the raider scoring points by stopping them from returning to their side of the court.

FENCING

Based on the traditional skills of swordsmanship, fencing as a sport has been around since the 18th century. Fighting with swords dates back way before it was a competitive sport, developing from military battle. It became organised in Italy in the 1900s before being refined in France into the sport we know today.

The aim is to hit your opponent with a sword in a one-on-one battle without being hit yourself. Each competitor wears equipment which is fitted with a buzzer that sounds when it is struck or touched, indicating that a point has been scored.

It requires all-round fitness, agility, unwavering concentration and lightning-quick reactions.

FACTS OF THE MATTER

- Fencing is one of only four sports to have been at **EVERY SINGLE** modern Olympic Games – along with swimming, gymnastics and cycling.
- It is thought that the tip of a fencing sword is the **SECOND-FASTEST** moving object in sport, slower only than a bullet in shooting.
- Fencers always wear **WHITE** – and not just because it looks good! Before the electronic scoring system was brought in (1936), sword tips were soaked in ink and would show up on the white uniform to indicate that a point had been scored.
- **TIME LIMITS** were not introduced in fencing until the 1930s. They were brought in after a match in New York lasted for seven hours!
- **BARON PIERRE DE COUBERTIN**, who helped found the modern Olympic Games, was a fencer.

RULES

» Fencers are equipped with a sword, all of which are blunt.

» One point is awarded each time a fencer touches an opponent with their weapon in the target area.

» The target area is different for different matches. There are three types of matches.

» A match is made of three separate bouts lasting three minutes each. And the first to score 15 points is the winner.

» Points are also awarded for forcing an opponent outside the back of the 'piste'.

MASK
Protects the face and is made of metal mesh so a fencer can see easily.

SWORD
There are three types of sword used in fencing, and matches are scored depending on what type is used in a match.

PISTE
The piste is where the bout takes place, it is 14 metres long.

SWORDS

FOIL

The lightest of all the swords, it is fitted with a sensor on the tip. In matches using a foil sword, the target area is very small. The tip must be pushed onto the opponent's trunks to score a point. Strikes to the head or arms do not count.

ÉPÉE

Slightly heavier and stiffer than the foil, in an épée match, a point is scored for hits anywhere on the body.

SABRE

This is the shortest sword of all three and folds back when it touches an opponent. In sabre fencing, the target area is restricted to the torso only.

TAEKWONDO

Taekwondo is the art of hand and foot fighting. Broken down the word literally means: 'tae' – kick or smash with the feet; 'kwon' – fist or to punch; 'do' – art or way.

Although punching is allowed in Taekwondo, the main emphasis of a bout is on head-kicks, jumping and spinning kicks and combinations of kicks. The best in the business are extremely agile, quick and possess vast amounts of power in their arms and legs.

It originated in Korea in 1945, when a new martial art schools opened in Seoul in the aftermath of World War II and combined karate with various other Chinese martial arts.

It is now part of the Olympic Games, making its first appearance as a demonstration sport in 1988.

RULES

» Bouts last three rounds and fighters score points by landing punches and kicks.

» Blows landed to the torso are worth one point, while two points are awarded for kicks to the head or neck. Three points are awarded for knocking an opponent down.

» Bouts can also be won by knockout – when judges decide to stop the fight if it is extremely one-sided.

» It is stopped automatically if one fighter is 12 points in front at any point.

» Points are deducted for fouls, such as hitting below the belt.

» A sudden-death round is fought in the event of a tie.

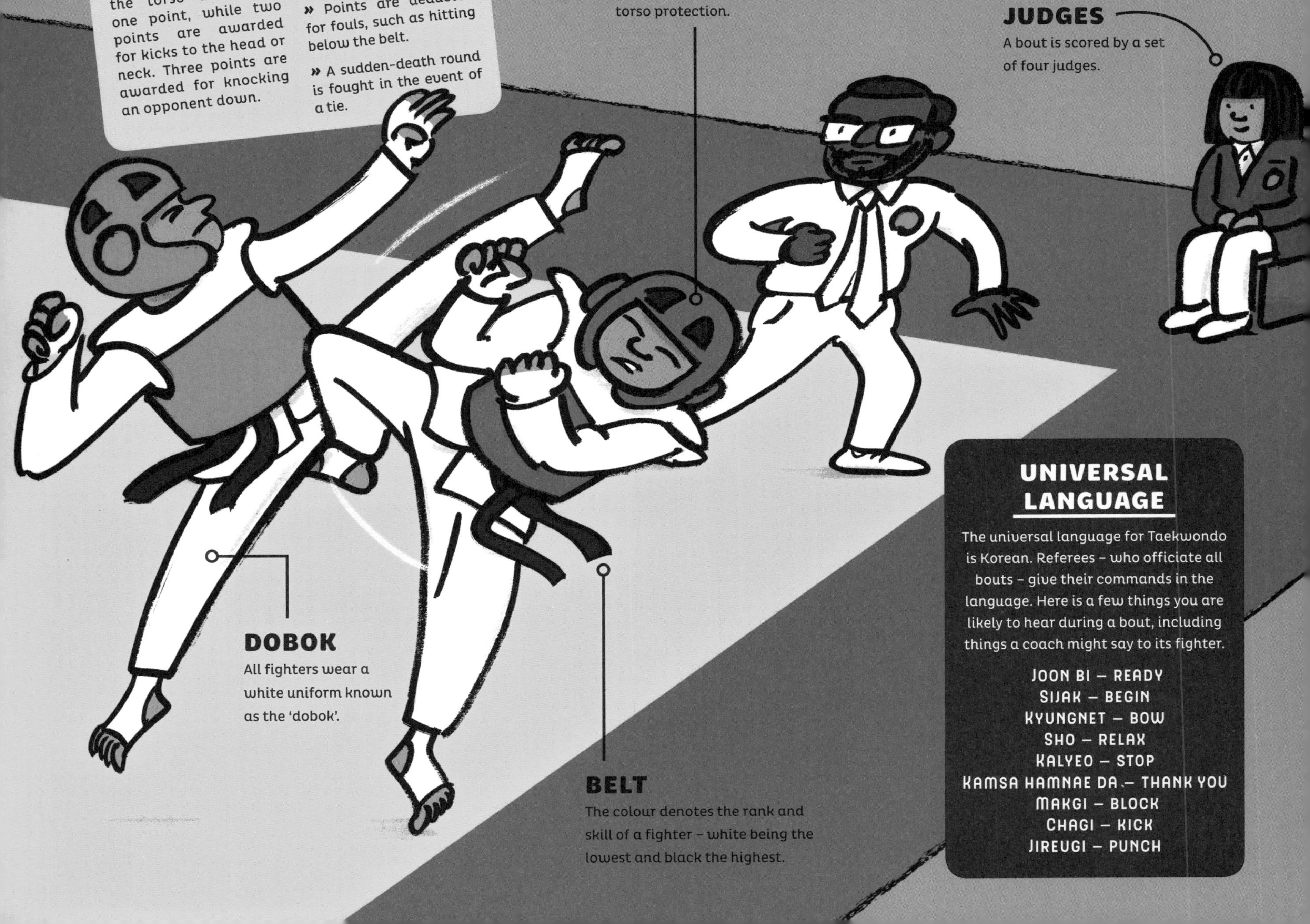

FACTS OF THE MATTER

- Taekwondo is practised by more than **70 MILLION PEOPLE** in 188 countries.
- Four million fighters have reached the highest level and wear a **BLACK BELT** to show their rank.
- There are different degrees to each rank. For example, to become a Taekwondo **MASTER**, a fighter must be a sixth-degree black belt, and be invited by the International Taekwon-Do Federation, the governing body of the sport.
- Men and women in the South Korean **MILITARY** learn Taekwondo as part of their initial training. In fact, a number of other militaries across the world have introduced it as part of their programmes.
- **SOUTH KOREA** have won 12 gold Taekwondo medals at the Olympic Games – more than any other nation – and have 19 medals in total.

SAFETY GEAR
Fighters wear headgear and torso protection.

JUDGES
A bout is scored by a set of four judges.

DOBOK
All fighters wear a white uniform known as the 'dobok'.

BELT
The colour denotes the rank and skill of a fighter – white being the lowest and black the highest.

UNIVERSAL LANGUAGE

The universal language for Taekwondo is Korean. Referees – who officiate all bouts – give their commands in the language. Here is a few things you are likely to hear during a bout, including things a coach might say to its fighter.

JOON BI – READY
SIJAK – BEGIN
KYUNGNET – BOW
SHO – RELAX
KALYEO – STOP
KAMSA HAMNAE DA – THANK YOU
MAKGI – BLOCK
CHAGI – KICK
JIREUGI – PUNCH

KARATE

Practised by an estimated 50 million people around the world, Karate is an ancient Japanese martial art that promotes self-defence.

Various forms have been around since the early 1300s and it was brought to mainland Japan from the Island of Okinawa by Gichin Funakoshi, founding father of the modern sport, in 1922.

Competitive bouts are now full-contact, involving punches, kicks, open-handed attacks and sometimes grappling.

However, karate is not all about combat. Nurturing discipline in training and improving spiritual awareness is perhaps more important. In fact, Funakoshi's theory was to never attack first. Instead his main aim was to encourage people to 'become better human beings', something that is still a cornerstone of karate today.

FACTS OF THE MATTER

- Karate has never been part of the Olympics. But that is about to change. It will feature as part of the official programme for the **FIRST TIME** ever at the 2020 Games in Tokyo.
- The sport has inspired a whole host of **MOVIES**. The *Karate Kid* (1984) series, which follows Daniel on his journey to become a karate master, is probably the most popular.
- 'Karate' is a combination of two words: 'Kara' (empty) and 'Te' (hand). That means the definition of karate is to fight **WITHOUT WEAPONS**.
- The sport is hugely popular among **CELEBRITIES**. Actor Sean Connery, pop legend Elvis Presley and TV's survival star Bear Grylls all have black belts in karate.
- To earn a **BLACK BELT** will normally take around three to seven years of training – sometimes even longer than that!

DOJO
The place where karate is practised is known as the dojo. The top karateka at any dojo is known as the 'sensei'.

KARATEKA
People who take part in karate are known as 'karateka'.

BELT
The colour of a karateka's belt indicates experience – white being the lowest and black the highest.

GI
A karateka's outfit is called a gi. It is normally white but other colours can be worn.

MAT
Bouts take place on a mat that measures 8 metres across. Karatekas are disqualified if they step into the safety area more than once in a bout.

RULES

» Bouts for male competitors are three minutes long and female bouts last two minutes.

» Points are awarded for landing blows on your opponent and the karateka with the most points at the end of the bout is the winner.

» One (Yuko), two (Waza-ari) or three points (Ippon) are awarded depending on what type of blow is landed. Ippon is awarded for landing a high kick or any move that puts your opponent on the floor.

» If a fighter is eight points ahead at any one time in a bout, they are automatically declared as the winner.

» Bouts can also end in disqualification or knockout if one fighter is unable to continue.

JUDO

Despite being a contact sport, the word judo translates as 'gentle way'.

Founded by educator Jigoro Kano, the sport's origins can be traced back to 1885 Japan. As a child, Kano was an avid fan of the Japanese martial art jujitsu, mainly because he was bullied at the English-speaking school he attended in Tokyo.

But jujitsu became increasingly unfashionable and hard to find, so Kano merged the sport's techniques with Japan's much-loved sumo style of wrestling to create the hugely popular sport we now know.

FACTS OF THE MATTER

- A judo bout takes place on a mat padded with tatami, which was originally made from compressed **RICE STRAW**.
- Judo's official rule book says competitors must cut their nails short and tie long hair back. They must also be clean, dry and **NOT SMELLY**!
- Judo became an **OLYMPIC SPORT** in 1964, when Tokyo hosted the Games.
- The smallest score used to be **KOKA**, awarded for throwing your opponent onto their **BUTTOCKS**, but this was removed in 2008.
- The sport is broken up into seven **WEIGHT CLASSES**: from extra lightweight (-60 kilograms) at the lowest level to heavyweight (100+ kilograms), which is the highest level.

JUDOGI

Worn by all judoka, the kit includes a heavy jacket, lighter trousers and a cotton belt.

REFEREE

The referee judges the bout from inside the contest area. The start the bout by shouting 'Hajime!'

DANGER AREA

Judoka are penalised for standing in the metre-wide red area around the edge of mat for more than five seconds.

BELT

The colour of the judoka's belt indicates their rank and skill. The top level is black.

EXTERNAL REFEREES

External referees support the main referee through video playback.

MAT

The bout takes place on a 14 x 14 metre mat (including the danger area).

RULES

- » A judo bout involves two fighters, who try to win 10 points through various throws and holds.
- » Competitors, known as judoka, use technique and cunning tactics rather than brute strength.
- » Bouts last for up to five minutes.
- » The bout is won when one judoka reaches 10 points.
- » If scores are level after five minutes, it enters 'golden score', where the next point wins.

IPPON

The 'perfect throw'

SCORE: 10 points

OUTCOME: immediate victory

HOW TO BE AWARDED ONE:
Throw your opponent onto their back.
Perform a 'technically perfect' move.
Your opponent submits to a hold.
Pin your opponent to the floor for 25 seconds.

SPORTING

EVENTS

THE OLYMPIC GAMES

THE Olympic Games is the world's biggest sporting spectacle.

Held every four years, this two-week blockbuster event showcases thousands of star athletes – all representing their country – while almost every sport in this book is featured in the Olympics, or has been at some stage!

All are fighting for an Olympic gold medal – the ultimate prize in any athlete's career. More than 200 nations compete in over 300 events, which are attended by thousands of fans and watched by billions more at home.

The event is constantly evolving – the host city changes each time and new sports are included. The first modern Olympics took place in Athens, Greece, in 1896 following the founding of the International Olympic Committee by Pierre de Coubertin. These were born from and inspired by the ancient Games, that took place in Greece thousands of years ago. Nowadays it is known as 'the greatest show on earth'.

From the elaborate opening ceremony to the stunning closing ceremony, this is the ultimate feast for any sports fanatic: records are broken, history is made, and stories to inspire generations for years to come are told.

BIKE

The bikes used at the Olympics are incredibly lightweight so they can reach high speeds.

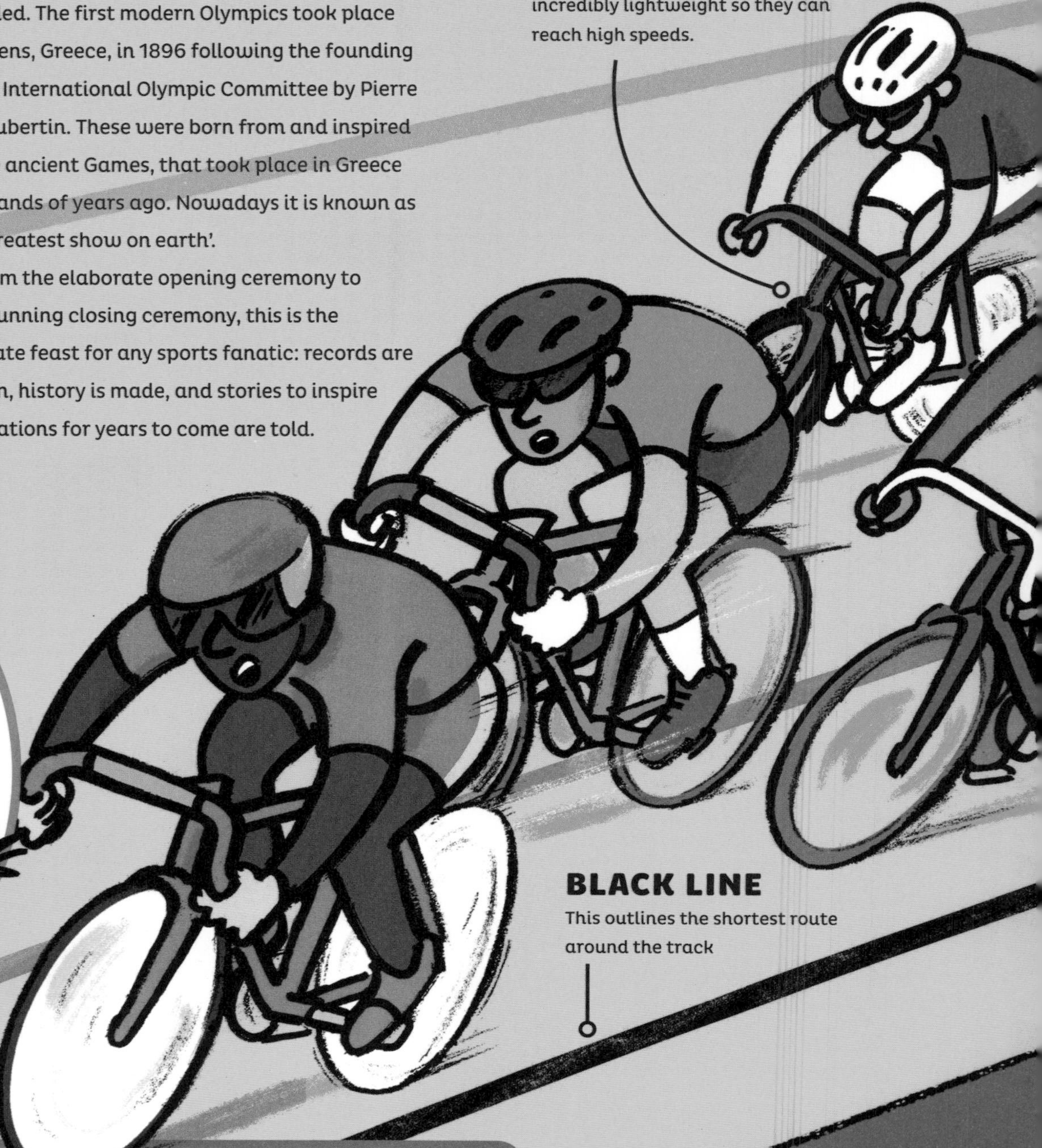

TRACK AND FIELD

Arguably the most popular part of the Olympic Games, all events take place inside the Olympic stadium, which is the main focus of the games. Events include throwing, jumping and running events. The 100-metre is the most popular, attracting millions of television viewers. It usually taking place on the final weekend of the Games.

BLACK LINE

This outlines the shortest route around the track

AS OLD AS TIME

While nobody can say for certain exactly when the first ancient Olympic Games took place, it originated in Greece around 3,000 years ago. The Games were held every four years – as the modern Games are still today – and featured sports such as running, jumping and wrestling, as well as more traditional events such as chariot racing. One notable difference from today's Games, however, was that the athletes competed naked!

The event was held in honour of the Greek god Zeus and was originally part of the Panhellenic Games, made up of four separate sports festivals held in ancient Greece. These were the Pythian Games, the Nemean Games, the Isthmian Games and the Olympics, all used to help measure time.

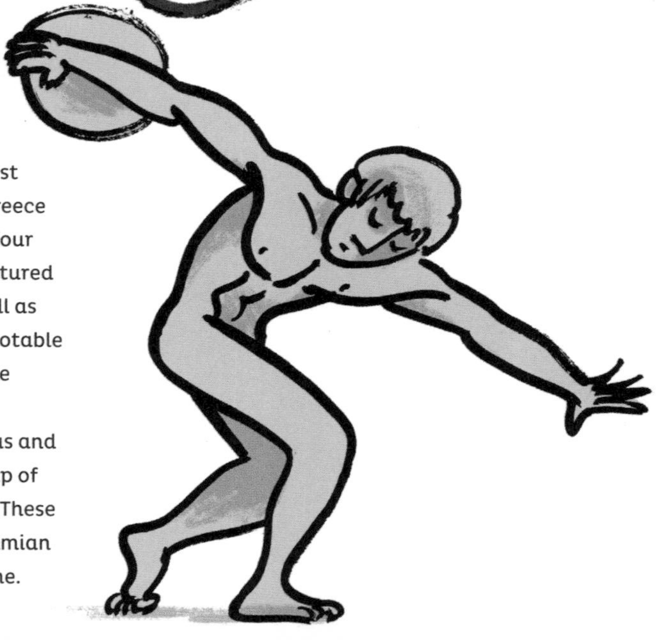

ON THE ROAD

Outside the velodrome, road races are held, sometimes over huge distances, and require incredible stamina and precise tactical planning.

Cycling and the Olympics have gone hand in hand since the first-ever games in 1894. The majority of races take place on a track inside a specially-built stadium known as a velodrome - featuring some of the most tightly-contested and exciting events in the Olympics. Races can be head-to-head contests or timed events, with those at the top level reaching breakneck speeds of up to 96 km/h.

RED LINE

Known as the sprinter's line, riders must go around this to overtake.

BRAKES?

Nope, not on an Olympic bike!

TRACK

Olympic standard velodromes are a minimum 250 metres in circumference. The track is banked up to a maximum of 45 degrees to allow riders to fly around without having to slow down.

LIST OF HOST CITIES FOR MODERN GAMES

1896	ATHENS, GREECE
1900	PARIS, FRANCE
1904	ST LOUIS, UNITED STATES
1908	LONDON, UNITED KINGDOM
1912	STOCKHOLM, SWEDEN
1920	ANTWERP, BELGIUM
1924	PARIS, FRANCE
1928	AMSTERDAM, HOLLAND
1932	LOS ANGELES, UNITED STATES
1936	BERLIN, GERMANY
1948	LONDON, UNITED KINGDOM
1952	HELSINKI, FINLAND
1956	MELBOURNE, AUSTRALIA
1960	ROME, ITALY
1964	TOKYO, JAPAN
1968	MEXICO CITY, MEXICO
1972	MUNICH, WEST GERMANY
1976	MONTREAL, CANADA
1980	MOSCOW, SOVIET UNION
1984	LOS ANGELES, UNITED STATES
1988	SEOUL, SOUTH KOREA
1992	BARCELONA, SPAIN
1996	ATLANTA, UNITED STATES
2000	SYDNEY, AUSTRALIA
2004	ATHENS, GREECE
2008	BEIJING, CHINA
2012	LONDON, UNITED KINGDOM
2016	RIO DE JANEIRO, BRAZIL
2020	TOKYO, JAPAN
2024	PARIS, FRANCE

FACTS OF THE MATTER

- Just four countries have sent athletes to **EVERY GAMES**: Great Britain, Greece, Australia and France.
- In the early years, only **AMATEUR** athletes were to compete at the Olympics, but these days it features the best athletes on the planet. Individuals have to go through qualifying events and must meet a minimum standard before being able to compete.
- Each athlete must meet a certain requirement to **QUALIFY** as an Olympian. That means some countries take hundreds of athletes while others take very few. In 2016, the United States had 554 representatives, while Liberia only had two.
- Olympic gold medals are not made from real gold – if they were, each medal would be worth around £20,000! Instead they are made up of other metals and covered in **GOLD PLATING**.
- There were no Games in 1916 due to **WORLD WAR I** and the Olympics were cancelled in 1940 and 1944 because of **WORLD WAR II**.
- London **HOSTED** the Olympics for the third time in 2012. That is more than any other host city. Paris will equal that record when they play host to the Games in 2024.
- The United States are the most **SUCCESSFUL** athletics team in Olympic history by some distance. Up to 2016, they claimed a whopping 335 gold medals and 801 overall. Second-place Soviet Union does not even come close. They have won 64 golds and 193 in total.
- Boxing legend **MUHAMMAD ALI** won a gold medal in Rome 1960. Despite being one of the most fearsome fighters on the planet, he was so scared of flying he wore a parachute on his flight from the United States to Italy!

THE ULTIMATE PRIZE

Athletes train their entire careers just to get a shot at winning an Olympic medal. Three medals are awarded for each event – gold for finishing 1st, silver for 2nd and bronze for 3rd. Medals are awarded to athletes at a ceremony after the event is finished, where the national anthem from each of the winning athlete's country is played.

HORSING AROUND

Horse sports are an integral part of the Games having been included in all but one since 1900. Humans had been riding horses long before it became a sporting spectacle and, as such, it is etched in history. The roots of dressage (loosely known as horse ballet) can be traced back to 430 BC, when the Greek military trained their horses to perform intricate movements in order to evade attack in battle.

OPEN WATER

Horses must not touch the water when jumping over an obstacle with open water.

OXER JUMP

A wider jump which features two obstacles, one after the other.

WINNING STREAK

The rider who completes the most obstacles cleanly is the winner, while if more than one rider completes all obstacles cleanly, the fastest time wins.

SHOW JUMPING

Show jumping features highly-skilled riders, who also showcase extreme bravery. It involves jumping over up to 13 obstacles – all in order and often at high speeds – which are placed around a course.

HORSE

The horses are specifically bred to take part in competitions. They must clear the obstacles cleanly without knocking them over or refusing to jump.

OLYMPIC FLAG

Created in 1914, it features five interlocking rings, which symbolise the five significant continents which participate in the Games – Africa, the Americas, Asia, Europe and Oceania.

OLYMPIC CAULDRON

Commemorates the theft of fire from the Greek god Zeus. This is lit at the start of every Olympic Games.

OLYMPIC TORCH

A torch relay takes place in the build-up to the Games. It always starts in Greece and is carried to the host city by torch bearers. Once at its destination, it is used to light the Olympic flame.

DRESSAGE

As well as being a sport, many consider dressage to be an art form. It involves the rider commanding their horse to perform movements, which include walking, trotting and cantering. Routines are pre-determined and marked by a set of judges, who award points for obedience, flexibility and balance. Essentially, it is all about showing the judge you can get your horse to do what you want.

FALL FROM GLORY

In the event that a horse falls, they are disqualified from the competition.

EVENTING

This is the ultimate test, featuring a mix of show jumping, dressage, as well as cross country. It features obstacles but over a much longer course – 5.9 kilometres and involves gruelling jumps and water traps.

GOING FOR GOLD

Riders earn points for each event and the one with the most accumulated points is declared the winner.

OLYMPIC FLAME

Sits on Olympia, Greece and is lit every two years. The Olympic torch is lit from here before making its way to the Olympic cauldron.

FACTS OF THE MATTER

- The 1908 Games were due to be held in Rome, but moved to London after Mount Vesuvius **ERUPTED**.
- Greek gymnast Dimitrios Loundras won a bronze medal as part of the Greek team in the parallel bars at the first-ever modern Games in Athens in 1896. He remains the **YOUNGEST** ever Olympic medal winner to this day.
- In the 1900 **PARIS OLYMPICS**, athletes were not awarded medals. Instead, they were given paintings or works of art (including some cups and trophies), which the French thought were more valuable.
- France were obviously forward-thinkers. In fact, the 1900 Games were the first-ever where **WOMEN** were allowed to compete. Until then, the Olympics was strictly men only.
- There are many examples of countries refusing to send athletes to certain Olympic Games for political reasons. This is known as a **BOYCOTT**. For example, the United States and 64 other countries did not go to Moscow in 1980 due to the Soviet Union invasion of Afghanistan. The Soviet Union responded by boycotting the Los Angeles Games in 1984.
- **SPONSORSHIP** is vital to help with the cost of running the Olympic Games. The first-ever sponsor was Coca-Cola, in 1928.
- For the duration of the Games – and some time before – athletes live in the **OLYMPIC VILLAGE**: a specially-built accommodation facility that only athletes and their families and friends are allowed into.
- **SHOW JUMPING** is one of the most unique events at the Olympic Games, with both men and women competing directly against each other. Sailing is the only other Olympic sport where this is the case.

ALL SPORTS AT 2020 GAMES

ARCHERY
BADMINTON
BASEBALL
BASKETBALL
BOXING
CANOEING/KAYAKING
CLIMBING
CYCLING
DIVING
EQUESTRIAN
FENCING
FOOTBALL
GOLF
GYMNASTICS
HANDBALL
HOCKEY
JUDO
MODERN PENTATHLON
ROWING
RUGBY 7S
SAILING
SHOOTING
SKATEBOARDING
SOFTBALL
SURFING
SWIMMING
SYNCHRONIZED
TABLE TENNIS
TAEKWONDO
TENNIS
TRACK & FIELD
TRIATHLON
VOLLEYBALL
WATER POLO
WEIGHTLIFTING
WRESTLING

THE PARALYMPIC GAMES

Paralympics means parallel Olympics as it runs alongside the main Olympic Games, taking place for just over a week immediately after the main Games. The main difference? It features athletes with various disabilities, from those who have amputated limbs to others with impaired vision or movement.

Most sports on show are the same or slight variations on those we know and love from the Olympics, and others are exclusive to the Paralympics.

The event was born when German neurologist Dr Ludwig Guttmann organised an archery competition for injured World War II veterans from the Stoke Mandeville Hospital in 1948. That was the catalyst for the first-ever organised Paralympic Games, which took place in Rome after the 1960 Olympic Games.

Since then, it has become a huge event in its own right and gone onto inspire millions of people who refuse to let their disabilities get in the way of their love of sport.

CATEGORIES

Paralympians are split into different classifications depending on the type of disability they have. This means athletes with similar disabilities are pitted against each other and ensures events are fair and as competitive as possible. There are six main categories, with various sub-categories, including those who have had limbs amputated to others who are in wheelchairs.

ON THE TRACK

Athletics are some of the most exciting and popular events at the Paralympics. Competitors are split into five main categories. Category F means field athletes and T stands for track athletes. They then have a number after their letter to determine their classification.

11-13: Visually impaired athletes

20: Intellectual or learning disability

31-38: Cerebral palsy

41-46: Amputees and other athletes with dwarfism

51-58: Wheelchair athletes, place on the track inside the Olympic stadium

WHEELCHAIR RACERS

Athletes who have lost limbs or the use of them race in wheelchairs. Races can be short sprints or even marathons.

PARALYMPIC-ONLY SPORTS

Goalball and boccia are two sports that are unique to the Paralympics. They feature some of the most inspirational athletes you will see at any sporting event.

GOALBALL

This involves two teams of three blind and visually impaired athletes, who try to roll a ball into the other team's net. The opposition defenders then try to block the ball with their bodies, usually by lying down on the floor.

BLADE RUNNER

Lots of Paralympians are missing parts or all their legs. But does that stop them running? Absolutely not. Most use prosthetic limbs made from carbon fibre called blades. Known as blade runners, they can reach incredibly high speeds. So much so, some Paralympians have even crossed over to run in the able-bodied Olympics.

PARALYMPIC SYMBOL

The Olympic flag is not connected with the Paralympics. Instead, the symbol is made up of three 'agitos', which are red, blue and green. They represent the Paralympic motto 'spirit in motion'.

FACTS OF THE MATTER

- American swimmer Trischa Zorn – who was blind from birth - is the most **SUCCESSFUL** Paralympian of all time, winning 41 gold medals from 1980-2004.
- Just 5,000 fans watched the opening ceremony for the first Paralympic Games in 1960 in Rome. The fact that **80,000 FANS** crammed into London's Olympic stadium to watch the 2012 opening ceremony shows just how far it has come.
- **MASCOTS** have been an important part of the Paralympics ever since it started. At the 2012 Games, the official mascot was named Mandeville to commemorate the patients from Stoke Mandeville Hospital who started the Paralympic movement.
- Paralympians stay in the same Olympic Village as athletes from the Olympics Games. However, it takes a huge effort to make it **ACCESSIBLE** for those with disabilities. At London 2012, it took five whole days to turn the Olympic Village into the Paralympic Village.
- The Paralympics has always been held in the same year as the Olympics. But it was not always in the same city. That tradition started in 1988 in **SEOUL**, South Korea, and has carried on ever since.
- Although the Paralympics hosts those with all sorts of disabilities, **DEAF** athletes cannot compete. Instead they have a separate competition called the Deaflympics, which takes place every four years.
- **TOKYO** will host the Paralympics for the second time in 2020, becoming the first city to do so twice. An incredible 2.3 million tickets will be available.
- **BADMINTON** has a longstanding tradition as an Olympic sport, but is yet to be featured in the Paralympics. However, that is about to change. It will be introduced to the Paralympic programme for the first time in 2020.

BOCCIA

Boccia is played by the most disabled athletes at the Paralympics. It is similar to bowls, with players throwing or kicking a ball and trying to land it as close as they possibly can to a smaller, target ball. It was initially introduced for athletes with cerebral palsy, but is now played by people with a wide range of disabilities.

THE WINTER OLYMPICS

The Winter Olympics is the world's biggest sports competition on snow and ice.

Like the main Olympic Games, it takes place every four years and awards medals – gold, silver and bronze – in exactly the same way.

Originally, winter events were incorporated into the summer Olympic Games. That was before the International Olympic Committee approved what was known as a winter sports week, which took place in Chamonix, France, in 1924. That became known as the Winter Olympics, with the first featuring just five different sports.

Since then, it has gone from strength to strength, attracting huge crowds and appealing to a wide audience. Traditional sports such as skiing have been part of the programme from the very start, while others are being added all the time.

Some of the more unique winter sports such as bobsleigh and skeleton involve hurtling down an ice track at incredibly high speeds!

ANCIENT HISTORY

Skiing has been practised for thousands of years, with primitive carvings in Sweden dating back to 5,000 BC depicting scenes of men on skis. The word 'ski' itself comes from a Norwegian word meaning a split piece of wood, which is how skis were first made. Originally a method for transporting items across the snow, skiing became popular as a pastime in the 19th century, and today it drives a multi-million pound tourism industry.

LIST OF HOST CITIES FOR MODERN GAMES

1924	CHAMONIX, FRANCE
1928	ST MORITZ, SWITZERLAND
1932	LAKE PLACID, UNITED STATES
1936	GARMISCH-PARTENKIRCHEN, GERMANY
1948	ST MORITZ, SWITZERLAND
1952	OSLO, NORWAY
1956	CORTINA D'AMPEZZO, ITALY
1960	SQUAW VALLEY, UNITED STATES
1964	INNSBRUCK, AUSTRIA
1968	GRENOBLE, FRANCE
1972	SAPPORO, JAPAN
1976	INNSBRUCK, AUSTRIA
1980	LAKE PLACID, UNITED STATES
1984	SARAJEVO, YUGOSLAVIA
1988	CALGARY, CANADA
1992	ALBERTVILLE, FRANCE
1994	LILLEHAMMER, NORWAY
1998	NAGANO, JAPAN
2002	SALT LAKE CITY, USA
2006	TURIN, ITALY
2010	VANCOUVER, CANADA
2014	SOCHI, RUSSIA
2018	PYEONGCHANG, SOUTH KOREA

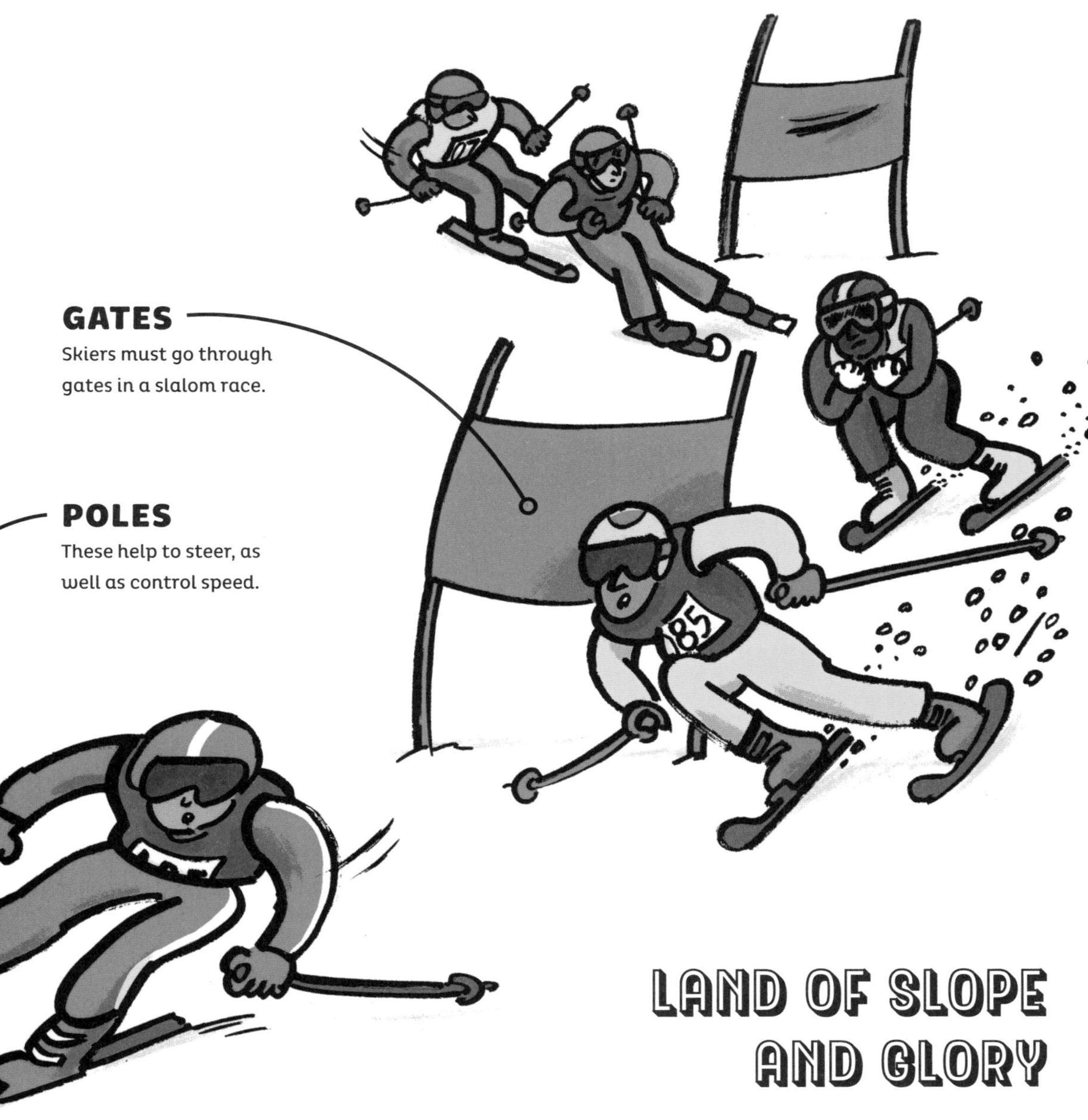

LAND OF SLOPE AND GLORY

Snow sports are the lifeblood of the Winter Olympics. The slopes play host to some of the most popular and exciting sports of the Games. Skiing is always a highlight and a number of events, with a number of events that test endurance, skill and speed. In slalom, for example, skiers must race down the slope as fast as possible, while negotiating obstacles at extremely high speeds. Cross-country skiing takes place over long distance and is a test of stamina, while some events combine daring jumps. In fact, ski jumping, which involves going down a huge runway and trying to jump as far as possible, is an event in its own right.

FACTS OF THE MATTER

- The United States have hosted the Winter Olympics a record **FOUR TIMES** – Lake Placid (1932 and 1980, Squaw Valley (1960) and Salt Lake City (2002).
- When it comes to Winter Olympic medals, no other country is quite as decorated as **NORWAY**. They have won a record 329 medals overall (including 118 golds). Next best is the United States, with 282 medals.
- **JAMAICA** entered a bobsleigh team for the first time ever at the 1988 Games in Calgary, Canada. They were considered the ultimate underdogs and captured the hearts of millions of sports fans. So much so, in fact, it inspired the popular movie *Cool Runnings*, which was released in 1993.
- Only one person in history has won gold medals at both the Summer and Winter Olympics. American **EDDIE EAGAN** won top prize in light-heavyweight boxing in 1920 and went on to do likewise as part of the USA bobsleigh team in 1932. A true all-rounder!
- While the host city changes every four years, the Games has never been held by a country in the Southern Hemisphere. Why? Because the weather is normally **WARM** in that part of the world.
- At the first Winter Olympic Games in 1924 in Chamonix, France, only 258 athletes from 16 nations took part. Now it is huge. At the 2014 Games in Sochi, Russia, **88 COUNTRIES** sent more than 2,800 people to compete in a whopping 98 events.
- Like the Summer Olympics, the Winter Games also starts with a ceremonial **TORCH RELAY** of the Olympic flame. The last one in 214 lasted 123 days and included a stop in the North Pole. It was even fired into outer space via a rocket!
- Each Winter Olympic Games has a **MASCOT**, which is a symbol meant to give good luck to the event. The last Games in 2014 featured a bear, a bunny and a leopard.

ALL A-BOARD

At the 1998 Games in Nagano, Japan, five new sports were added to the programme. Snowboarding was one of them. Despite its modern-day popularity, it was known as a 'fringe' sport before then. Now some of the most highly-skilled daring sports stars on show at the Games can be found in the snowboarding events. Slalom snowboarding is the same as it is in skiing. In the half-pipe event, snowboarders perform tricks in a semi-circular ramp that is built into the snow. At the next Games in 2018, a new event called 'big air' will be introduced. This involves launching off a huge ramp and performing audacious tricks in the air.

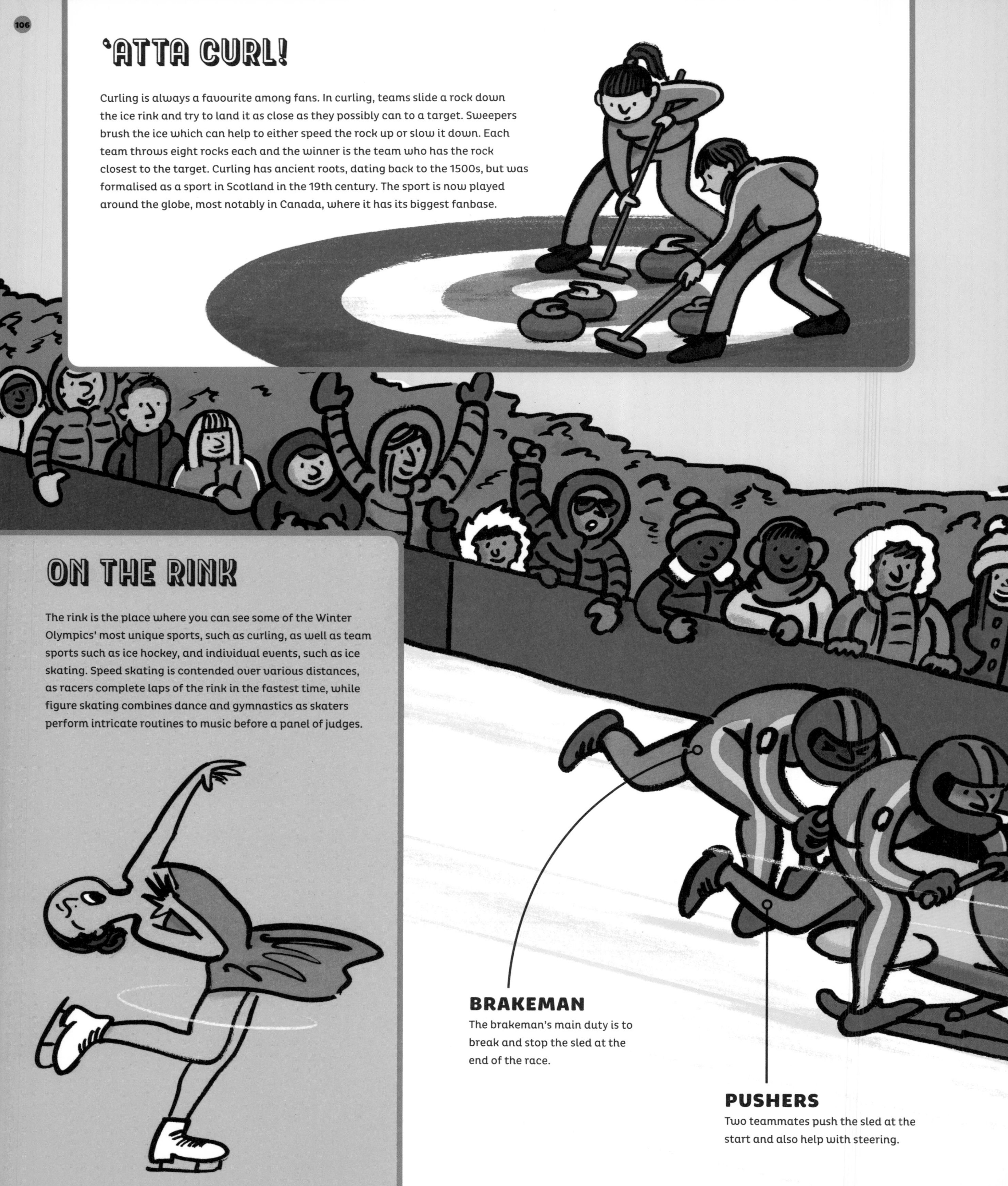

'ATTA CURL!

Curling is always a favourite among fans. In curling, teams slide a rock down the ice rink and try to land it as close as they possibly can to a target. Sweepers brush the ice which can help to either speed the rock up or slow it down. Each team throws eight rocks each and the winner is the team who has the rock closest to the target. Curling has ancient roots, dating back to the 1500s, but was formalised as a sport in Scotland in the 19th century. The sport is now played around the globe, most notably in Canada, where it has its biggest fanbase.

ON THE RINK

The rink is the place where you can see some of the Winter Olympics' most unique sports, such as curling, as well as team sports such as ice hockey, and individual events, such as ice skating. Speed skating is contended over various distances, as racers complete laps of the rink in the fastest time, while figure skating combines dance and gymnastics as skaters perform intricate routines to music before a panel of judges.

BRAKEMAN

The brakeman's main duty is to break and stop the sled at the end of the race.

PUSHERS

Two teammates push the sled at the start and also help with steering.

HAVE A NEED FOR SPEED?

Then the bobsleigh course is where you'll want to be. Here, the Games' fastest events – bobsleigh, luge and skeleton – take place. In bobsleigh, a team of racers drive a sled down an iced track, negotiating twists and turns at speeds of up to 150 km/h. It is often referred to as Formula 1 on ice!

If it's possible, skeleton might be even more extreme. It is an individual sport, where the racer lies face-down on a sled while taking on the course head-first. Luge is similar to skeleton but features two teammates who lie face up.

ALL SPORTS AT 2018 GAMES

ALPINE SKIING
FREESTYLE SKIING
SNOWBOARDING
BIATHLON
CROSS-COUNTRY SKIING
SKI JUMPING
NORDIC COMBINED
BOBSLEIGH
LUGE
SKELETON
ICE HOCKEY
FIGURE SKATING
ICE HOCKEY
SPEED SKATING
CURLING
SHORT-TRACK SPEED SKATING

FACTS OF THE MATTER

- The 1964 Games in Innsbruck, Austria, were almost cancelled due to a lack of snow. However, the **AUSTRIAN ARMY** came to the rescue by taking 40,000 cubic metres of snow and ice from the tops of nearby mountains and packing it down on ski slopes with their hands and feet.
- American snowboarder **SHAUN WHITE** is the world's best-paid winter sportsperson. He has pocketed around £15 million in sponsorship money to date and won Olympic gold in the snowboarding half-pipe in 2006 (in Turin) and 2010 (Vancouver).
- It cost an estimated £37 million to host the 2014 Winter Olympics in Sochi, Russia – making it the most **EXPENSIVE** Games of all time. The bill for the 2018 Games in Pyeongchang is around five times smaller.
- There will be a record **102 MEDALS** on offer at the 2018 Games, in 15 different disciplines.
- Norwegian cross-country skier **OLE EINAR BJØRNDALEN** has won more Winter Olympic medals than anyone – eight golds, four silvers and one bronze.
- Speed skater Kim Yun-mi won a gold medal as part of the South Korean relay team in Lillehammer, Norway, in 1994... when she was just 13! She remains the Games' **YOUNGEST-EVER GOLD MEDALLIST**.
- The 1998 Games in Nagano were badly affected by a **FLU EPIDEMIC** that had spread across Japan. Around 900,000 people were taken ill in the country, while huge numbers of athletes withdrew.
- The 2014 Sochi Games were watched by **1.2 BILLION PEOPLE** either in venues or on TV. But it has not always been that popular. The International Olympic Committee actually paid around 10,000 people to watch the first-ever event in 1924!

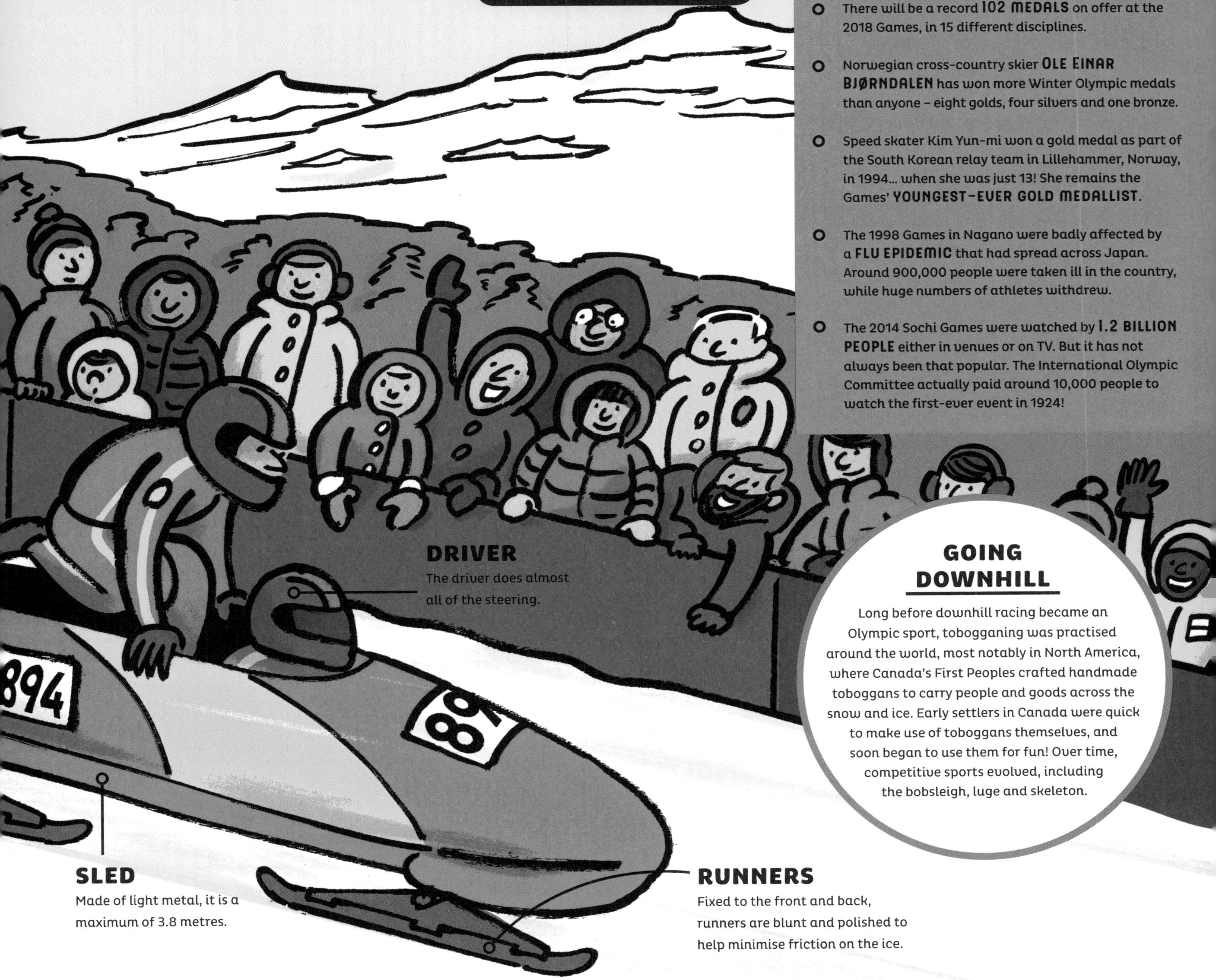

DRIVER
The driver does almost all of the steering.

894

SLED
Made of light metal, it is a maximum of 3.8 metres.

RUNNERS
Fixed to the front and back, runners are blunt and polished to help minimise friction on the ice.

GOING DOWNHILL

Long before downhill racing became an Olympic sport, tobogganing was practised around the world, most notably in North America, where Canada's First Peoples crafted handmade toboggans to carry people and goods across the snow and ice. Early settlers in Canada were quick to make use of toboggans themselves, and soon began to use them for fun! Over time, competitive sports evolved, including the bobsleigh, luge and skeleton.

INDEX

Brimming with creative inspiration, how-to projects, and useful information to enrich your everyday life, Quarto Knows is a favorite destination for those pursuing their interests and passions. Visit our site and dig deeper with our books into your area of interest: Quarto Creates, Quarto Cooks, Quarto Homes, Quarto Lives, Quarto Drives, Quarto Explores, Quarto Gifts, or Quarto Kids.

First published in 2018 by Wide Eyed Editions, an imprint of The Quarto Group
The Old Brewery, 6 Blundell Street, London N7 9BH, United Kingdom.
T (0)20 7700 6700 F (0)20 7700 8066 **www.QuartoKnows.com**

A catalog record for this book is available from the British Library.

ISBN 978-1-78603-084-9

The illustrations were created in mixed media
Set in Pluto, Hipton Sans, and Brevia

Published by Jenny Broom and Rachel Williams
Designed by Nicola Price
Edited by Jenny Broom

Manufactured in Dongguan, China TL0618

9 8 7 6 5 4 3 2 1

PRINCIPAL FLOOR

GARDEN TERRACE

THE QUEEN'S GALLERY

AMBASSADORS' ENTRANCE

QUADRANGLE

FORECOURT

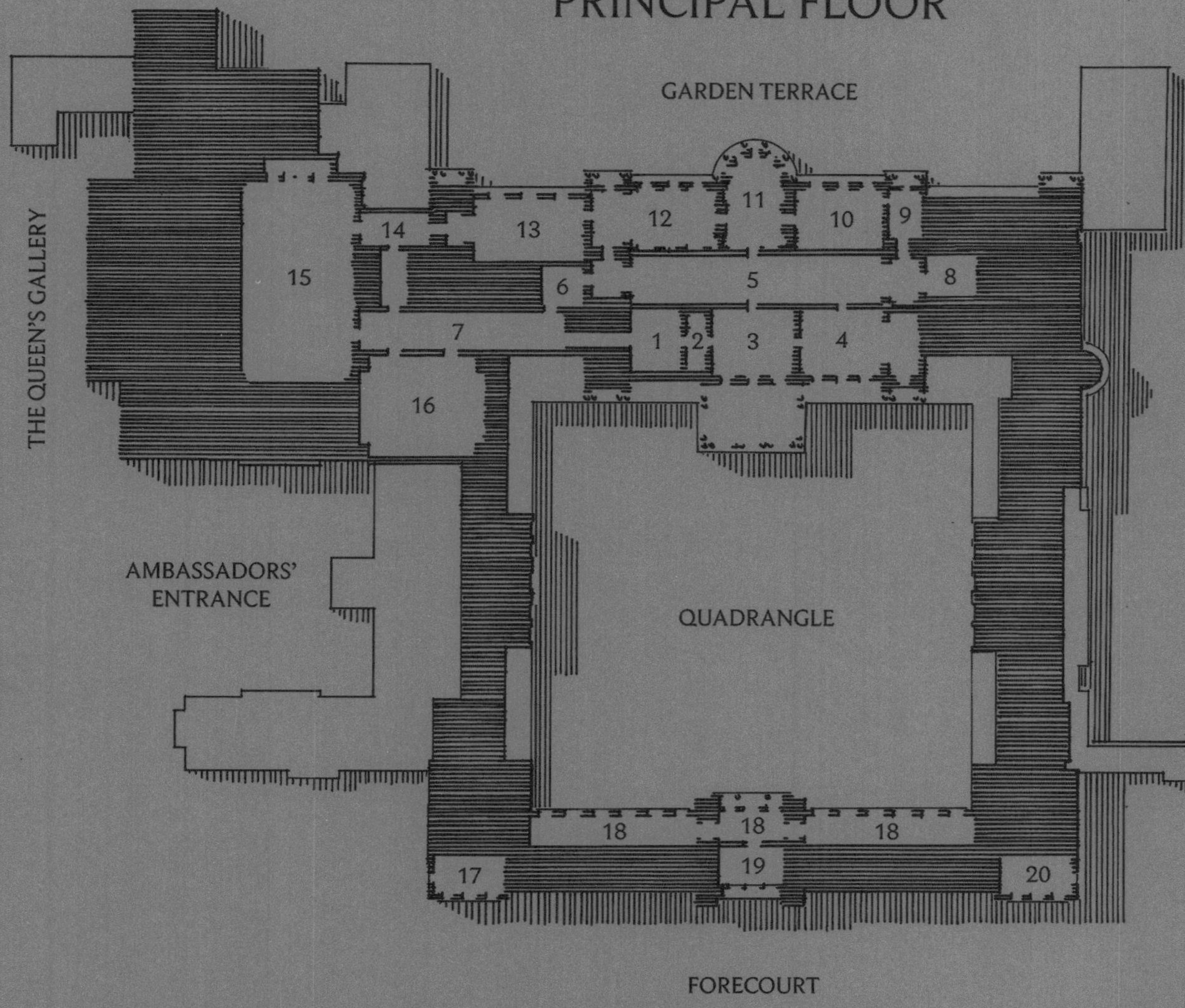

1 GRAND STAIRCASE
2 GUARD CHAMBER
3 GREEN DRAWING ROOM
4 THRONE ROOM
5 PICTURE GALLERY
6 SILK TAPESTRY ROOM
7 EAST GALLERY
8 MINISTERS' STAIRCASE
9 ROYAL CLOSET
10 WHITE DRAWING ROOM
11 MUSIC ROOM
12 BLUE DRAWING ROOM
13 STATE DINING ROOM
14 WEST GALLERY
15 BALL ROOM
16 BALL SUPPER ROOM
17 YELLOW DRAWING ROOM
18 PRINCIPAL CORRIDOR
19 CENTRE ROOM
20 CHINESE DINING ROOM

BUCKINGHAM PALACE

◇

THE INTERIORS

BUCKINGHAM PALACE

◇

THE INTERIORS

TEXT AND PHOTOGRAPHS BY

ASHLEY HICKS

New York Paris London Milan

IN ASSOCIATION WITH ROYAL COLLECTION TRUST

CONTENTS

The
author
and publishers
wish to express their
great sense of gratitude to

Her Majesty The Queen

for her most gracious permission to
prepare this description of the
decoration and contents of
Buckingham Palace
in this 67th year
of her reign
2018

CLARENCE HOUSE

It is exactly fifty years since the last major volume on Buckingham Palace was published. John Harris, Geoffrey de Bellaigue and Oliver Millar's magisterial tome has become a classic and continues to be a useful reference work for all who are fascinated by the remarkable interiors of the Palace and the spectacular paintings and works of art which embellish those splendid spaces. This was followed in 1995 by John Martin Robinson's heroic official history of the Palace, which focused on the building history. I am delighted that Ashley Hicks has now brought his informed perspective and creativity to respond to these rooms, marvellously captured in his atmospheric photography, and supplemented by a fresh history of the Palace.

Unlike Windsor Castle, where many interior arrangements have evolved over time and changing requirements, the *mise-en-scène* in the State Rooms at Buckingham Palace was largely arrived at, and to a surprisingly high degree settled upon, in the 1830s. While the picture hang has changed, especially in the Picture Gallery, the arrangements of works of art in other State Rooms, were happily brought together under the careful eye of Queen Adelaide, consort of King William IV, who lived at Clarence House. It is a tribute to Queen Adelaide's rather undervalued eye and skills that these combinations have largely endured down to the present day. Some placings suggested themselves conveniently, with green-ground Sevres porcelain vases placed in the Green Drawing Room, and blue-ground Sevres placed in the Blue Drawing Room. Many other combinations have stood the test of time, such as the happy pairing of the two remarkable *pietre dure* commodes in the Green Drawing Room, one of which carries the Sevres *pot pourri à vaisseau*, which belonged originally to Madame de Pompadour; or the gathering of the giltwood seat furniture by Gourdin in the White Drawing Room. The State Rooms and those in the East Wing of the Palace represent some of the finest and best preserved interiors of late Regency and Victorian England, the State Rooms having been created for King George IV by his architect John Nash, and those in the Victorian East Wing created for, and largely by, Prince Albert and his architect Edward Blore.

The Palace has now been seen by over ten million visitors who, since 1993 when the Palace first threw open its doors, come during the annual Summer Opening of the State Rooms. It is my hope that this book will bring the interiors to the attention of a new audience who may be inspired by these very beautiful rooms.

Charles

FROM THE QUEEN'S HOUSE TO BUCKINGHAM PALACE

Deep within the walls of Buckingham Palace lies the original house built from 1702 to 1705 for John Sheffield, 1st Duke of Buckingham and Normanby, by the gentleman architect Captain William Winde, probably using designs from William Talman of Chatsworth fame. It was constructed on land partly owned by the Crown, on which a succession of houses had stood since the land was used briefly as a mulberry garden to breed silkworms around 1605. Buckingham House, as it was known, was erected on a fresh part of the site, centred on the Mall, the elm avenue planted in 1615 under James I alongside St James's Palace.

The Mall, named after the French ball game Pelle-Melle already played there in the 1630s, had become a popular walking spot and centre of social life after Charles II opened St James's Park to the public in the 1660s. When the Duke built his new house, it was a country mansion on the edge of the city, but more importantly it was in a most significant position. On the entrance front of the house was the Latin inscription 'Sic siti laetantur lares', meaning 'The household gods delight in such a situation'.

The interior of the Duke's house had all the splendour of a great noble mansion of its time. From the Saloon, its main entertaining room, in the centre of the first floor, there was a magnificent view over the avenue towards the City of London. The double-height room was crowned by Orazio Gentileschi's ceiling painting of Apollo and the Muses, made for George Villiers, 1st Duke of Buckingham, Charles I's favourite, at York House in 1627. After the Sheffield Duke's death his widow, an illegitimate daughter of James II, nicknamed 'Princess Buckingham' by Horace Walpole, held court here for another two decades, and finally in 1762 the house was sold to the newly-wed and crowned King George III and Queen Charlotte.

Facing: The Great Staircase, Buckingham House, 1818, by James Stephanoff, showing wall paintings by Louis Laguerre and William Oram with James Wyatt's new staircase, all about to be swept away.

Above: Queen Charlotte's Saloon and George III's Octagon Library, both 1818, by Stephanoff.

Left: The Prince of Wales and Prince Frederick in Queen Charlotte's 'Warm Room', 1765, by Johan Zoffany.

Above: Queen Charlotte at her dressing table, 1765, shown by Zoffany by the garden door from the King's rooms downstairs at Buckingham House, with the Prince of Wales dressed as Telemachus and Prince Frederick as a Turk.

Traditionally, consorts of reigning monarchs have held their own separate courts, with distinct households. Anne of Denmark, Queen of James I, was given Somerset House on the Thames as her residence in 1603. The last queen to live there was Charles II's widow, Catherine of Braganza, ninety years later, but it remained legally the property of the King's wife or mother. George III's young and spirited Queen, Charlotte of Mecklenburg-Strelitz, disliked St James's Palace, so it was decided to give her Buckingham House in exchange for Somerset House, which was rebuilt to house the Royal Academy and other institutions.

The new Queen's House, as it became known, was the perfect home for George III, a king of unassuming, modest tastes, academic interests and great dedication to work. The King had studied architecture as a nineteen-year-old prince from 1757 under Sir William Chambers, who was appointed Joint Architect to the Office of Works in 1761 and worked on the Queen's House, officially in tandem with Robert Adam. George III saw too much gilding and 'gingerbread' in Adam's work and decided 'mere simplicity will always bear the preference', so that Adam's input was severely limited.

The King himself lived downstairs, in plain, panelled rooms opening onto the garden, apparently unaltered from

Above: Queen Charlotte's Breakfast Room (with the Duke of Buckingham's japanned panelling) and Crimson Drawing Room (with ceiling by Robert Adam and doorcases by George III), 1817, by Stephanoff.

the Duke's day. He refused to have them carpeted, believing the warmth of carpet unhealthy. The Duke's great staircase remained, with its baroque painted walls and ceiling by Louis Laguerre. The simplicity of the King's rooms did not extend to the Queen's upstairs, and she immediately had the Saloon redecorated to modern taste. This included a ceiling painted by Giovanni Battista Cipriani, continuing the gilt and grisaille Neoclassical motifs of the rest of the room's new decor.

The Saloon walls were initially hung with one of the treasures of Charles I's art collection, the seven Raphael Cartoons commissioned by the Medici Pope Leo X in 1515 for tapestries for the Sistine Chapel. Brought from Hampton Court, they were here until 1787, when they went to Windsor Castle, and are now on loan to the Victoria and Albert Museum. In 1787 the Saloon walls were given grisaille decoration like the ceiling, and eight large looking glasses in gilt frames, and with this decor the room was used for the formal 'Drawing Rooms' that the Queen held here rather than at a fire-damaged St James's Palace after the start of the Regency in 1811.

Downstairs, the Duke's severely architectural hall was hung with sixteen Canaletto views of Venice and Rome bought in 1763 by George III from Consul Smith, the great English art dealer in Venice. Together with the pictures, the King bought Smith's vast library, and it was this purchase that prompted him to have Chambers begin a series of large book rooms forming a new south wing of the Queen's House. The West, South, Octagon and East Libraries followed each other in quick succession over the next decade, the only entrance to them being through the King's rather small bedroom.

Chambers was simultaneously working on Carlton House, home to the King's mother, the widowed Augusta, Princess of Wales, extending and remodelling it until she died in 1772. The house stood empty until 1783 when it was given to the new Prince of Wales, George, just turned twenty-one and needing a house of his own. He and his

Above: Queen Charlotte's Green Closet at Buckingham House, recorded by Stephanoff not long before her death for publication in William Henry Pyne's 'History of the Royal Residences', 1819.

Above: Henry Holland's 1787 front of Carlton House on Pall Mall. Demolished in 1827, its Corinthian columns now grace the façade of the National Gallery in Trafalgar Square.

Above: The Grand Staircase, Carlton House, 1817, by Charles Wild, with one of the Prince's liveried footmen approaching his newly acquired clock supposedly from Versailles, which is in the Palace's Silk Tapestry Room today.

brother Frederick, Duke of York, had been inseparable, kept apart from their thirteen siblings, living a strictly governed life of study from which they seized any chance to escape. This ended when Frederick was sent to university in the ancestral home of Hanover in 1781, leaving George caught between his disapproving parents' parochial home life and the enticing social whirl of London.

Carlton House stood on the other side of St James's Palace from the Queen's House, set back on Pall Mall, with a large garden bordering St James's Park. Nearby, on St James's Street, a bright young architect named Henry Holland had built Brooks's Club five years earlier, a new home for the smart young men known as Macaronis who had made the Grand Tour and learnt to love Continental fashions and reforming politics. They had long been members of Almack's Club and were looking for a place of their own to indulge their taste for wining, dining and gambling, chief among them Charles James Fox, the charismatic leader of the opposition Whig party.

The Prince of Wales became a member of Brooks's in 1783 and was often seen in shockingly high spirits on the balcony over Holland's original porch with his friends, all ardent Whig supporters, outraging the King's Tory sympathies. The work to turn Carlton House into a suitable residence for the Prince was quickly wrested from the hands of Sir William Chambers and given to Henry Holland, whose style was modern and Francophile, satisfying the Prince's love of French fashions, furniture and even cosmetics, inspired by his friendship with Louis XVI's dangerous cousin, the duc d'Orléans.

Carlton House would be a work in progress for forty years. From 1787 to 1789 Holland remodelled it inside and turned a jumble of old houses into a chaste, Neoclassical palace with a Corinthian portico and Ionic screen on Pall Mall. The house became at once a symbol of the Prince's taste and elegance, of his outrageous spending and hedonistic lifestyle, and of the Whig party itself, who for the next twenty years would centre their plays for power on 'the Carlton House Set'. Work stopped and started with each lurching movement in the Prince's finances, as his vast debts were repeatedly exposed to a horrified public and paid off by a reluctant Crown or Parliament.

In the house the Prince first showed interest in the Chinese style that would so obsess him. Was this sparked by the painted Chinese figures shown behind his mother's lacy dressing table in Johan Zoffany's picture of him, aged three, in fancy dress as Telemachus with Frederick dressed as a Turk? The Chinese Drawing Room at Carlton House, opening onto the garden and designed by Holland in 1789, became so well known that furniture designer Thomas Sheraton published two prints of it in his 'Drawing-Book' four years later.

This Chinese obsession found its ultimate expression at Brighton. The Prince first visited the little seaside resort of Brighthelmstone when he turned twenty-one, staying

Above: The Chinese Drawing Room, Carlton House, with its heated sofa, published in Sheraton's 'Drawing Book', 1793.

Below: The Throne Room, Carlton House, in its final splendour, 1817, with the furniture by Georges Jacob now in the Palace's Music Room.

Above: The Royal Pavilion, Brighton: the Prince of Wales's fantasy palace is revealed in this sectional view from John Nash's 'Views', 1826.

Left, above: The Saloon, Brighton, as redecorated in 1816 using Chinese wallpaper, which was removed in 1822 and is now in the Palace's Yellow Drawing Room.

Left: The Banqueting Room, Brighton, which was later re-created on a more domestic scale by Queen Victoria as the Palace's Chinese Dining Room.

with his naughty uncle the Duke of Cumberland who took him racing, gambling and dancing: everything the King loathed. Extended stays were prompted by doctors' prescriptions for sea bathing and by financial crises, and in 1787 the Prince bought a farmhouse, which Holland turned into a French classical-style jewel of a 'Marine Pavilion' with a columned rotunda, surmounted by Coade stone statues, housing a Saloon hung with Chinese wallpaper.

Holland continued to add to the Pavilion until 1802, including an extraordinary Chinese Passage Room with walls of etched glass oil-painted with flowering trees, birds and butterflies by Frederick Crace, lit from behind by daylight from outer windows or by lamps at night. Holland and his successor William Porden both made unbuilt designs for the exterior in the Chinese style. Porden did build the vast Indian-inspired Stables, their dome completed in November 1804, looking like a page from Thomas and William Daniell's 'Views in Hindoostan', published the previous January.

The Prince was a man of extraordinary contrasts. He always remained like a spoilt child but one with enormous charisma. No one who met him failed to record his delightful, infectious charm, although many also noted his inappropriate tearfulness and self-indulgent moods. His life was one long drama played out in the public eye: a succession of mistresses; his not-so-secret marriage to

Maria Fitzherbert; his disastrous official one to his cousin Caroline of Brunswick, the Queen who was locked out of his Coronation; and her scandalous 'trial' in the House of Lords and the dangerous riots it caused.

By 1809 the rooms of Carlton House, all of Holland's simple, noble interiors in restrained Neoclassical taste, had been smothered in crimson velvet and gold fringes by Walsh Porter who lived at Craven Cottage, Chelsea, which he made wildly exotic with a 'sofa Camel' and other features too outré for even his royal patron's liking. When the cruel illness of porphyria took its final hold on George III, making him too deranged to properly function as monarch, the Prince became Regent in 1811. He took his responsibilities as Regent and later King with great seriousness, but nothing could stop his incessant spending.

John Nash, the architect son of a Lambeth millwright, was ten years older than the Prince. Nash had a disastrous early career in London followed by a successful interlude building houses in Wales, after which he moved back and became, in 1806, an architect to the Office of Woods and Forests, the department that managed the royal estates. By 1813 he was architect to the Prince Regent, developing Regent's Park and the Crown Estate in the West End, constructing the Royal Lodge at Windsor and directing work at Carlton House, including the creation of a new Gothic dining room.

Nash's earlier business partner, the garden designer Humphry Repton, had made unbuilt Indian-inspired designs for the exterior of Brighton Pavilion soon after Porden's Indian-style dome for the Stables went up in 1804. In 1815 Nash went to Brighton to start the remodelling of the Pavilion to create the building we know today. This seven-year campaign, as a result of which Holland's original house and stables were engulfed, provided the vast entertaining spaces desired, topped with a forest of onion domes and minarets, innovatively designed with cast iron.

Queen Charlotte died in 1818. The Prince had long felt that Carlton House's situation on a public street was beneath his dignity and made it too easy for the mob to get at. He now decided to move and make his London residence in the Queen's House. From the moment of his mother's death he pressured the government for funds to make it fit for him to live in. The job should by rights have gone to Sir John Soane, the architect responsible for the site, but the Prince, who became King George IV in 1820, insisted it go to Nash instead and had the plans sent to him a week after his astonishingly lavish Coronation in July 1821.

Whereas work at Brighton and at Windsor, where Jeffry Wyatville was busy rebuilding the Castle, was largely funded from the King's Privy Purse, money for Buckingham Palace (as the King decided it should be called) would have to come from the Treasury, subject to intense public and parliamentary scrutiny. It took until 1825 for funds to be found. The King had intended to sacrifice St James's Palace in order to raise money, but instead chose to demolish Carlton House, leaving an empty space as the focus of Nash's new Regent's Street, which had been planned to centre on Holland's portico.

Above: Buckingham Palace, John Nash's design complete with the Marble Arch, as recorded in 1846 by Joseph Nash before the addition of Edward Blore's East Wing.

Nash would have preferred to build a new palace on a new site, but the King insisted that he must have 'a pied-à-terre' at Buckingham House, his concept of a pied-à-terre being of course somewhat grander than most. Early associations, he said, endeared him to the spot. He was advised now on all artistic matters by Sir Charles Long, who had drawn up the brief for Windsor and now turned to Buckingham Palace. This would combine the residence of the Sovereign with a national monument to British military victories, using a programme of sculpture to adorn the building.

Between Nash, the King and Long a scheme was worked out to enlarge the central block of the old house, keeping large parts of its bones, as we will see when examining the Palace room by room. Long proposed including galleries of sculpture on the ground floor and of pictures above. He had spent time in Paris in 1817 and the Tuileries Palace, as completed for Napoleon, informed features of the design, such as the triumphal Marble Arch in the Forecourt (removed in 1850 and partly re-erected at the top of Park Lane) and the Grand Hall fireplace. The suggestion of French precedents can only have delighted a king as Francophile as George IV.

From its beginning the project was controversial. While many had complained for years that London had lacked a proper palace for its Sovereign since Whitehall had burned down in 1698, the medieval jumble of St James's being considered far from ideal, others had regarded four decades of notoriously extravagant work on Carlton House with horror, and the King's great unpopularity in London did not bode well for the new palace. Matters were made worse by the King's insistence that it was to be his private residence.

However, in December 1826 when the King visited the site, now roofed-in and with the rooms taking shape, he told Nash, 'the State Rooms you have made me are so handsome that I think I shall hold my Courts there.' Nash protested that he had not planned for this, that there was no space for the requisite offices and that the state rooms were insufficient and unsuitable, but the King would not be moved. Nash then had to improvise changes, squeezing in a tiny Guard Chamber and altering the already completed wings to add offices upstairs, but it would be years before the Palace was truly usable for court occasions, long after architect and king were both dead.

By 1828 there were already major rows over the expense of the Palace project and its design. Nash was questioned in the House of Commons over his practice of buying materials and selling them on to the contractor, which in fact saved the Crown money, and features like the dome over his bow-fronted garden façade, which peeped over the front portico 'like a common slop-pail [or chamber pot] turned upside down', were greatly criticised. When the King died in 1830 Nash, aged almost eighty, was hauled before a new Parliamentary Committee and eventually fired, a scapegoat for yet another public building scandal.

The new King, George's brother William IV, was not eager to live in the now rather tainted Palace, still far from completion. At one point, he offered it to house Parliament when the Palace of Westminster burned down in 1834. Lady Caroline Lamb's brother Lord Duncannon was appointed by the Prime Minister Earl Grey to get the palace finished, a task that he saw to the end, through various changes of government from 1831 to 1837. Queen Adelaide took some interest in the decoration, but on the whole the detailed scheme that George IV and Long had devised was adhered to.

The new architect was Edward Blore, cattily known as Blore the Bore, whose competent, if dull, work got the building finished on budget with little complication, mainly because the passionately interested but erratic George IV was no longer involved. Additions were made to Nash's design to house the Queen and Guards, and the work was nearly completed when William IV suddenly announced he would move out of Clarence House in 1836 and into the Palace. A desperate rush to finish it ensued, only for the King to die in June 1837. In consequence it was his niece, the young Queen Victoria, who drove in state from her childhood home of Kensington Palace on 13 July to take possession.

The Queen married her first cousin Prince Albert of Saxe-Coburg and Gotha in 1840, and five years later was telling Sir Robert Peel, her Prime Minister, that 'our little family, which is fast growing up' required more room, and furthermore the Palace lacked a proper Ballroom. In these projects she had her own artistic adviser in her husband, whose passionate interest in the arts was driven by more selfless and generous instincts than her uncle's had been, but who had, for a time, an equally strong impact on the interiors of the Palace. The space the Queen needed was provided by the East Wing, built by Blore to enclose the Quadrangle in 1848, followed in 1855 by the South Wing and Ballroom, added by Nash's stepson, Sir James Pennethorne.

Above: The Grand Staircase, 1843, painted by Douglas Morison, showing Nash's simple, clean design with walls of Siena scagliola.

These additions were financed in part by the sale of Brighton Pavilion, from which all contents and fittings had been removed in the expectation of it being demolished and the site developed. In a spirit of economy, the Prince was keen to use as many of the furnishings and fittings from the Pavilion as possible in the new rooms. Prince Albert's other significant contribution to the Palace, a neo-Renaissance polychrome scheme of decoration, was sadly almost entirely obliterated by his son King Edward VII in 1902, who found it 'a duty and a necessity' to modernise and redecorate the building, almost unused since Albert's death forty years earlier.

After Queen Victoria's epic reign at the height of British power, it was decided to create a memorial to her in the form of a completely reshaped approach to Buckingham Palace. A vast monument to the Queen in front of the Palace was matched at the other end of the Mall with Admiralty Arch, providing an apartment for the First Sea Lord around a triumphal arch opening into Trafalgar Square. As the 1848 façade of the Palace had been misguidedly built by Blore

Facing, above: The Royal Family on Blore's new balcony as the Guards return from the Crimea, July 1856, by William Simpson.

Facing, below: Queen Victoria and Prince Albert with wounded Grenadiers in the Grand Hall, 1855, by George Housman Thomas.

Above: Dinner in the lilac-painted Picture Gallery, June 1853, after Prince Leopold's christening, by Louis Haghe.

Below: The Queen's birthday table at Buckingham Palace, 24 May 1846, by Joseph Nash.

using Caen stone, which weathered very badly and had to be painted repeatedly, this, too, was refaced as part of the overall memorial to the Queen.

Sir Aston Webb designed the whole scheme using Portland stone, with the monument itself and sculptures on the Arch by Sir Thomas Brock. The new Palace façade, all made off-site, was put in place in just over three months in 1913 without breaking a single pane of glass in the existing windows around which it fitted. On King George V's accession in 1911, his wife Queen Mary had taken charge. Every bit as passionate about furniture and objects as her own great-uncle George IV had been, she had a huge impact on the interiors, noting ruefully that 'many things were changed … much too quickly by our predecessors'.

The more recent history of the Palace has centred on its preservation and restoration. Most importantly, it has been opened up to enormous numbers of visitors. Every year, some fifty thousand guests from all walks of life are invited to functions and events, while more than ten million visitors have toured the state rooms over the last twenty-five summers. At the same time, great treasures from the Royal Collection are shown year-round in changing thematic exhibitions at the Queen's Gallery, first opened in 1962, built on the site of Queen Victoria's chapel. Buckingham Palace may have begun as a pied-à-terre for the private enjoyment of a luxury-loving, connoisseur king, but it has now long been the symbolic heart of the British nation as well as the home of its Sovereign.

Above: Queen Victoria's bedroom (top) and sitting room, 1848, and the bedroom prepared for Napoleon III, 1855, by James Roberts.

Facing: Queen Victoria in white marble lit by the morning sun on Sir Thomas Brock's memorial.

VICTORIA
REGINA

PART I

GRAND HALL • GRAND STAIRCASE • GREEN DRAWING ROOM
THRONE ROOM • PICTURE GALLERY • EAST GALLERY

GRAND HALL

Grand Hall and Staircase • 1843 • Douglas Morison

Visitors' first impression of the state rooms of the Palace is of this expansive but surprisingly low-ceilinged space, built on the foundations of the Entrance Hall of the original Buckingham House, which had felt loftier, broken up as it had been with fluted columns supporting the Saloon above. Nash cleared these away and raised the floor of the surrounding space and the long, low Marble Hall beyond, forming pedestal bases to his new columns at the same level, in order to give more height to the basement offices below, which he had found very cramped.

The Grand Hall was redecorated by King Edward VII's decorator C.H. Bessant in 1902, who removed the wonderful coloured paintwork designed by Ludwig Grüner for Prince Albert in the 1840s, altered the centre of the ceiling and added gilded wall mouldings out of keeping with the restrained, marmoreal dignity of the original Nash design. What had been a sombre, plain basement in sharp contrast to the magnificence upstairs became just one in a sequence of white and gold rooms. The gilding, formerly limited to the bronze capitals, was suddenly everywhere.

Grüner had the walls painted by the firm of C.H. Moxon with green faux marble in place of Joseph Browne's buff scagliola from the Nash period, which had cracked, supposedly beyond repair, after twenty years. Both buff scagliola and green paint let the subtly grey-veined, milky white marble of Nash's columns, floor and fireplace shine, while Bessant's pale cream paint makes it look very grey. The fireplace, probably designed by Nash, is a virtuoso piece carved by Joseph Theakston, a pupil of John Flaxman and Sir Francis Legatt Chantrey, and set with the first of the Palace's many clocks by Benjamin Lewis Vulliamy.

Around the walls stand mahogany hall chairs and benches made by Marsh & Tatham in 1802 for the Entrance Hall at the then Prince of Wales's Marine Pavilion, Brighton. Like most hall seating, they were painted with the owner's coat of arms, here on a turquoise ground with the Prince's badge in ovals beside it. They came here with much of the rest of the Pavilion's contents in 1846 after it was sold by Queen Victoria.

26: Spode cistern mounted in gilt bronze by Vulliamy, probably to Robert Jones's design, for the Banqueting Room, Brighton, 1820, now in the Grand Hall.

28–29: The Grand Hall, looking from the fireplace towards the Grand Staircase leading up to the East Gallery. In the gilded niches are statues of Hyacinthus and Flora, bought by Prince Albert for Osborne and placed here by Queen Mary.

30: An 1802 hall bench from Brighton (left), with Richard James Wyatt's 'Nymph of Diana' given by Queen Victoria to Prince Albert for Christmas, 1850. Flanking the fireplace topped by a garlanded bust of George IV are wall lights by Pierre-Philippe Thomire, bought by Queen Mary in 1929.

31: The fireplace, carved to Nash's design by Joseph Theakston, full of classical scrolling foliage in emulation of Percier & Fontaine's work for Napoleon.

32: One of a pair of French bronze-mounted granite vases, *c.*1780, bought for George IV by Sir William Knighton, the society '*accoucheur*' who became his indispensable, often hated, advisor and Keeper of the Privy Purse.

GRAND STAIRCASE

Buckingham House Staircase • 1817 • Richard Cattermole

Nash's dramatic, sweeping staircase for King George IV replaced the short-lived one built in 1800 by James Wyatt for the King's parents, George III and Queen Charlotte. This was based on Sir William Chambers's unexecuted 1776 design for a symmetrical 'Imperial Stair' to replace the Duke of Buckingham's original staircase that had wrapped around the walls in the conventional way. Chambers had included a door from the landing directly into the Queen's Saloon, which had previously been entered in a roundabout way through other rooms. This door was framed by painted trompe l'oeil architecture that was added by William Oram to the Duke's murals by Louis Laguerre.

The old, generous landing had to be sacrificed to form a miniature, symbolic Guard Chamber when the King told Nash in 1826 that he wished the house to be his ceremonial Palace rather than the 'pied-à-terre' that he had begun building. The staircase, as a result, became rather abrupt and tightly curved, with the writhing, florid scrolls of Samuel Parker's gilt-bronze balustrade sweeping upwards vertiginously. A new half-landing pierced the side wall of the Duke's old house with a grand arch framing another flight of stairs up to the East Gallery, but the ceremonial route turns to climb back towards the Guard Chamber.

The Grand Staircase's walls are inset with sculpted reliefs of the Seasons by Thomas Stothard. The original scagliola wall surface was replaced with polychrome paintwork by Ludwig Grüner into which Queen Victoria set framed portraits of her immediate antecedents and relations. Edward VII's decorator Bessant moved the portraits up enough to add more of his gilded swags and bows, but preserved the arrangement that remains to this day. The windows are blocked up and the space is top-lit by a huge glass dome, intended symbolically to lead the visitor up into the light of the royal presence.

The little Guard Chamber itself is one of Nash's most perfect spaces, a momentary but significant pause between his austere Grand Staircase and the sumptuous Green Drawing Room, which precedes the Throne Room itself. It, too, is top-lit, by curved, oval plates of glass engraved by Wainwright & Brothers with Garter Stars framing crowns. The last of the marble columns and gilt-bronze capitals are here, and presumably it also once had walls of scagliola.

34: Richard James Wyatt's marble of Diana's nymph tending to a hound's paw, commissioned by Queen Victoria for Osborne House in 1850.

36–37: The drama of Nash's Grand Staircase and his arched entrance to the further flight leading to the East Gallery.

38: The soaring, top-lit volume of Nash's staircase, still open to the Hall fireplace, as it was in 1818 (see p. 10).

39: Eugène Lami's view of guests arriving at a state ball in 1848, the staircase just redecorated by Prince Albert and Ludwig Grüner.

40–41: A copy of Benvenuto Cellini's Perseus by Clemente Papi, bought by Prince Albert at the Paris Exhibition of 1855, on a turning base. Behind, Queen Victoria's mother, the Duchess of Kent.

42: The Guard Chamber with a statue of Queen Victoria's granddaughters, Princesses Victoria and Maud, later Queen of Norway, 1877, by Mary Thornycroft.

43: Robert Burns's beloved 'Highland Mary', *c.*1853, by Benjamin Edward Spence, and Queen Victoria in Grecian drapery, 1844–7, by John Gibson, in the Guard Chamber.

44: Sumptuous gilt-bronze capitals and balustrade made by Samuel Parker, now surrounded by Edward VII's excessive gilding.

GREEN DRAWING ROOM

Green Drawing Room • 1843 • Douglas Morison

Originally built between 1702 and 1705 as the Duke of Buckingham's Saloon, this is essentially the same room that Queen Charlotte used as her Drawing Room and in which courts were held. Nash had built his deep portico outside, which blocked the upper windows and shaded the lower, and he made a door into his new Throne Room beyond, but otherwise the space is unchanged. It has been called the Green Drawing Room since 1834 when it was hung with green silk tabinet from Ireland at the suggestion of Queen Adelaide, who was moved by pity for impoverished Irish silk workers.

In Queen Charlotte's day the room was hung with the Raphael Cartoons until 1787, when they were replaced by eight large looking glasses and the walls were decorated in grisaille by Cipriani to designs probably by Athenian Stuart and Sir William Chambers. Nash's design keeps the deep coving to the ceiling and the walls divided by flat pilasters, so that it must have seemed very familiar to his client George IV, despite the very different, bold detailing of his new plasterwork.

The 1843 watercolour shows the room as first finished and, indeed, almost exactly as it is today, with the same paintings and seat furniture but with a green carpet rather than the red that is there now. The sofas and chairs are from a huge set of fifty-six pieces, among them twelve sofas, ordered by George IV from Morel & Seddon in 1826 for Windsor Castle. The great French *ébéniste* François-Honoré-Georges Jacob-Desmalter was invited over from Paris specially to help Nicholas Morel design the furniture for Windsor.

Other treasures in the room include: the Neoclassical lamp pedestals from the Throne Room at Carlton House, probably made in France; the famed boat-form Sèvres pot-pourri vase most likely bought by Madame de Pompadour in 1759; and two Parisian cabinets from around 1780 set with old *pietre dure* panels, one by Adam Weisweiler with inlaid botanical panels from the Opificio in Florence and the other by Martin Carlin with panels from the Gobelins workshop in Paris. On the walls hang Allan Ramsay's great Coronation portrait of George III, from which so many copies were produced, and the enchanting group of his youngest daughters by John Singleton Copley.

F. COTES. R.A. 1767

46: A detail of Morel & Seddon's splendid sofa, part of a set made for Windsor Castle in 1826.

48: Allan Ramsay's portraits of George III, *c.*1761–2, and Queen Charlotte with her two eldest sons, *c.*1764–9, flanking the door to the Guard Chamber, over which is a portrait from 1618–19 of three children of Elizabeth of Bohemia, James I's daughter whose grandson was the first Hanoverian, George I.

49: A French gilt-bronze candelabrum from Carlton House on one of the fireplaces.

50: A cabinet made *c.*1785 by Adam Weisweiler, using pietre dure inlays of a tulip and a crown imperial produced in Florence *c.*1600, bought for Carlton House from Dominique Daguerre's sale in 1791.

51: Below John Singleton Copley's wonderfully spirited image of George III's daughters, Princesses Mary, Amelia and Sophia, 1785, is a commode made by Martin Carlin, *c.*1778, using early eighteenth-century Gobelins *pietre dure* panels, for the scandalous opera singer Marie-Joséphine Laguerre.

52: Candelabra made by Benjamin Vulliamy in black marble and gilt bronze for Carlton House, 1811.

53: Chair made for Windsor, 1826, and pedestal from Carlton House, *c.*1795.

54: The famed Sèvres 'Vaisseau à Mât' potpourri vase, 1758–9.

55: Detail of the extraordinary gilt-bronze-mounted mirrored mahogany doors, twelve feet high, used throughout Nash's state rooms.

56: Curtain tassels made for Queen Mary with green silk Tudor roses.

THRONE ROOM

Investiture of the Order of the Bath • 1855 • Louis Haghe

Here, on a crimson-carpeted dais, is the literal Seat of the Sovereign: the throne, or rather the Chair of Estate, used by Her Majesty The Queen at the beginning of her Coronation in 1953, made by royal decorators White Allom & Co. in an exuberant 1660s' style inspired by the Coronation Regalia. Beside it sits a matching chair for The Duke of Edinburgh, produced slightly later. Each has their own cipher embroidered onto silk damask.

In 1984 the walls were hung with red silk, as they had been when the room was completed in 1833, before Edward VII's desire to paint everything white took its toll. Queen Mary had them painted a light stone colour in 1928. As seen in the 1855 watercolour, the only white in the original scheme was on door frames and sculptures, such as Edward Hodges Baily's friezes of the Wars of the Roses and Francis Bernasconi's winged Victories garlanding the cipher of George IV, which stood out splendidly against the mellow stone colour of everything else.

Flanking the throne canopy are four giltwood trophies of the Seasons of around 1785, said to have come from the Throne Room at Carlton House. Below the trophies, beside the 1937 Coronation Throne Chairs, are the massive, gilded Roman-style chairs, carved with sphinx arms and chariot backs, made for Carlton House in 1812 and later seen in the Throne Room there.

Facing the throne, the door from the Green Drawing Room still has its crowning tympanum within which, modelled after the Grand Hall fireplace, Victories crown William IV, whose actual military valour was a somewhat distant memory when he became King in 1830, having been a midshipman of fifteen at Cape St Vincent in 1780. All made in scagliola, this was painted white and gilded for Edward VII.

58: Her Majesty The Queen's Chair of Estate from her Coronation in 1953 on the dais; below, Queen Elizabeth The Queen Mother's Throne Chair from the 1937 Coronation.

60–61: From the entrance door, the Royal Alcove framed by George IV's cipher garlanded by Francis Bernasconi's winged figures of Victory. By the window, Baron Carlo Marochetti's marble of Prince Arthur, aged three, 1853.

62: Mid-Georgian stools with a gilt gesso table by James Moore, *c.*1720, made for George I's Kensington Palace.

63: Doorcase, in scagliola now painted white, with a bust of William IV garlanded by Victories.

64: The father of the Horatii brothers passing them swords as they take their oath to defend Rome, on Claude Galle's clock of around 1805 based on Jacques-Louis David's great painting of 1785.

65: The ceiling of the main room, dominated by a colossal star.

66: The Horatii clock and a pair of cornucopia candelabra, all by Claude Galle, stand on the marble fireplace carved with military trophies and George IV's cipher.

67 and 68: Giltwood Seasons trophies of *c.*1785 probably carved for Carlton House to Holland's designs by Jean Prusserot, and a sphinx-armed Roman-style chair for its Throne Room, made soon after the Regency was established in 1812.

PICTURE GALLERY

Picture Gallery • 1843 • Douglas Morison

Central to Nash's design of the new Palace was this 'spine' made up of all of Queen Charlotte's rooms on the garden front of old Buckingham House knocked into one long, top-lit gallery and enabling him to add a whole new range beside it, looking over the garden. Nash roofed this huge space with a beautiful and complicated structure of timber and cast iron holding three rows of circular roof lights, with seventeen above each long wall forming linked domes, seeming to float on pendant arches reminiscent of Sir John Soane's work.

When Nash was sacked, the central part was altered by Blore, but it was not until 1914 that it was swept away entirely and replaced with the interior, designed by Sir Frank Baines of the Office of Works, that can be seen today. The old roof leaked, but it was also thought in bad taste at a time when chaste Georgian elegance was all the rage, and with it went the elaborate, sculpted door-surrounds, to be replaced by carved festoons in the style of Grinling Gibbons. The only surviving features of the original space are the fireplaces, each carved with a different artist wreathed in laurels by standing angels: Leonardo, Dürer, Titian and van Dyck, with Rembrandt exiled to the East Gallery nearby.

In 1914 the gallery walls were hung with olive-green damask after George V's Master of the Household told the Office of Works, 'The King expressed his dislike of gold walls and favours green'. They now have pink flocked paper on which hangs a selection of masterpieces from the Royal Collection, above Queen Charlotte's Saloon sofas. On pier tables with mirror backs, probably made by Weisweiler in Paris for Carlton House around 1790 and later 'improved' to satisfy the jaded eye of George IV by having Vulliamy add ormolu acanthus scrolls, are arranged the King's collection of old Japanese gold-lacquer bowls with French gilt-bronze mounts.

A door at the south end of the Picture Gallery leads to the Silk Tapestry Room, named after George IV's pieces from the Barberini workshop in Rome that once hung here, one of which is now in the Picture Gallery proper. Here, instead, the walls are now hung with pink damask and an unlikely trio of superb portraits: George IV when Prince of Wales, by John Russell; his loathed wife Caroline, by one of her many supposed lovers, Sir Thomas Lawrence; and the Prince's great friend 'Handsome Jack' St Leger painted, together with a companion piece of the royal patron now at Waddesdon Manor, by Thomas Gainsborough.

J. RUSSELL, R.A.

SIR T. LAWRENCE

JOHANNES VERMEER. A LADY AT THE VIRGINAL WITH A GENTLEMAN

70: The Picture Gallery, remodelled in 1914 with marble columns to suit George V's preferred green wall hangings.

72: The Prince of Wales in the uniform he designed for the Royal Kentish Bowmen, 1791, by John Russell, above a Weisweiler *pietre dure* table.

73: The Princess of Wales at her harp with Princess Charlotte, 1801, by Sir Thomas Lawrence. The picture was an object of rumours at her 'trial' six years later.

74: 'Handsome Jack' St Leger, 1782, by Thomas Gainsborough, above a Morel & Seddon table made for Windsor, 1825. A posthumous bust of Princess Charlotte; chair by François Hervé, 1792.

75: Clock by Jean-Baptiste Farine, Paris, *c.*1735, bought by George IV as being from Versailles and placed on the staircase at Carlton House.

76: One of George IV's old gold-lacquer Japanese bowls mounted in gilt bronze in Paris, *c.*1760.

77: Johannes Vermeer's *A Lady at the Virginal with a Gentleman*, early 1660s, bought by George III in 1762.

78: Leandro Bassano's 1592 portrait of sculptor Tiziano Aspetti and Lorenzo Lotto's of collector Andrea Odoni, 1527.

79: On one of four fireplaces, a black Sèvres chinoiserie vase, *c.*1791–2, and a candelabrum, both from Carlton House.

80: 'Annunciation' silk tapestry, Barberini factory, Rome, *c.*1650, above Sir Francis Chantrey's group of William IV's mistress Mrs Jordan with two of their illegitimate children, commissioned by him as King in 1831.

CHARLES, 1ST

EAST GALLERY

The Promenade Gallery, Buckingham Palace • 1873 • Hills & Saunders

From the Silk Tapestry Room we emerge into this space, designed by Nash as a short gallery linking his Grand Staircase to the Chapel, which he planned in the upper part of George III's Octagon Library. When that made way in 1855 for Queen Victoria's new Ball Supper Room, its architect Sir James Pennethorne lengthened this space to make it into a Promenade Gallery along which guests could stroll between dances. Part of the elaborate Ballroom scheme by Prince Albert's Ludwig Grüner, it was painted in trompe l'oeil as a marble-walled arcade with vases overflowing with summer flowers.

The only elements of this decorative scheme visible today are the painted friezes, in grisaille on gold grounds, of parading putti by Nicola Consoni, an Italian who also painted the interior of the Royal Mausoleum at Frogmore to Grüner's designs. The flowered arcades are still there, but covered up by cream damask as a background to some of the grandest portraits in the Royal Collection. Hanging here in the photograph, but usually at Windsor, is van Dyck's great equestrian portrait of Charles I with M. de St Antoine.

Here also are Queen Charlotte, painted by Benjamin West with the Queen's Lodge at Windsor behind, where she and George III lived before the Castle was repaired; her granddaughter Queen Victoria, in her Coronation portrait by Sir George Hayter, and his huge picture of the Coronation itself, the Queen just crowned, trumpets blowing and the assembled peers, including the distinctive figure of the Duke of Wellington, about to don their own coronets; and Franz Xaver Winterhalter's initial English commission, Victoria and Albert with their first five children around them.

From the East Gallery we turn back towards the Grand Staircase, across which we see the curved balcony outside the Guard Chamber, and descend the stairs, heading straight for the fireplace on the other side of the Grand Hall. Much of Nash's design concerned picturesque vistas that would lead the eye and imagination on, and here they are at full play.

SIR GEORGE HAYTER · QUEEN VICTORIA

QUEEN VICTORIA
PRINCESS ALICE
PRINCE ALBERT
PRINCESS HELENA
PRINCESS ROYAL
Winterhalter

82: Anthony van Dyck's great equestrian portrait of Charles I, 1632. Painted for the end of the Gallery at St James's, it must have seemed the King was riding into the space. Beside him, riding-master M. de St Antoine, who came with a gift of horses to Charles's brother Henry from his godfather Henri IV of France in 1603.

84–85: Gold-ground friezes of triumphant putti, painted by Nicola Consoni, are all that remain visible of Grüner's elaborate decoration of 1855.

86: Sir George Hayter's 1838 Coronation portrait of Queen Victoria is reflected in mirrored doors copied faithfully from Nash's originals. Clock by 'de la Croix', which, according to legend, was won by George IV from Charles X of France in a wager; candelabrum ordered by the King from Thomire, Paris, 1813.

87: One of five fireplaces designed by Nash for the Picture Gallery, each with a different artist's portrait, garlanded by angels holding palettes, carved in Carrara by Italians for Joseph Browne. Rembrandt was at the north end, moved here by Blore when he opened up the space for his Ministers' Staircase. The pair of porphyry-ground Sèvres vases dates from 1792–3.

88: Victoria and Albert, on chairs now in the Green Drawing Room, painted with their first five children by Franz Xaver Winterhalter, 1846, beside Victoria's grandmother Queen Charlotte by Benjamin West, 1779: Buckingham Palace's first occupant with Buckingham House's last.

PART II

MARBLE HALL & MINISTERS' STAIRCASE • ROYAL CLOSET

WHITE DRAWING ROOM • MUSIC ROOM • BLUE DRAWING ROOM

STATE DINING ROOM • WEST GALLERY • BALLROOM

MARBLE HALL & MINISTERS' STAIRCASE

Hall, Carlton House • 1817 • Charles Wild

The Marble Hall, named because it was planned as a sculpture gallery in the tradition of English galleries of ancient statues or 'marbles' as they were known, follows the lines of the Picture Gallery above it. It, too, is formed of the garden-facing rooms of old Buckingham House knocked into one by Nash to make a connecting 'spine' off which additional rooms could be built out into the garden. In this sense it is hugely successful. As a gallery, it is slightly less so, as its only daylight is filtered through from the Grand Hall.

Like the Grand Hall, it was originally all golden tan scagliola, polychromed by Grüner in 1848 and then whitewashed in 1903. Edward VII's decorator Bessant had great fun here enlivening the dull expanses of plain wall between Nash's columns with all manner of gilded plasterwork moulding, dangling Georgian-ish trophies and even installing, above the pair of exquisitely simple, Neoclassical marble fireplaces designed by Henry Holland for Carlton House, the overscaled, carved festoons, possibly remnants of the Duke of Buckingham's original Saloon of 1702, that had more recently decorated Queen Victoria's Tapestry Drawing Room, now the Centre Room, in the East Wing.

Flanking the central door to the Bow Room, in the key vista from the Grand Entrance, are the official portraits of Queen Victoria and Prince Albert by Winterhalter from 1859, the Queen with the Imperial State Crown beside her and Westminster Abbey, where she was crowned, in the distance. At the north end of the Marble Hall is the Ministers' Staircase, built by Blore in 1838. Against it, dramatically lit from above, is the sculpture of *Mars and Venus* commissioned from Antonio Canova by the Prince Regent in 1815 while Napoleon's favourite sculptor was visiting London to see the Elgin Marbles.

On the wall of the Ministers' Staircase now hangs John Hoppner's 1796 portrait of George IV when Prince of Wales. Originally there was a large window here, which in 1905 was replaced with a huge stained-glass memorial to the Duke of Clarence commissioned by Queen Alexandra, showing her eldest son, who had died aged twenty-eight, as St George in armour. This was damaged in the bombing of 1940 and removed. At the top of the stairs is an octagonal vestibule, formed under Edward VII in 1902, which leads into the Picture Gallery and, by means of a jib door in Bessant's faux Georgian panelling, into the Royal Closet.

EODORE PRINCESS HOHENLOHE LANGENBURG
and PRINCESS ADELAIDE

ALEXANDER CUMMING LONDON

92: The Prince of Wales, 1789, by his brother the Duke of York's painter Mather Byles Brown, with Antonio Canova's 1820 *Nymph Dirce* from Carlton House.

94–95: Holland's 1788 marble fireplaces from Carlton House stood here against Nash's plain walls of scagliola, now crowded with gilt mouldings.

96 and 97: Flanking the central door, Winterhalter's 1859 portraits of Victoria and Albert, 1701 gilt tables by Jean Pelletier for Hampton Court and early nineteenth-century perfume-burners with green-stained walnut imitating malachite.

98: Giovanni Antonio Pellegrini's Augustus, Duke of Sussex, 1811, with Canova's *Fountain Nymph*, placed in the Gothic Conservatory at Carlton House in 1819.

99: The combined barometer and clock of 1763–5, by Alexander Cumming, was one of George III's favourites.

100–01: Blore's 1838 Ministers' Staircase, flanked by gilded torchères ordered by Walsh Porter in 1807 from Bogaerts & Storr for the Throne Room, Carlton House.

102: Canova's *Mars and Venus*, commissioned by the Prince Regent to celebrate the peace of 1815.

103: John Hoppner's portrait of George IV when Prince of Wales in full Garter robes, 1796.

104: The octagonal vestibule between the Picture Gallery and the Ministers' Staircase. Winterhalter's portrait of Princess Alice aged eighteen, painted in June 1861 before her father Prince Albert's death. Next year she married the Grand Duke of Hesse and died in Darmstadt on the anniversary of Albert's death, 1878.

ROYAL CLOSET

Apollo Clock in the Pictorial Inventory
*c.*1830 • Office of Augustus Charles Pugin

In the octagonal vestibule between the Ministers' Staircase and the Picture Gallery, a discreet jib door is hidden in the panelling. Hung with a copy of Winterhalter's portrait of Prince Albert painted in enamel on porcelain by Carl Schmidt, it opens to reveal this small room designed for and still used by the Royal Family to assemble before going in procession to state functions. From it another jib door leads to the White Drawing Room, where guests will occasionally be surprised by its opening, concealed as it is by an enormous mirror and *pietre dure* inlaid ebony cabinet, which swing into the room as if by magic.

The Closet itself has one of Nash's most inventive and beautiful ceilings with a coving of giant, freestanding flowers, but it is the fireplace that is the real star. This is one of a pair supplied by Parisian *marchand-mercier* Dominique Daguerre for the Prince of Wales's Carlton House around 1787, installed in the Great Drawing Room, which later became the Throne Room. Daguerre and his partner Martin-Eloy Lignereux had been the leading purveyors of luxury furniture and ornaments in Paris, official suppliers to the Royal Family since 1778, Wedgwood's Paris distributor from 1787 and entrusted by Marie-Antoinette with her personal collection to sell after the French Revolution.

Daguerre opened a London showroom on Piccadilly in 1786, and worked with the Prince's architect Henry Holland on supplying pieces for Carlton House and Brighton, and for Holland's other projects at Althorp and Woburn. The chimney piece, in white marble with extremely fine bronze mounts including large figures of female satyrs, follows a 1781 design by Parisian architect François-Joseph Bélanger for the duchesse de Mazarin, the figures modelled by Jean-Joseph Foucou and the bronzes made by Pierre Gouthière. The Prince's chimney piece, with bronzes by François Rémond, is of extraordinary quality, and flanked by equally perfect cabinets, combining similar bronze mounts, ebony and Japanese lacquer, produced by Bernard Molitor some fifteen years later and bought by the Carlton House Clerk Comptroller of the Kitchen, John Baptiste Watier, in post-Empire Paris in 1816.

Also in the Closet are two elegant, gilded vitrine tables holding eighteenth-century scent-bottles and other precious objects, and a glass cabinet in the window with a collection of carved hardstones, jade and amethyst assembled by Queen Mary. When the Palace was first lived in, by Queen Victoria, the Closet contained Prince Albert's collection of small, Early Renaissance paintings, 'Primitives' as they were known, densely hung in the traditional manner of cabinet pictures.

54

106: Carl Schmidt's 1859 enamel copy of Prince Albert's portrait by Winterhalter hangs on the jib door to the Royal Closet, hidden in Edward VII's panelling.

108 and 109: Matching arched mirror frames, probably from Grüner's time when Prince Albert arranged the Closet with early Italian pictures. The side chair is from the Saloon, Brighton.

110 and 111: Part of Queen Mary's collection of bibelots sits in a pair of gilded vitrines, while on the chimney she placed candelabra with gilded palm-bearing angels bought in Paris by the Prince Regent's pastry chef François Benois, 1814.

112–13: The Louis XVI chimney piece from the Throne Room of Carlton House, slightly spoiled by its clumsy lining of fifty years later but enhanced by being flanked by Bernard Molitor's cabinets with Japanese lacquer.

114 and 115: Queen Mary's jade collection by the window and the exquisitely chased and gilded female satyr and Bacchic ornament on the fireplace.

116 and 117: The most elaborate jib door imaginable, through which the Royal Family enter the state apartments on official occasions after gathering in the Royal Closet. Fixed to the door is one of four *pietre dure* cabinets, topped with a Sèvres vase between a pair of Louis XVI candelabra.

118: Nash's wonderful ceiling, edged with full-relief flowers on stalks.

WHITE DRAWING ROOM

Crimson Drawing Room, Carlton House • 1816 • Charles Wild

This is the first of the run of state rooms on the garden front of the Palace and the first of John Nash's three new reception rooms opening off his Picture Gallery, to all of which he gave strong architectural form through inventive ceilings held on grand columns or pilasters of strongly coloured scagliola. These survive intact only in his Bow Drawing Room, now the Music Room. Here in the White Drawing Room, his pilasters were originally Siena yellow; in the Blue Drawing Room, the columns were 'raspberry-coloured' imitation porphyry.

The pilasters here, with Mughal Indian–inspired floral bases and capitals featuring Garter Stars, originally framed walls hung with gold and white figured damask. In 1860 the silk went, the walls were embellished with plaster festoons and overdoors, and the pilasters with recessed panels of ornament, all of it painted cream. The huge mirrors in their baroque gilt frames were designed by Blore when he was completing Nash's rooms for William IV in 1831. The placing of the ebony and *pietre dure* cabinets below them, one of them fixed to the jib door from the Royal Closet, is just the sort of extravagant conceit that would have appealed to George IV.

In pride of place is one of the finest pieces of furniture in the Royal Collection, the desk by Jean-Henri Riesener bought by George IV in 1825, then said to have belonged to Louis XVI. Almost everything in the room was acquired or commissioned by him, from the candelabra-stands of cranes that stood in the Crimson Drawing Room at Carlton House and the sofas from its Blue Velvet Room, to the Roman-style military candelabra by Napoleon's favourite bronze-maker Pierre-Philippe Thomire, purchased by the then Prince Regent in 1813, at the height of the war with France.

Over the fireplace hangs a sumptuous *fin-de-siècle* portrait of Queen Alexandra, famed royal beauty, painted by Edward Hughes for her to give to her father, the King of Denmark. When Hughes's picture was finished, the story goes, the court all declared the portrait too beautiful to leave England, and so the Queen gave it to Edward VII on their wedding anniversary in 1904 and had Hughes paint a copy for her father. The picture has hung in its present position since 1907, seen throughout the magnificent vista formed by the enfilade of Nash's state rooms.

120: Queen Alexandra surveying the room, as she has since 1907, below the plaster friezes of putti, made by William Pitts in 1828 to symbolise poetry and music but described by Parliament as 'The Sports of Boys, costing £800'.

122: Sèvres vases on one of the pair of fireplaces probably carved by Richard Westmacott inspired by John Flaxman, who had advised on the Palace before he died in 1826.

123: Nash's vigorous ceiling and a portrait by Sir Peter Lely installed with a festooned frame in 1860, then thought to show Anne Hyde, James II's wife and mother of Queen Anne.

124–25: 'The Superfine Axminster carpet for the North Drawing Room [as it was known then] 119 yards square, at 34/6…£205. 5s. 6d.' supplied by Messrs Watson, Wood and Bell of Old Bond Street in 1834 has been replaced by a modern copy.

126: Queen Mary's wartime Christmas present from her family, 1943: a pair of Louis XVI candelabra by Pierre Gouthière.

127: A giltwood sofa and crane torchère, made by Tatham & Co. for Carlton House in 1812.

128 and 129: Probably made by Jean-Henri Riesener around 1775, the desk was bought by George IV in 1825, described as having belonged to Louis XVI.

130: Military trophy candelabra, ordered from Thomire in Paris by the Prince Regent, 1813.

MUSIC ROOM

The Saloon, Buckingham Palace • 1843 • Douglas Morison

Nash's 'Bow Drawing Room' is the least changed of his three new state rooms. Its great columns of scagliola imitating lapis lazuli, which cost £900 in 1828 and an additional £315 for the 'metal granula being introduced' into the mixture, are the only surviving pieces of Joseph Browne's scagliola work that was such a feature of the original interiors of the Palace. Recently restored by Hayles & Howe, the columns, with their gilt-bronze capitals and mouldings by Samuel Parker, give an air of Imperial Roman splendour to the domed space.

The dome itself, and the half-dome that covers the elegant bow sticking into the garden, have trellis plasterwork studded with the English, Irish and Scottish national emblems of rose, shamrock and thistle, above tympana filled with groups of putti sculpted by William Pitts representing Harmony, Eloquence and Pleasure. If the carpet is pulled back, the superb parquetry floor is revealed, with George IV's cipher bound in laurel wreaths, all in tulip and rosewood inlaid into satinwood and white holly, by cabinetmaker George Seddon.

The room is furnished with a set of *fauteuils* and four sofas made around 1780 by the great Parisian *ébéniste* Georges Jacob and supplied for the Great Drawing Room at Carlton House around 1790 through Daguerre, whose label is still fixed to some of the pieces. They can be seen in the view of the room (p. 15) after it became the Throne Room in 1811, the chairs around the table and the sofas in their original positions each in a columned alcove, which suggests they were ordered expressly for the room. Were the mirror-filled recesses in Nash's new room at the Palace designed to accommodate these treasured sofas, which fit them so perfectly?

Today the Jacob furniture is covered in cerise silk damask. The walls, now painted cream, were originally hung with bright yellow silk in a Palace that was very definitely not colour-shy, although already by 1843, as seen in the watercolour by Douglas Morison here, the silk had gone and the parquetry floor was completely hidden by plain crimson fitted carpet. At the same time, the furniture was all covered in scarlet slipcovers, under which we can recognise the Jacob sofas but not the chairs.

132: Part of the suite of Jacob chairs and sofas bought by the Prince of Wales for his Great Drawing Room at Carlton House *c.*1780, their cerise silk glorious against the lapis lazuli scagliola columns.

134: Seen in the mirror, Nash's half-dome over the bay projecting from his garden front.

135: Sèvres vase in a 1764 garniture bought by Lord Yarmouth in Paris and received at Carlton House in 1818.

136: Potpourri vase in deep blue Sèvres porcelain, mounted in gilt bronze by Napoleon's *bronzier* Thomire, ordered from him by the Prince Regent and placed in the Blue Velvet Room at Carlton House, June 1812.

137: Nash's dome, tympana with plaster figures by Pitts, and endless reflections in the mirrored recesses.

138–39: The only surviving scagliola in the state apartments, which was such a feature of their original design.

140: Nash's plasterwork, a trellis filled with national flowers and a frieze of Masonic triangles (the Prince of Wales had his own lodge, 1787–1820), with one of Parker's gilt-bronze capitals.

141: A marble chimney piece with a gilt-bronze gallery.

142: The parquetry floor with its wreathed ciphers of George IV.

BLUE DRAWING ROOM

Blue Velvet Room, Carlton House • 1816 • Charles Wild

The last and largest of Nash's three new state rooms, then called the South Drawing Room, served as the ballroom until Queen Victoria had her new one built in 1855. It has been known as the Blue Drawing Room since being hung with flocked paper, turquoise on a buff ground. The colour has faded to the dove grey seen today and only the turquoise silk upholstery and curtains recall the scheme, 'altogether delightful in colour' according to Clifford Smith, Keeper of Furniture at the Victoria and Albert Museum, who assisted Queen Mary with decoration work and wrote the definitive history of the Palace in 1931.

Nash's raspberry-red scagliola columns, imitating a bright porphyry, with their gilt-bronze capitals, were combined with crimson silk on the walls when the room was first completed, an explosion of red whose only surviving element is the ground of the immense Axminster carpet, a recent copy of the one ordered in 1834 from Watson, Wood and Bell's carpet warehouse on Old Bond Street, priced at £263 plus £22 for the design. The scagliola columns were painted to look like onyx in 1860 when these rooms were redecorated under Prince Albert's supervision, not long before his death.

The muscular, bracketed ceiling is one of Nash's most inventive and frames sculptural reliefs on the end walls by William Pitts celebrating Edmund Spenser, William Shakespeare and John Milton. The gilded sofas and chairs were all produced for George IV, some for Carlton House, some for Windsor, while four Louis XIV–style tables in ebony, lapis lazuli and gilt bronze made by Alexandre Louis Bellangé in Paris around 1823 and bought by the King for Windsor were rejected by him and only brought out of storage and placed here after his death when Lord Duncannon was charged with furnishing the rooms.

The star of the room, however, is the famous Table of the Great Commanders of Antiquity, ordered by Napoleon from Sèvres in 1806 as one of a set of four tables topped by single, metre-wide porcelain plaques set in gilt-bronze mounts by Thomire. The set, designed by Imperial architect Charles Percier, included a modern equivalent to this, with Napoleon surrounded by his marshals, which is today at Malmaison. After the Bourbon Restoration Louis XVIII, made aware that this table was much coveted by George IV, presented it to him, upon which the King had Sir Thomas Lawrence include it in his Coronation portrait.

144: Nash's columns, originally in porphyry scagliola but painted in faux onyx, probably by C.H. Moxon for Grüner and Prince Albert, 1860. An X-frame chair by Morel & Seddon for Windsor, 1828: a fashionable design inspired by ancient Roman curule chairs reserved for dignitaries.

146: Clock in marble, gilt bronze and enamelled porcelain by Jean-Antoine Lépine, bought from him by the Prince of Wales, 1790, with a beaded marble base added later by Vulliamy for the Blue Velvet Room, Carlton House.

147: Table of the Great Commanders of Antiquity, designed by Charles Percier for Napoleon, given to George IV by Louis XVIII. The top, a single piece of Sèvres porcelain, can be rotated.

148 and 149: A phoenix in a *pietre dure* tabletop and a candelabra probably by François Rémond, from the Great Drawing Room at Carlton House.

150–51: The Axminster carpet, a modern copy of the original, with a red ground from the original colour scheme of crimson silk wall hangings and porphyry scagliola columns. The state portraits of George V by Sir Luke Fildes and Queen Mary by Sir William Llewellyn were painted in 1911.

152: The leonine arm of a sofa made by Tatham & Bailey for the Crimson Drawing Room, Carlton House, 1810.

STATE DINING ROOM

State Dining Room • 1843 • Douglas Morison

This room was intended by Nash as a single-height Music Room, set back from the main garden elevation with Ionic columns in scagliola and a flat ceiling below an upper floor. It was rebuilt by Blore in 1833 in line with the rest of the west front as a double-height State Dining Room, replacing one Nash had built on the ground floor. Blore designed a new interior with a rather clumsy version of one of Nash's vaulted ceilings, which was not finished until Queen Victoria's reign when her cipher was added alongside that of her uncle William IV. The only Nash features remaining are the music-themed fireplaces, carved in white marble by Matthew Cotes Wyatt, son of James Wyatt, the architect of Queen Charlotte's short-lived staircase.

When the room was first completed, as seen in the 1843 watercolour view, the large alcove at the far end, with doors to the service areas behind, was home to a great buffet displaying gold plate in the classic manner. This was swept away in 1855 when Pennethorne opened the back wall into his West Gallery leading to the new Ballroom. The room is hung with George IV's Coronation portrait by Lawrence, his hand resting on Napoleon's Sèvres table now in the Blue Drawing Room, flanked by his parents, grandparents and great-grandparents in strict ancestral order, an arrangement decided by Queen Victoria in 1841.

On the fireplaces stand two of George IV's vast collection of clocks. Below his portrait is one made for him in 1811 by Benjamin Vulliamy, his long-time clockmaker, with a Derby biscuit porcelain group of figures representing Time and Astronomy around a broken column; the other is a spectacular creation by French Imperial bronze-maker Thomire, bought in 1810 for the Crimson Silk Drawing Room at Carlton House, with Phaeton crossing the heavens in his father Helios's chariot, its spoked wheel forming the clock face.

The clock was moved to Royal Lodge, Windsor, and then to the Pavilion at Brighton, where it was when Vulliamy replaced its movement in 1834, explaining that 'the works of the clock are good for nothing and the case is very dirty ...'. Flanking the Thomire clock is a pair of candelabra by François Rémond bought for George IV in Paris in 1820, by his pastry chef François Benois. These are raised on bases added for the King by Vulliamy in Griotte marble with gilt-bronze mounts, like that of the clock. This is the end of the great enfilade of state rooms on the garden front; from here we move into the 1855 extension built by Pennethorne for Queen Victoria.

H.M. QUEEN CHARLOTTE.
ALLAN RAMSAY.
H.R.H. FREDERICK.

Vulliamy

154: Queen Alexandra's distant gaze along the enfilade from the White Drawing Room.

156: Thomire's gilt-bronze clock, *c.*1800, with Phaeton, son of the sun god Helios, recklessly driving his father's chariot across the heavens sits on a marble fireplace designed by Nash for his intended Music Room.

157: All the door frames have oak leaf and acorn ornament in gilt bronze by Parker.

158–59: Blore's State Dining Room, now an awkward end to Nash's enfilade of state apartments. Nash had planned this as a pilastered Music Room lower, narrower and with a flat ceiling, centred on the Picture Gallery, with the Dining Room on the ground floor, below it.

160: Candelabra by Rémond, *c.*1785, bought for George IV by Benois in Paris, 1820, with Griotte marble bases added by Vulliamy.

161: The parade of ancestral portraits includes George IV's mother Queen Charlotte, by Ramsay, and his grandfather Frederick, Prince of Wales, by Jean-Baptise van Loo, in frames designed by Blore with their ciphers.

162: Derby biscuit porcelain figures around a broken marble column, the gilt-bronze scroll inscribed 'Design'd for His R.H. ye P. of WALES by B. Vulliamy'.

WEST GALLERY

Approach Gallery, Buckingham Palace • 1873 • Hills & Saunders

Here we enter the Ballroom extension, built for Queen Victoria in 1855 by her 'excellent and worthy man, Mr Thomas Cubitt', the greatest London builder of the time, with Nash's stepson, architect Sir James Pennethorne. The State Dining Room's plate alcove was opened up and linked by this space, then known as the Approach Gallery, to the huge new Ballroom, also reached by the parallel Promenade (now East) Gallery, the two connected by a smaller Cross Gallery. All of this was to provide proper entertaining space in a palace where balls had formerly been held in the Blue Drawing Room and great dinners in the Picture Gallery.

The West Gallery is a perfect space designed in Nash's grand manner by Pennethorne, top-lit through engraved glass in the barrel vault, reminiscent of the Guard Chamber. Above the doors are deep classical reliefs showing Venus, borne on a seashell and bringing armour to Achilles, aptly enough for the proud home of the ruler of the sea, as Queen Victoria was at the time of the Royal Navy's greatest strength. Set in the wall panelling are four Gobelins tapestries with scenes from Don Quixote within flowered borders, given when new in 1787 by Louis XVI to the artist Richard Cosway in gratitude for a gift of four cartoons thought to be by Giulio Romano.

Cosway was the then Prince of Wales's neighbour, living in high style at Schomberg House with his glamorous wife Maria and a household including Ottobah Cugoano, a Ghanaian ex-slave (and famed anti-slavery campaigner) whom they dressed like Vatican footmen in crimson Genoa velvet. Given the Gobelins tapestries, 'so sumptuous as to be Princely', by Louis XVI, Cosway presented them in 1788 to the Prince whose favourite artist he then was, signing his work 'Primarius Pictor Serenissimi Walliae Principis'. The tapestries were said to be 'one of the chief embellishments of Carlton House'.

Also from Carlton House are four large Chinese porcelain vases in celadon turquoise decorated with Buddhist auspicious emblems, imported to London when new around 1800, bought by the Prince and mounted in gilt bronze by Vulliamy with intertwined snake handles and festooned mounts on marble bases. These were installed in the Blue Velvet Room in September 1814 but moved to Brighton five years later. The adjacent Cross Gallery is mainly interesting for the surviving fragments of Ludwig Grüner's decorative painting, including soffits to the doorways with the Prince of Wales's badge and motto.

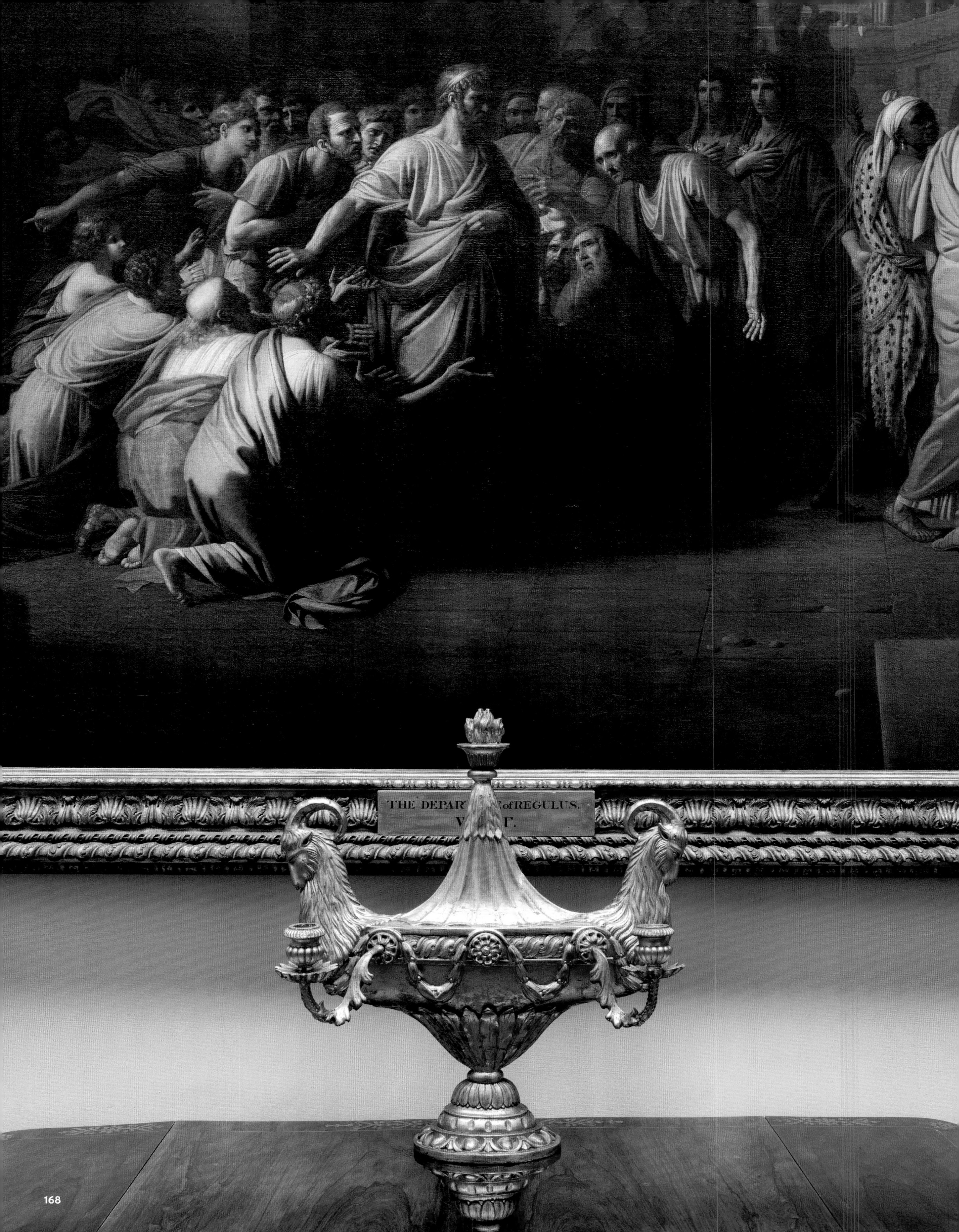
THE DEPAR of REGULUS.

164: Over the door, William Theed's 1855 *Venus Descending with the Armour of Achilles*. Below, four Chinese porcelain vases covered in Buddhist emblems, imported new to England and mounted by Vulliamy with snake handles and marble bases in 1814 for the Blue Velvet Room, Carlton House.

166: Theed's 1855 *Birth of Venus* over the door to the Ballroom.

167: Boulle-work 'Bureau Mazarin' *c.*1710, bought for the Prince of Wales in 1807. Its pair, with the marquetry reversed, is in the Wallace Collection. It was the Prince of Wales's dressing table at Brighton. The Chinese landscape vases, *c.*1800, were a Diamond Jubilee gift to Queen Victoria from the Dowager Empress Cixi.

168 and 169: The Cross Gallery, connecting the West and East Galleries, preserves snippets of the decorative painting by Moxon & Co., designed by Grüner for Prince Albert, 1855, elsewhere painted out by Edward VII. Two big Neoclassical canvases by Benjamin West face stacked dining chairs, some from the set of sixty made by Tatham & Bailey for Carlton House, 1813.

170: Above a pair of mirrored mahogany doors mounted with gilt bronze is a painted soffit designed by Grüner with the Prince of Wales's feathers and motto.

BALLROOM

Children's Fancy Dress Ball [Ball Supper Room] • 1859 • Eugenio Agneni

This huge space, used today for state banquets and, more often, investitures, was built by Queen Victoria in 1855. Its great height probably arose from the need to get daylight in on both sides, achieved with clerestory windows that have since been reduced and partly obscured by new buildings. Nash's stepson Sir James Pennethorne was architect, but the interior was very much a collaboration between him, Prince Albert and Ludwig Grüner, whose fascination with the Renaissance dictated its original style, recorded with great precision in Louis Haghe's 1856 watercolour view.

The largest of all of the Prince Regent's relics from the Pavilion at Brighton had to be accommodated in the new Ballroom: the organ, supposedly the largest and most powerful in England, built by Henry Cephas Lincoln for £3,014 in 1818, originally in a case designed by Frederick Crace in line with the rest of his extravagantly Indo-Chinese decorative scheme. Pennethorne gave the ends of his space vast arched alcoves and sat the organ, in a new columned case, in one with a corresponding throne canopy in the other. The whole room was painted to Grüner's elaborate designs, full of quotations from Raphael such as his Parnassus above the throne.

Edward VII, far from enamoured with his father's tastes, felt the Ballroom needed a radical transformation, and gave it one. Out went the richness of colour and detail, the careful scaling of the architecture and the high-minded aspirations of the old scheme, replaced by a giant order of pilasters and colossal door frames in a design by the architect Frank Verity, much altered and carried out by the White Allom decorating company. The resulting space is uncompromisingly magnificent.

Queen Mary brilliantly added a throne canopy using the gold-embroidered Shamiana hangings that had shaded her and King-Emperor George V from the blazing Indian sun at the Delhi Durbar of 1911. Designed by the Mayo School of Art in Lahore and embroidered there with Mughal-inspired designs, they were reused to make this domed canopy designed by Sir Edwin Lutyens in 1916, when he was meeting the King and Queen frequently to discuss the new Viceroy's House, then under construction in New Delhi. In 1967 the canopy was altered and simplified, removing most of the Indian embroidery, which had become very worn over time.

MDCCCLV.

172: The Ballroom ready for an investiture. The standing candelabra, made in Paris in 1855 by Ferdinand Barbedienne to Grüner's design, were removed under Edward VII, and later put back with very florid arms replacing the originals, which were made into chandeliers by Maurice Escaré for the Principal Corridor in 1911.

174: The Ball Supper Room retains its vigorous Grecian plasterwork but lost all of Grüner's complex painted decoration in 1902, seen in the 1859 watercolour (p. 173).

175: The chimney piece celebrating naval triumphs came from the Armoury formed by Nash out of George III's Octagon Library.

176: Queen Victoria is seated on her throne beneath the arch in Louis Haghe's watercolour of the second ball held in the new room, 17 June 1856, showing the luxury and balance of Grüner's neo-Renaissance decoration.

177: The organ from Brighton up in its loft.

178–79: Sir Edwin Lutyens's 1916 throne canopy was much simplified in 1967. Framed in the side wall panelling are two duplicate Gobelins tapestries from the 1776 'Story of Jason' set bought in 1825 for Windsor.

180: Edward VII's throne from his 1902 Coronation, made by the Parisian decorators Carlhian & Baumetz under the direction of Sir Joseph Duveen, art dealer to the King's circle, who also lent tapestries and carpets to dress Westminster Abbey for the occasion. The scrolling Indian embroidery behind is the only remnant of the Imperial Shamiana from Delhi, 1911.

PART III

AMBASSADORS' ENTRANCE • BOW ROOM • 1844 & 1855 ROOMS
YELLOW DRAWING ROOM • PRINCIPAL CORRIDOR • CENTRE ROOM
CHINESE DINING ROOM

HONY SOIT CVI MAL Y PENSE

AMBASSADORS' ENTRANCE

The Entrée, Ambassadors' Entrance • 1924

Here we are in the Entrée, built as the privileged entrance for diplomats and other notables to escape passing through the Forecourt, and since 1993 also used by paying visitors during the Summer Opening of the Palace. The exterior was built with a curved colonnade and central portico by Nash, then altered by Blore who removed the curves and set the columns against the wall, and again later when the small portico was turned into a *porte-cochère* to protect the ambassadors from London rain. Stepping inside, we find ourselves in 1924, when it was remodelled for Queen Mary by royal decorator Sir Charles Allom.

This is the only complete Palace interior we see of this date, which makes it rather fascinating. It was done in the year of the British Empire Exhibition, where Queen Mary's Dolls' House, just completed by Sir Edwin Lutyens, was shown and for which gift the Queen wrote to her architect thanking him for 'this wonderful work of art'. Indeed the space feels rather like one of the rooms of the Dolls' House, which is on display at Windsor Castle, its miniature fantasy interiors complete with working Rolls-Royce cars, Purdey shotguns and an exquisite wind-up gramophone with records such as 'God Save the King'.

Over the *brocatello* marble fireplace is a mirror decorated with beautifully carved, silvered festoons and draperies hanging from a royal cipher on a wreath of laurel and oak, from which is suspended a large Garter Star framing a clock. The whole delicious confection is a masterpiece of 1920s' decoration and the perfect response to George IV's grandiose carved marble fireplace and clock in the Grand Hall of the Palace, the emblems of successive Georges separated by exactly a century. The cipher here of course is not merely GR but GMR, with the Queen's central M very dominant indeed.

In front of the fireplace is one of the three big Chinese porcelain jardinières made around 1760 and mounted with bold, vaguely Chinese gilt-bronze handles and bases by Vulliamy for the Banqueting Room at Brighton in 1820 together with four similar bowls in plain brilliant blue glaze produced by Spode, now in the Grand Hall. In the glazed corridor beyond hang portraits including a startlingly modern-looking canvas that is in fact a fragment of a barely begun studio copy of Hayter's Coronation portrait of Queen Victoria, bought by that imaginative collector Queen Elizabeth The Queen Mother in 1949.

184: Echoing the Grand Hall where George IV's elaborately carved marble fireplace includes a Vulliamy clock, in George V's Ambassadors' Entrance of 1924 is this clock made by Charles Frodsham & Co., which succeeded as Royal Clockmakers on Vulliamy's death in 1854. The white-gilded Garter Star setting appears to float on the mirror.

186: The Ambassadors' Entrance, altered from Nash's original design of curving, open colonnades, retains his beautifully carved Ionic columns of Bath stone, rearranged against straight walls and forming now a *porte-cochère*.

187: The bolection fireplace surround, carved swags and royal cipher quoting Kensington and Hampton Court are all very much to the taste of Queen Mary whose watchful eye supervised this addition to the Palace. The Chinese porcelain jardinière of 1750 was mounted by Vulliamy for Brighton.

188: Fragment of an unfinished studio copy of Queen Victoria's Coronation portrait by Hayter now in the East Gallery. Dozens of copies were made for British Embassies. This was bought by Queen Elizabeth The Queen Mother in 1949.

BOW ROOM

Bow Room, Buckingham Palace • 1873 • Hills & Saunders

From the Entrée we pass on to the central three rooms off the Marble Hall, designed by Nash as libraries adjoining what would have been George IV's private apartments, modest versions of George III's three huge book rooms added by Sir William Chambers, entered directly from the King's bedroom at the south end of Buckingham House. These rooms lost their bookcases when William IV decided to move the Royal Library entirely to Windsor Castle and were not given any real identity until the 1850s.

George IV had always loved a bow window looking at a garden: this arrangement at Carlton House had been preserved through all of Henry Holland's changes there, so that Nash's central bow here was very much to the King's taste. The Bow Room is used as the main entrance to the Palace gardens to this day, both for the formal Garden Parties held on the lawns in early summer and for the tourists visiting later on, during the Summer Opening.

The bones of the room's decoration date from when Queen Victoria and Prince Albert arranged the portraits of her family, gathered for Prince Leopold's 1853 christening, in oval frames set into the walls within elaborate neo-Renaissance plasterwork by Ludwig Grüner. At that time the curved recesses towards the outer wall were glazed and admitted daylight. They now form vitrines for china display, which has rather darkened the room. Grüner's decoration was lost in Edward VII's great whitewashing campaign of 1902.

The twin fireplaces were replaced by Queen Mary with the present ones of around 1800 in black basalt with gilt-bronze mounts by Vulliamy, who was the source of so many of George IV's treasures, made for Lord Bridgewater's house at 7 Grosvenor Square. In the curved vitrines set into the walls is displayed the famous Mecklenburg Service of porcelain, commissioned from the Chelsea factory by Queen Charlotte for her brother the Duke of Mecklenburg around 1763. The service was given to Queen Elizabeth The Queen Mother in 1947 by the industrialist James Oakes.

F. WINTERHALTER 1853.

MDCCCLIII

MDCCCLIII

PRINCESS AUGUSTA
STRELITZ
MELVILLE
F. WINTERHALTER

190: The sweeping curve of the Bow Room. The gilded torchère is one of a pair, probably made for Queen Charlotte's Crimson Drawing Room upstairs at Buckingham House, *c.*1812.

192: In oval frames set into the walls are eight portraits of Queen Victoria's extended family, who came to London in June 1853 for Prince Leopold's christening. Here is one of the godparents, Augusta, Princess William of Prussia and future German Empress, painted by Winterhalter with the sash of the Prussian Order of the Red Eagle. She was opposed to Otto von Bismarck's Prussian military growth and delighted when her son William married Victoria and Albert's daughter Princess Victoria. Her grandson, however, was William III, the Kaiser of the Great War.

193: On the black basalt fireplaces installed by Queen Mary are four verde antico vases, *c.*1790, bought by Benois for George IV while on a shopping trip to Paris after Napoleon's fall, July 1814.

194–95: The curved glass vitrines that replaced George IV's bookcases now hold the Mecklenburg Service of Chelsea porcelain.

196: Princess Augusta of Cambridge, Duchess of Mecklenburg and Queen Mary's aunt, copied for the room by Alexander Melville in 1853 from Winterhalter's portrait.

CUYP · TROOPER·WITH A GREY HORSE

1844 & 1855 ROOMS

1844 Room, Buckingham Palace • 1849 • James Roberts

These two rooms bear the dates of their occupation by the grandest of visitors: Russian Tsar Nicholas I in 1844 and French Emperor Napoleon III, with his Empress Eugénie, in 1855. Both rooms were built as part of George IV's library but decorated for Queen Victoria. The finished 1844 Room, with its portraits of the Tsar and other fellow royalties set into elegant red and gold plaster frames on pale blue walls, was recorded in a watercolour view for the Queen in 1850. The 1855 Room's pilasters and dado were painted in dark faux marbre before being whitewashed like the rest of the Palace for Edward VII.

The 1855 Room today still has Queen Victoria's arrangement of pictures of the events and personalities of the year set in gilded frames in the walls. The most important were painted by George Housman Thomas, who was engaged by the Queen to record the events of 1855 some four years later, when the room was decorated. We see Napoleon III made a Knight of the Garter at Windsor in April 1855 and, in August the same year, entertaining Queen Victoria and the Prince Consort on their return visit to Paris with a review of troops on a dusty Champ de Mars.

Here is the Queen at the tomb of Napoleon I, her host's uncle, at Les Invalides, and reviewing her own troops at Woolwich and the Royal Navy at Spithead. On the floor of the 1855 Room is a carpet made by Southwell's of Shropshire in 1897, a Diamond Jubilee gift to the Queen Empress from 'the Ladies of England', with her cipher VRI and a floral border with, in its corners, animals representing the four corners of the Empire: tiger, kangaroo, beaver and elephant.

The 1844 Room now contains more of the suite of sofas and chairs made by Morel & Seddon for Windsor in 1828, all gilded lions' masks and paws, covered in a vibrant blue and gold silk. The Tsar has gone, but George IV and Frederick, Duke of York, painted as children in the robes of Garter and Bath knights by Richard Brompton, hang in handsome frames with carved crests. The star of the room, however, is the splendid Neoclassical mechanical desk by David Roentgen, unsigned but unmistakable, bought for George IV in Paris, 1820.

AUGUST 24TH 1855 C.H.THOMAS

198: The 1844 Room today with Aelbert Cuyp's 1652 *Cavalry Trooper Decorating His Dappled Grey* over the desk by David Roentgen, bought by George IV in 1805 and 1820 respectively. On the desk are bronze binoculars sculpted by Janie Beardsall, presented to Her Majesty The Queen by Sir Peter O'Sullevan in 2002 in recognition of a lifetime's contribution to horse racing.

200 and 201: Richard Brompton's portraits of George, Prince of Wales in Garter robes and Prince Frederick in Bath ones, in frames crested by ostrich feathers and the mitre of the Bishop of Osnabrück, which the younger brother had become at the age of six months. The malachite candelabra by Thomire was bought by Benois in Paris for George IV, 1828.

202–03: On the 1844 Room's ormolu-mounted Portoro marble chimney piece stands a clock of 1795–99 signed by former royal clockmaker 'Robin à Paris', bought by George IV's friend Lord Hertford in Paris, whose son gave it to Wellington's amanuensis Colonel Gurwood. It was bought by Queen Mary for the Royal Collection in 1938.

204 and 205: George Housman Thomas's views of the reciprocal visits of Napoleon III and Empress Eugénie to London, and Victoria and Albert to Paris, still set in their wall frames in the 1855 Room.

206: One of the scrapbook-style walls of portraits and scenes from 1855.

207: A figure of Dawn unveiling herself on a clock made in Paris around 1810 by André-Antoine Ravrio.

208: The empire-themed carpet made by Southwell's of Shropshire in 1897, a Diamond Jubilee gift to Queen Empress Victoria from 'the Ladies of England'.

YELLOW DRAWING ROOM

Yellow Drawing Room, Buckingham Palace • 1855 • James Roberts

We have now returned upstairs, to the East Wing added for Queen Victoria when she protested that the Palace, built for George IV to live in alone, was far too small for her growing family. Blore closed Nash's courtyard, running an airy corridor along it with new suites of rooms looking out over the Forecourt and over the trees of the Mall. He was made by Prince Albert, rather against his will, to use decorative elements from George IV's beloved Pavilion at Brighton, which lift his very ordinary rooms into the realm of the extraordinary.

The Yellow Drawing Room, named for the yellow silk on its walls when completed in 1850, sits at the south-east corner of the Palace, where Nash's Household Corridor meets Blore's Principal one. The yellow silk is restricted to curtains and chairs now, for Queen Mary had it hung with Chinese wallpaper in the late 1920s, paper found in the Palace stores that it seems had been used for the Brighton Pavilion's Saloon when redecorated by Frederick Crace in 1816, before George IV grew tired of the look and opted for a more exotic, Indian-inspired scheme in red and gold eight years later.

The astonishing fireplace was made for that final, red and gold, Saloon at Brighton, designed like the rest of the room by the mysterious Robert Jones who worked in tandem with Crace on the Pavilion from 1815, contributing many of the more idiosyncratic and fantastic designs. The marble was carved by Richard Westmacott and the gilt-bronze mounts produced by Samuel Parker who would go on to do all the bronze for the Palace. He was here brought in by Nash, beating Vulliamy's quote of £1,500 for the work with his own of £840, including the cold-painted bronze Chinese figures, fire irons and fender.

Jones's fireplace design incorporated the garniture atop it today, centred on the fantastic 'Kylin' clock, a French rococo confection of old Chinese porcelain and new bronzes, with gilt sunflowers added by Jones and Parker in 1823, framed by the massive candelabras, each made up of two Chinese vases joined and mounted with writhing dragons and painted figures of Chinese court officials standing in sunflowers. Further items of Brightonalia include the pair of vase pedestals en suite with the fireplace and the set of extraordinary chairs from the Music Room, also presumably designed by Jones.

210: The Chinese wallpaper, apparently used in the Saloon, Brighton, 1816, and rehung here by Queen Mary in the 1920s, with a new scalloped border made by White Allom to fill the space at the top. The turquoise porcelain vase, mounted by Vulliamy, stands on the white and gold Indo-Chinese open pedestal designed for it by Jones en suite with the fireplace now also here.

212 and 213: Jones's fabulously elaborate fireplace from his redecoration of the Brighton Saloon, all in gilt-bronze-mounted white marble including his new base for the rococo 'Kylin' clock. The figures in court costumes are English painted bronze, reminiscent of Queen Charlotte's painted clay Chinese export ones in Zoffany's painting (p. 12).

214: One of the 'Kylins', in fact lions, munching on ormolu foliage from the original clock, unlike the extra sunflowers added in 1823 by Parker.

215: A Chinese figure sprouts like Venus from a scallop shell in a sunflower on green enamel waves, in a moment of sublime decorative madness from Jones.

216: One of four extraordinary armchairs made with twelve side chairs by Bailey & Sanders for Brighton, 1817, all fretwork and batwings, possibly early designs by Jones.

PRINCIPAL CORRIDOR

Music Room, Brighton • 1838 • John Agar (drawn by James Stephanoff)

This was known as the Princesses' Corridor in 1857 when Queen Victoria's daughters had rooms off it and it was painted by James Roberts in a wedding album given by the Queen to her eldest daughter Victoria, who married the future Emperor Frederick III of Prussia, the next year. In 1860 the end walls were covered with the mirror glass panels that remain today, although the overdoor portraits added then, in gilded, carved oval frames with festoons of fruit and flowers, matching those that can still be seen in the White Drawing Room, have since been removed. What were built as the Princesses' bedrooms are now suites of guest rooms.

The space was painted celadon green for Queen Mary when she moved into the Palace in 1911, and newly lit by gilt-bronze chandeliers made by Maurice Escaré using the arms of the giant 1855 candelabra, produced by Ferdinand Barbedienne in Paris to Ludwig Grüner's design for the Ballroom, until they were removed in 1902. The crimson carpet and curtains have been renewed many times but were probably first used under Edward VII.

Almost all of the furniture and objects are from George IV's collection, with a strong Chinese theme and including the star pieces, dating from around 1789, from his first exotic interior, the Chinese Drawing Room at Carlton House: the pier table and open cabinet made by Adam Weisweiler and acquired from Daguerre. These masterpieces blend Neoclassical forms with Chinese-inspired detail in ebony and gilt bronze. The pier table's legs have painted bronze Chinese caryatids with long moustaches, which also appear on the room's fireplace, now in another part of the Palace. Both table and cabinet were copied by Edward Bailey in 1819 to make pairs for Brighton and all four pieces stand in this corridor today.

Here, too, are the suite of chairs from the same room made by émigré *menuisier* François Hervé at his workshop off the Tottenham Court Road, amazingly light and delicate pieces with fretwork frames and hollow arms, alongside massively heavy sofas with Chinese motifs from the last phase at Brighton. The corridor also contains the set of Indian engraved ivory-veneered chairs and sofa that George III bought as a gift for Queen Charlotte when he was passing a house sale held by James Christie at Marlow in 1781. When the Queen's possessions were sold by Christie's in 1819, George IV purchased the set for Brighton.

MARRIAGE OF H.R.H ALBERT EDWARD, PRINCE OF WALES, K.G. WITH H.

QUEEN ALEXANDRA

218 and 220: The Principal Corridor runs the full length of Blore's East Wing, lined with George IV's treasures from his Royal Pavilion, Brighton.

221: A chair by Hervé with pierced rails and arm-supports, topped by Chinese seated figures, for Carlton House, 1789.

222 and 223: Weisweiler tables supplied by Daguerre for the Chinese Drawing Room at Carlton House, *c.*1787–9, and copied by Edward Bailey in 1819 to make pairs for the North Drawing Room at Brighton.

224: A dragon in tones of gilding on a curtain pole from Brighton.

225: The mirrored end walls of the Corridor, probably done shortly before the Prince Consort's death in 1861, with two of four Chinese porcelain pagodas built up with Spode plinths to a sufficient scale for the Music Room at Brighton in 1817.

226: A massive chinoiserie sofa from Brighton below William Frith's painting of the Prince of Wales's wedding to Alexandra of Denmark in 1863, with young Princes Leopold and Arthur in kilts.

227: More chinoiserie and Chinese treasures.

228–29: The north end of the Corridor.

230: Queen Alexandra's state portrait, 1905, by Fildes, by the door into the Centre Room.

CENTRE ROOM

Tapestry Drawing Room prepared for Empress Eugénie • 1855 • James Roberts

When the Royal Family is seen on the balcony of the Palace on some great occasion, they have stepped out from this room. There is sometimes a brief glimpse of an exotic-looking chandelier, but nothing more to suggest that behind Sir Aston Webb's eminently respectable Palace façade lies this unseen fantasy room, relic of the Prince Regent's yearning for aesthetic adventure. The chandelier is one of eight that surrounded a giant one in the Music Room at the Royal Pavilion, Brighton, all painted with Chinese motifs on etched glass, edged with glass 'pearls'.

When built for Queen Victoria this was the Tapestry Drawing Room, a curious mixture of elements from Brighton like the Banqueting Room fireplaces, giant pagodas and towering Chinese vases on Spode bases, with the carved and gilded festoons in the Marble Hall today and two Gobelins tapestries now on the Ministers' Staircase. Under Edward VII the room was painted white, of course, and hung with portraits of his fellow monarchs in uniform.

The room was redecorated by Queen Mary around 1922 in a Chinese vein and became known as the Centre Room. From the Palace stores came six panels of Chinese Imperial yellow silk embroidered with landscape scenes, possibly ones sent by the Emperor of China to Queen Victoria on her Diamond Jubilee in 1897. These were hung on the walls from gilt poles within Chinese fretwork, like the rest of the room mixing old pieces from Brighton with new work created by the Queen's decorator Sir Charles Allom. Curtains were made using old Chinese embroideries found in the stores.

Designed by Robert Jones, sideboards with gilded dragons hold Chinese porcelain vases mounted by Vulliamy with more dragons, all from Brighton. Four of the yellow silk panels, now very faded, have been replaced by four of Jones's painted panels of Chinese figures on patterned backgrounds, made for the Banqueting Room at Brighton, and the wall colours have been refreshed in brighter colours drawn from Jones's panels. On the two fireplaces are two pairs of chinoiserie candelabra and a clock from the Chinese Room at Carlton House, rounding off this exotic fantasy room so improbably located behind the balcony.

232: Giant porcelain oil lamps and sideboard with dragons from Brighton, designed by Jones who painted the Chinese figures above for the walls of the Banqueting Room there in 1817.

234: The door through which the Royal Family emerge onto the balcony on state occasions, with the gilded top of the Victoria memorial.

235: Curtains made up by White Allom for Queen Mary, using old Chinese fabrics found in the Palace stores.

236–37: The sublime chinoiserie madness behind the sober façade: fireplace, paintings and sideboards all from the Brighton Banqueting Room, while the silk hanging was hung for Queen Mary.

238: Chinoiserie doors and mouldings from Brighton.

239: The Chinese Drummer clock by Charles-Guillaume Manière supplied by Daguerre for Carlton House, *c.*1787–90.

240: Chinese musician figure, part of a candelabrum made for Carlton House *c.*1787–90.

241: A marble Chinoiserie clock, *c.*1780, by David-Frédéric Dubois, which was once owned by George IV's brother Adolphus, Duke of Cambridge, and bought by Her Majesty The Queen in 1977.

242: A bell push added by White Allom when redecorating for Queen Mary in 1929. Pushing the tongue would summon a footman.

CHINESE DINING ROOM

Pavilion Breakfast Room, Buckingham Palace • 1850 • James Roberts

Created for Queen Victoria in 1849 as the Pavilion Breakfast Room, this is the least changed of her new rooms. Located in the north-east corner of the Palace, at the opposite end of the Principal Corridor, it still serves as a private dining room. The curtains are no longer in the yellow silk of 1849, nor is the carpet still the central part of one from the Brighton Music Room, but otherwise it has remained unchanged for 170 years since James Roberts painted the charming breakfast scene with two-year-old Princess Louise's high chair in the corner.

The room is a reduced version of the 1818 Banqueting Room at Brighton, using original fittings from it like the pagoda-painted doors with their gilded Indian-inspired crestings, four of Robert Jones's painted panels of Chinese groups, the dining chairs (from a set of forty-eight supplied by Bailey & Sanders in 1817, most of which are now back in Brighton), and even the fretwork cornicing with bells. All of this was, of course, only thirty years old at the time. The trompe l'oeil Chinese railing dado was carefully reproduced, and one of the Brighton Music Room chandeliers hung from a ceiling newly painted with a dragon fighting a snake against a cloudy sky.

Also from the Music Room came Jones's spectacular fireplace, a colossal confection with a giant dragon, wings outstretched, carved with the shelf from a single huge block of white marble by Westmacott, the whole thing embellished with details in gilt bronze by Vulliamy and costing in all £1,684. Between the windows are four of the six giant oil lamps from the Music Room which combine Chinese export porcelain vases made around 1720 for the duc d'Orléans with new parts produced by Spode and Vulliamy in about 1820.

On the fireplace sits the monumental rococo gilt-bronze 'Rock Clock', made in Paris around 1750, that sat on it in Brighton. Like those in the Centre Room the curtains were produced by White Allom & Co. in 1922 for Queen Mary, using old Chinese embroideries from the Palace stores, leftovers from George IV's decorating mania, as with so much of the interior of Buckingham Palace. It is a delightful irony that the exotic, ever-changing tastes and unbridled extravagance of the King, derided and vilified as both were for most of his life, should have left such an enduring monument, serving his successors so well to this day.

244: Looking out on the gilded memorial to Queen Victoria, who would notice no changes, other than carpet and curtains, to what she called the Pavilion Breakfast Room.

246: Jones's madly exuberant fireplace from the Brighton Music Room.

247: Dining chairs from the set of forty-eight made for the Banqueting Room by Bailey & Sanders in 1817, most of which have now returned to Brighton. 'A dragon has been painted on the ceiling and harmonises with the rest' – Queen Victoria's diary, June 1849.

248: More of Jones's wall paintings of Chinese groups and one of his exotic Indian-inspired door crestings.

249: William Perry's chandelier, a water-lily form in oil-painted glass made in 1818 for the Brighton Music Room.

250: Curtain pelmets made for Queen Mary from Chinese embroideries found in store.

251: Painted dado and sideboard by Bailey & Sanders in 'very fine Rosewood, Snakewood and Satinwood'.

252–53: Above Westmacott's marble dragon there is a gilt bronze one on the huge rococo clock, *c.*1740, bought by Vulliamy in Paris in 1819 for Brighton.

254: A firedog, or rather dragon, supplied by stovemaker William Feetham in 1849 together with a new grate (required to fit the fireplace to Blore's inadequate hearth).

Ashley Hicks would like to thank everyone at both Royal Collection Trust and Rizzoli who helped make this book a reality, especially Jemima Rellie, Shruti Patel, Rufus Bird, Philip Reeser and Charles Miers.

First published in the United States of America in 2018 by
Rizzoli International Publications, Inc.
300 Park Avenue South
New York, NY 10010
www.rizzoliusa.com

ISBN: 978-0-8478-6319-8
Library of Congress Control Number: 2018938667

For Rizzoli International Publications:
Philip Reeser, Editor
Alyn Evans, Production Manager
Linda Schofield, Copy Editor

For Royal Collection Trust:
Tim Knox, Director
Elizabeth Silverton, Content Manager
Tom Love, Publishing Assistant

Design: Paul Sloman | +SUBTRACT
Printed in Italy
2018 2019 2020 2021 / 10 9 8 7 6 5 4 3 2 1

GROUND FLOOR

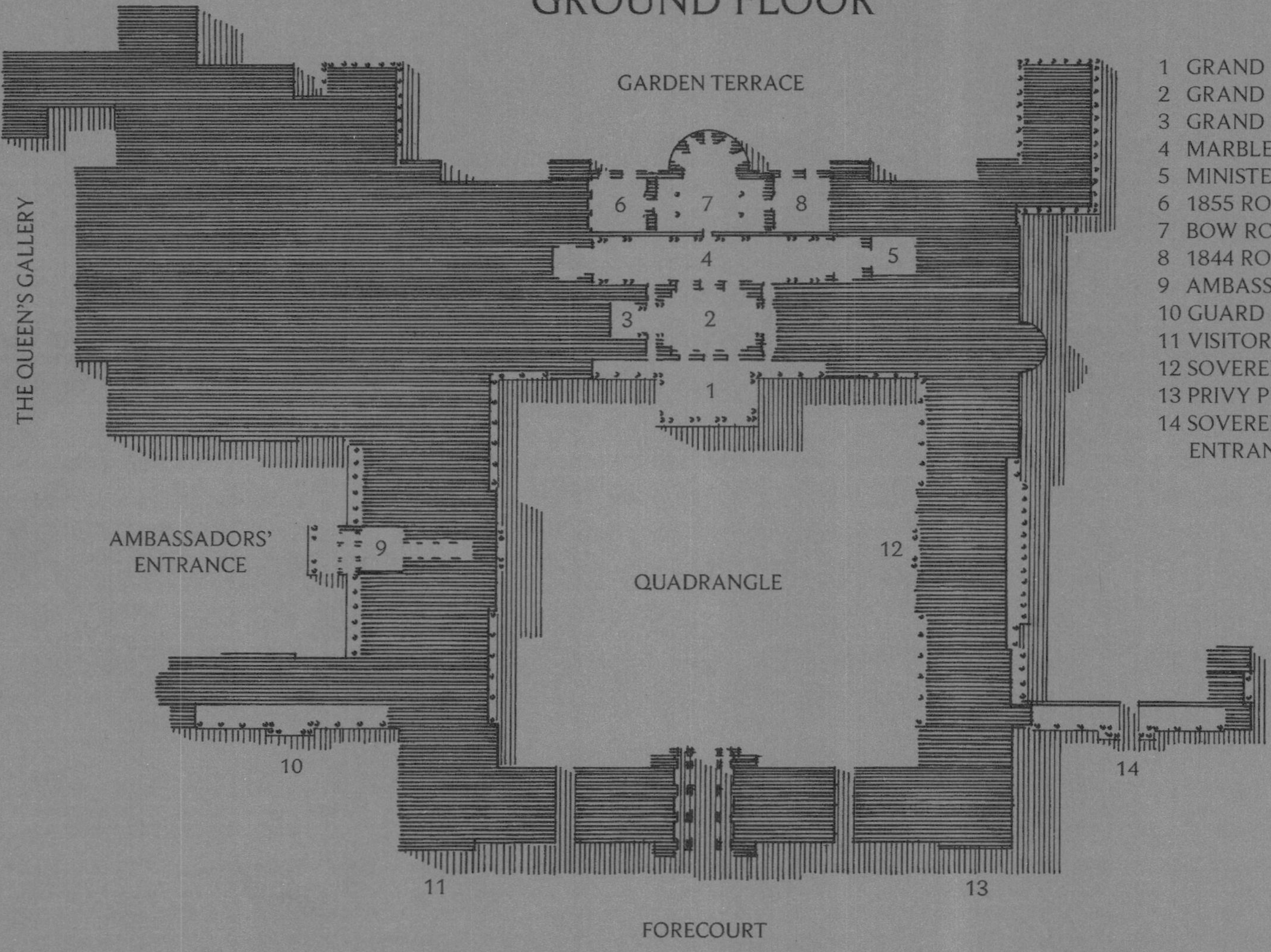

GARDEN TERRACE

THE QUEEN'S GALLERY

AMBASSADORS' ENTRANCE

QUADRANGLE

FORECOURT

1 GRAND ENTRANCE
2 GRAND HALL
3 GRAND STAIRCASE
4 MARBLE HALL
5 MINISTERS' STAIRCASE
6 1855 ROOM
7 BOW ROOM
8 1844 ROOM
9 AMBASSADORS' ENTRANCE
10 GUARD ROOM
11 VISITORS' DOOR
12 SOVEREIGN'S DOOR
13 PRIVY PURSE DOOR
14 SOVEREIGN'S GARDEN ENTRANCE